MEN I DATED SO YOU DON'T HAVE TO

The unveiled truths of
a London girl's dating life

Verity Ellis

Clink
Street

'There are all different kinds of love in this world,
but never the same love twice.'

F. Scott Fitzgerald

Chapter 1 – Pablo

Spain 2014
Tarragona train station

Coming from a sheltered upbringing doesn't mean you don't have dreams. I mean, look at me. I came from a sheltered upbringing, and I definitely had dreams. I had fantasised about a Mediterranean man sweeping me off my feet and serenading to me with a guitar, ever since I watched a clip of Enrique Iglesias singing 'Hero' to a female fan at one of his concerts. I vividly remember feeling love-struck, filled with lusty desire at the thought of being wrapped in the embrace of a hunky lothario. When Enrique kissed the fan at the end of the song, I was besotted. It only made sense, then, for my heart to skip a beat when Pablo Gonzalez and I matched on Tinder. My dream was coming true.

Pablo was Spanish, aged twenty-nine, with dark swishy hair, nice teeth and a passion for Amazon rainforest conservation. He was, in fact, my first ever Tinder date, but I didn't let him in on this. Since my Spanish doesn't transcend beyond GCSE grade C, I had to rely on google translate for the entirety of our Tinder conversation. Pablo's English was certainly better than my Spanish, but I quickly learned that he was bilingual and spoke a bit of French, too. I think that made him tri-lingual actually, or two-and-a-half-lingual. He liked to switch between them all in single sentences. For example, when I asked whether he went on Tinder dates often, he replied:

'Dating? Me? No... j'aime le Tinder to help con mi ingles.'

I decided to adopt the faithful British approach of sarcasm, asking Pablo whether I was his date or English tutor. He just replied with a question mark, triggering the start of a series of virtual misunderstandings. It got to the point where I was seriously considering cancelling the date altogether and joining the family I was au pairing for on their weekend trip to Barcelona Zoo. Maybe there would be a sexy lothario zookeeper there, helping the kids feed bananas to the giraffes. When I presented this conundrum to Naomi, my ex-boarding school bestie turned resident of Australia, she encouraged me to lie to the family I was working for and say that I am going to meet another au pair from a Facebook page. She told me to 'embrace the unknown' and 'expand my horizons,' justifying my date with the term 'YOLO.'

I consult Naomi for everything in life. She and I became friends after I let her borrow my spare skirt on the first day of Year 7 at Pipford Hall – a boarding school in the heart of Buckinghamshire still stuck in 1954. The uniform was a knee-length tartan skirt and a green knitted jumper with the school's eagle crest etched on the front. Naomi coloured in all the squares of her skirt with green and yellow highlighter pen during her first Maths lesson, giving the eagle a fluorescent pink beak so it matched the flamingo on her pencil case. The boarding mistress threatened her with suspension if she didn't change her behaviour fast. Of course, Naomi never did. She was expelled three years later after setting off the fire alarm with a deodorant can because she couldn't be bothered to re-sit her History mock.

That was almost five years ago. By the time I connect with Pablo, I am nineteen, and I have still never had a boyfriend. Or been in love. Not even remotely close. I've dreamt about it, of course. I decided that Dom, the guy I dated when I was sixteen, didn't count, even though it was he who had taken my virginity. Dom was from the local boy's grammar school who I met at a field party one Friday night after sneaking out of my boarding house. If you are not from a home county in the UK, then field parties may sound strange to you. It is just what millennials from Buckinghamshire used to do on Friday nights back then; congregate outside an off license in the latest Jack Wills collection, ask strangers to buy them a bottle of Lambrini Cherry and go and get wasted on an open plane of grass in the Chiltern Hills. If you're lucky, you will spark a romantic connection with a boy from a neighbouring school, chat on MSN for a few days and arrange to go down on each other the following Friday against a tree or a burrow of twigs.

My epic romance with Dom followed this paradigm. It lasted all of three weeks, before I discovered 'extreme fetishes' in his search engine when he shared a screen with me once during a Skype call after school. I lost sleep over imagining what they were. What if Pablo has 'extreme fetishes' too? He could do. I didn't know anything about him. He could abduct me, for all I know – whisk me away in a van and sell me as a sex slave. My passport photo will be plastered across the front page of the *Telegraph*; or worse, the *Daily Star*. I would be known by the nation as a sad, missing girl, who mistook a Spanish serial killer for a Tinder date.

I suppose there is always that risk with dating apps, although sadly, we Millennials don't have much of a choice. We are digital natives, born into a new wave of social media and technology that renders a pre-smartphone life inconceivable. We don't meet at bus stops, cafés and ballroom dances like people did in the olden days, nor do we attend in person book clubs, salsa classes or French lessons. Those bottled opportunities of serendipitous love hidden in the mundane of the everyday have been lost and forgotten. To where – I do not know. I have been searching for what feels like forever.

I took a deep breath and briefly entertained the possibility that the date with Pablo will go well. Maybe we will hit it off and realise that we are star-crossed lovers. Maybe he will be my soulmate – the epic love of my life, and recount this very first date of ours in his speech on our wedding day at the beach, just before our first dance. It will be the acoustic version of a romantic Latin song with the cocooning hush of maracas, played by a live band with flamenco dancers swaying in long ruffled skirts with roses in their hair.

I saw my train pulling in. It would take me ten minutes to arrive at Torredembarra – the town where Pablo and I had agreed to meet.

I looked up at the sky and prayed to the gods as it arrived.

Wish me luck, Venus, Zeus, Apollo and whatever the rest of your names are. And please let him be the doppelgänger of Enrique Iglesias.

Please.

By the time my train arrived at Torredembara, I was practically quivering with nerves. The air was thick, muggy, and suffocating. I wandered aimlessly across the platform, trying to locate the exit. When I eventually found my way outside, I could see that there was only one car waiting. It looked like a scruffy white rust bucket. I noticed a man inside, who (I thought) was Pablo.

'Buenos dias,' he smiled, as he wound down the window.

Yep. It's definitely him. He was wearing a loose grey vest like one of his pictures with a hair band and a peace sign necklace. He removed his seatbelt and stepped out of the car, whilst I stood there with my mouth half open like a gormless fish.

'Verity?' He said my name in a thick Spanish accent,

looking slightly dazed. I wondered if he was high. I could certainly smell weed.

'Yes?' I squeaked, sounding as if I was in trouble. 'Are you Pablo?'

'Si! Bonjour.'

He was attractive, but a tad sleazier looking than I had hoped. I was expecting Enrique Iglesias 2.0. Instead, I got a wannabe tribute act who looked as if he was about to audition for the Eurovision song contest in the year 2000, stoned.

'Just wondering, are we going to speak in English, Spanish or French, because I better–'

'Languages – I speak two,' he smiled, signalling the number with his fingers. 'Hablo Español y je parle Francais.'

'Yes, I know you do, but I need to work out which one to–'

'Paris, I live. Summer, I stay here. Avec mi familia. Torredembarra, where I am now,' he grinned. 'En las vacaciones. September, me back to Paris. Paris, like… une baguette, un crossaint… La Tour Eiffel. I fly… en avion,' he said, pointing to the sky. 'En el cielo.'

Looks like we're going for all three.

'Nice to… how you say… meet you!' He lowered himself to kiss me on either cheek. 'So small,' he laughed, patting my head.

'Yes,' I said, managing to respond with an awkward chuckle. I had never felt more stereotypically British in my entire life.

'Not hard to be small against you, is it?'

'Que?' He looked at me quizzically, as if I had suddenly morphed into an alien and grown a second head. This was proving to be a slight disaster, and we hadn't even left the station. I didn't know whether to attempt to respond in French, Spanish, or both. I decided to go for a mixture – just like him.

'Estoy… une petite femme!'

I beamed proudly, feeling impressed with my attempt. A concerned look spread across Pablo's face.

'Funny chica,' he smirked, walking me to his car. 'La voiture. We go to beach. Vamos a la playa.'

Before I could think twice, I was settling in the front seat. There was clutter everywhere; a torn open packet of cigarettes, a small stick of male deodorant, a tin of mints, a pair of mismatched flip flops and a bucket and spade. I relaxed in the knowledge that none of these items would be particularly useful in abducting a nineteen-year-old girl.

'So you make sandcastles, huh?'

I suddenly remembered that sarcasm doesn't always translate to people who aren't British. The same was true with metaphorical idioms. I was reminded of this last week, when Naomi had said 'an elephant in the room' on Facetime and the kids I am au pairing for started screaming hysterically. They thought that a real-life elephant had escaped from Barcelona Zoo into the apartment. Trying to calm them down had involved a family size packet of Haribo Starmix and allowing the boy to go to the park wearing a pink tutu.

'Sandcastle?' queried Pablo. 'What is sandcastle?'

I told him not to worry as we began driving off. Trying to explain the purpose of sandcastles to a man who spoke French in a Spanish accent, Spanish in a French accent and English in both would be like explaining the concept of a Rubik's Cube to a blind person.

'Ah,' he said, raising his eyebrows. 'Castillo de erena! My niece. Mon petite sobrina. She like them very much.'

I didn't know if his niece was called Sobrina, or if sobrina was Spanish for the word niece. This was all a terrible idea. I wanted to go home.

We had only just left the station. It wasn't too late to ask

Pablo to turn around. I thought about it for a second, but then there was the small issue of communicating it. Just then, 'Like A Prayer' by Madonna began playing. Maybe Pablo and I could bond over music instead.

'I love this song,' I squealed enthusiastically. 'Mind if I turn it up?' Pablo looked confused and began winding up the window.

'No, no, not the window,' I said. 'Window, down. Music, up!'

'Ah, ruidiso,' he said, adjusting the volume control. Seemingly this language barrier wasn't frustrating him to the same extent as me.

'Music,' he said. 'You like this?'

I nodded. 'The old stuff, mainly. From the eighties era. Queen. Elton John. Madonna. All the greats.'

'Madonna es muy bien. And Queen – très bien! Me encanta la musica,' he said. 'Tu es... Ginger Spice.' He stuck his tongue out and winked at me, pulling on a strand of my hair. He was decidedly impressed with himself at the comparison he had just made. I noticed then that his tongue was pierced. He had definitely not included this detail in any of his Tinder pictures. 'Which is your favourite Spice Girl?'

I asked the question in some tragic attempt to make a connection with Pablo, but his confusion persisted. Perhaps I would have to communicate through song. I broke into 'Wannabe', accompanied with some sort of interpretive jig at the same time. We stopped, waiting for a green light. I caught the eye of an old Spanish lady driving in the car next to us, who gave me a disconcerting glare and drove off.

'Me gusta Baby Spice. Emma Bunton,' said Pablo, over-emphasising the last two syllables of her surname so that it sounded more like 'button.' 'She is très... how you say... sexe.'

I was starting to wonder if Ashton Kutcher would spring up out of nowhere to tell me I had been Punk'd.

'Tu es hunger?'

'I ate several hours ago,' I said. 'But I could eat again.'

Eating would mean less time spent talking.

'In Spain, I eat. Many times. France the same. I know good place. Very good paella. C'est delicieux.'

I stared out the window and looked over at the Spanish coast. Every day of the summer had been beautiful, but today was exceptionally so. Even though the heat was slightly oppressive for a Brit, the breeze was cool, the skies were cloudless and the sea was iridescent. The fact I was with a man I had just met on Tinder who I could barely converse with, as opposed to the love of my life, was slightly gutting. I would have to suck it up. Just two hours, I told myself. I would eat lunch, then make an excuse to leave. Say that the family I was working for needed me urgently, and I had to go. He wouldn't be able to argue with that.

* * *

Twenty minutes later, we had arrived at a restaurant by the beach and were halfway through a bottle of wine. Pablo had ordered calamari, sardines and paella as well. I wondered if he might add a croissant and snails to the mix too, given that was the route we were going down. It was starting to get overwhelmingly confusing.

'Spain,' he said, topping up my wine. 'Aimes-tu? You like?'

'You mean, do I like Spain?'

'Oui. Correcte. Do. You. Like. Spain?'

'I love Spain,' I said, taking several large gulps of wine. 'Te amo.'

Pablo frowned. I quickly realised I had just said that I

love him in Spanish, as opposed to saying that I loved the country.

'Ignore that,' I said, topping my wine up again. 'I meant that I love Spain. I was working at a summer camp in Madrid and arrived here two weeks ago. I am working as an au pair for a family in Tarragona.'

Knowing whether or not he had understood a single word of that was a complete gamble.

'Oui. You like?'

'Sure,' I shrugged. 'I mean, I think I underestimated how hard it was going to be. Helping a mother with a new born baby and dealing with two five-year-olds is hard. Sometimes, I feel the person who really needs looking after is me.'

'Baby?' he asked, innocently. 'Baby Spice?'

I sighed, drinking more wine, feeling the cool, crisp alcohol pour down my throat and soothe my frustration.

'Not Baby Spice. A baby. A new born baby. The mother, I am working for, has a baby. Look, Pablo, I'm not sure if–'

'Ah,' he smiled. 'Je comprends. Un bebe. Muy dificil.'

'That's right,' I said. 'And tiring.'

I closed my eyes, pretending to snore. He paused for a moment, looking at me.

'You are very beautiful,' he smiled. 'Muy belle. Un fleur inglesa.'

I smiled, thinking of a way to pay him a compliment back. 'You are… in excellent shape! Do you, exercise?' I moved my elbows, attempting to mimic someone going on a run.

'Si. J'aime la gym. Running, every day, en la playa. Sunrise,' he smiled, gesturing to the sky.

'You run when the sun comes up!' I beamed. 'How lovely. Tougher on your legs, I imagine. You know – running on sand, and all that.'

'Yes,' he said, standing up to flex his calf muscles. 'Résistance!'

I couldn't believe we were finally making conversational progress. Maybe this date did have potential after all.

'Next week, we run?' asked Pablo. 'Then we make love in my car?'

Ok. Maybe not.

We were saved by a giant pan of paella which had just arrived at the table. The waiter served me a generous helping of fish and rice, topping me up with more wine. I drank it immediately, noticing he had a name badge which said Pierre. I was sure this was a French name. What on earth was going on?

'Mas vino por favor,' said Pablo to the waiter. 'Merci.'

The waiter smiled and nodded, not seeming remotely phased that Pablo had just thanked him in French. I remember someone once told me that only the French understand the French. I think what they had meant to say is that only the Europeans understand the Europeans, with the exception of the English.

'I won't drink anymore, Pablo. I'm a terrible lightweight. You know, une petite femme. Little old me!'

I rested my palm against my forehead in despair. This was, quite possibly, the worst thing I could have done. The waiter looked alarmed.

'Caliente?' He reached for the napkin and started to fan me down. 'Estas caliente?'

'No!' I said, urging him to stop. 'God, no! I'm not hot, I'm fine! I was referring to the wine!'

I pointed furiously to the glass, shaking my head at the same time, but it was futile. I just looked like I was doing the jive.

Pablo leaned his arm across the table to check my temperature. I tried to stop him, but it only served to fuel the confusion. A look of concern spread across his face as he touched my forehead.

'Oh merde. Tu es muy caliente, cariño.'

He began caressing my cheek with deep loving concern, like a devoted husband watching his wife wilt away on her death bed.

'You have fever. Ice, por favor!' Pablo shouted over to Pierre, who was taking the order of a couple that had walked in shortly after us. 'Cariño need ice!'

'Si, si, señor!' Pierre shuffled inside to the kitchen like an alarmed penguin.

'I'm fine, Pablo. I don't need ice, I just feel a bit tipsy. You know, dizzy.'

I spun my head in circular motions, which was a grave error. From Pablo's perspective, it probably looked like I was having a seizure.

'My god! El hospital! I drive!'

He stood up urgently and reached for his keys in the pocket of his shorts.

'No, Pablo! It's not necessary for a hospital, really, I just-'

'Madam!' shrieked Pierre. He was running over to our table, carrying an unnecessarily large bucket of ice over his head. 'Ice! I bring ice!'

He had brought another waiter with him, who was carrying a green first aid kit and a large stack of white towels. He had a thick, dark moustache and was incredibly podgy. They looked as if they were about to pin me down on the table and resuscitate me, right next to the paella. There was no time to waste. I had get out of here. Now.

I grabbed my bag hurriedly, preparing to leave the restaurant as quickly as I could. Pablo tried to stop me but I shoved him out of the way. I walked straight into Pierre, who lost balance and dropped the ice bucket all over the floor. I tried to push through, elbowing the podgy waiter out of the way, but it was hopeless. I slid on the ice, face planted the floor and lost consciousness.

Chapter 2 – Max

Six months later
University of Leeds, 2015

I placed the cake proudly onto the table and removed the foil.

I stood there for a moment, looking at it. A triple tier vegan carrot cake, with cream cheese frosting sandwiched between each layer. There are vegan versions for everything nowadays, but it had taken me a while to find a recipe for cream cheese frosting. I had to use coconut cream from an overpriced health store and soak up raw cashew nuts. The process had been costly, fiddly and meticulous, but it didn't matter. Doing nice things for Max never felt like a chore. Besides, I was pleased with how the cake had turned out. It had taken me almost four hours.

'You shouldn't have gone to all this trouble, Verity.'

I grinned. Max's tone was modest, but I knew he was secretly delighted.

'I know it was last week, but I'm still going to sing you Happy Birthday. Don't hate me for it.' I retrieved the number '2' candle that had sunk into the icing and propped it back up next to the '0', sparking my lighter. I'd had to awkwardly ask the sales assistant to go to the stock room and hunt around for a number '0' candle. It had taken me so long to find it, that at one point I thought it might be better to just pretend Max was still nineteen. We had partially agreed to write this year off anyway, given that his grades had been spectacularly atrocious and he was considering dropping out of uni. The feedback on Max's assignments was always the same. According to his tutor, Max writes too much like he speaks: colloquial, superfluous and American. He references arrogantly (barely ever), incorrectly (never adhering to the guidelines) and assumes his ideas are ground-breaking rather than a 'waffling regurgitation' of existing ones.

'Please don't sing, Verity,' he cringed. 'Birthdays are excruciating enough. Add a song to commemorate the day and it's pure torture.'

'But there's no audience,' I giggled. 'It's just me singing.'

'Exactly. That's worse.'

Ignoring him, I lit both candles and walked over to the kitchen wall to dim the lights. Max winced his eyes the entire time I sung, like someone afraid of needles being forced to have an injection. It made me laugh.

'Quick, make a wish!'

He blew out the candles in one go and stared at the cake without a word.

'What did you wish for?'

'If I tell you then it won't come true.'

He took a giant spoonful of the cake and shoved it inelegantly into his mouth, still managing to look gorgeous. I wondered how I had gone an entire summer of working with him in Madrid without noticing it.

Max wasn't exactly what you'd call classically good looking. His nose was big and ever so slightly crooked. His two front teeth sat a little too far apart, and there was the odd scar on his skin from his teenage years of acne. Still, his imperfections, combined with his dark hair and height somehow meshed together to form an unassumingly attractive guy. At least I thought so.

Since we had started our final year together, the two of

us were inseparable. We did everything together; cooked, snuggled, watched films, brushed our teeth, shared a bed and told secrets. My favourite thing of all that Max and I did was to wait for each other after lectures like parents picking up their kids from school, greeting one another with that same excitability and love.

We'd go raving, just the two of us, dance together until five in the morning and go and lie in a deserted park, watching morning devour the night. It never crossed my mind that it was unsafe. With Max, I felt everything but.

Last week was the first time we had shared a bed, falling asleep together after watching some indie Spanish film about a Syrian refugee. Max had said it would be useful to both our theses, but it was utterly pointless. In the morning, I had woken up to find his arms wrapped tightly around me. His embrace had felt so safe, so right. It was, in my eyes, a friendship that was blossoming into something more, which is how all the best kinds of relationships start.

'How does the cake taste, Maxy?'

'Delicious,' he smiled, wiping frosting from his mouth. 'You didn't need to do all this, really...'

'I'm just happy you like it,' I squealed, wrapping my arms around his neck. He sat there, still in my clasp.

'I was so worried the mini carrots wouldn't come in time, you know. Thank god they did.' This part had taken even longer than the icing. I had found the carrot decorations on Etsy, and placed them all neatly round the rim of the cake, ensuring an equal 3 mm distance between each one. I had even used a tape measure to check. Max's brain worked in symmetry. Noticing an uneven distance between each carrot was pedantic, but he wouldn't have missed it. He stood up to give me a hug.

'You truly are the best friend ever. Which reminds me actually – there was something I wanted to talk to you about.'

14

My heart jumped. This was it. The moment of truth. He was going to tell me he loved me.

'Hold that thought, please.'

I rushed upstairs to my bathroom. If Max was going to confess his feelings to me – which he was, I was absolutely sure of it – then I needed to look the part. I had made an effort this evening; worn my trusty sexy top on purpose, exposing the perfect amount of cleavage, with my favourite pair of jeans that made my bum look good. It was Max who had told me that. He came with me to buy them, waiting patiently on the chair outside the fitting rooms to review all of my outfit choices.

'He's a nice boyfriend, isn't he?' said the sales assistant. 'I wish mine was as enthusiastic as yours.'

I didn't correct her by saying that Max and I were just friends. If all went to plan this evening, I wouldn't need to correct anyone ever again.

I slung back some mouthwash and gurgled it in the back in my throat, just in case we ended up kissing. We had done it once already, drunkenly in a nightclub last weekend. Max didn't mention anything of it the next day, and I had been too nervous to attempt it again since. I reapplied deodorant furiously under my armpits and misted myself with more perfume, brushing the ends of my hair. I had even shaved. You know. Just in case.

Max's head was buried in his hands when I arrived back to the kitchen. They were trembling. I could tell he was nervous.

'What is it, Max?' I pulled up a chair to sit next to him, pushing the carrot cake aside. The candle '2' had plopped back down into the icing, but I didn't bother to retrieve it this time. 'Whatever it is, you can tell me.'

He paused. 'I've never met anyone like you, Vee. You make me feel like I can be anyone.'

'I feel the same.'

'I love how close we've become since Madrid. I feel like I can tell you anything; now more than ever.'

He was choking up as he said it. This was all unfolding like a beautiful firework display. Max had never opened up to me like this before. In fact, no guy had. This display of vulnerability was what I had always wanted – and now I was about to have it all, with my best friend.

'That's exactly how I always want you to feel, Max.'

He hesitated, looking up at me. His eyes were puffy and red, his nose swollen. He had been crying whilst I was in the bathroom. This was obviously a hard thing for him to admit. 'Verity, I think – – wait, what am I saying? I don't think, I know, that-'

'I love you too, Max.'

Neither of us said anything for a second.

'Phew,' I laughed, sighing with relief. 'It feels good to finally say it out loud. I've known for ages, but I think it was last week during that shitty film that really cemented it, you know? I watched you for a bit when you were still asleep, and thought, wow, how wonderful it is that we've found each other, and how crazy that we've been friends for so long and missed it the entire time. It was there all along, right under the tips of our noses! Yes, I know that's the premise of a cheesy cliché, and you hate cheesy clichés, but look at us, Maxy! We've fulfilled it.'

Max turned away and stared down at the floor, avoiding eye contact. Typical, I thought. He's never been good at talking about his feelings. I think it has something to do with the fact he was bullied in primary school. I grabbed his face and leaned into him, closing my eyes, preparing for a movie like kiss. I felt the weight of his hands against my shoulders as he edged me back.

'Verity…'

'What is it?' I said, opening my eyes. 'Do I have something in my teeth?' 'No, it's just that…'
'What?'
'I'm gay, Verity.'

Chapter 3 – Joe

One year later
Perth, Western Australia

Visiting Naomi in Australia was the biggest adventure I had embarked on since leaving Pipford Hall.

Pipford was a strange place. A quintessentially English boarding school in the middle of nowhere, with a refusal to shackle it's hundred-year values on women's education in the name of 'moving with the times.' From punishment skirts for girls who stood on the grass to lamb hotpot smothered in semi-dissolved gravy granules and dishwater; it upheld a set of traditions which hadn't changed since the school was founded after the Second World War. When I chose to go to Leeds over Oxbridge, it was almost as scandalous as when Britney and Madonna had French kissed at the 2003 VMAs.

'Are you sure you want to venture up north, Verity?' asked Miss Fielding, my English teacher.

'People are different up there, you know. Not like us.'

'That's exactly why I want to go, Miss.'

'I'm just not sure it's the right place for you,' she sighed. 'I've had a look at their English course, and I wasn't very impressed. The lives of the Brontës are missed out entirely, and they fail to include *Jane Eyre* in their module on Literary Heroines…'

'Leeds is far away, Miss,' I said, cutting her off. 'It's less about the course and more about me having a fresh start.'

She looked offended. It was as if I had just told her that the hideous shade of green she wore in every item of clothing was neither flattering nor her colour, and made her look rather like a stuffed vine leaf.

'A fresh start from what, exactly?' She let out a long, exasperated sigh. 'You're my brightest pupil, Verity. I'm fond of you, and have strong hopes for your future. You'd be better off choosing somewhere that will attract people of your kind. Academics who can nurture your abilities, and pupils from other schools, just like you.'

I caught a glimpse of her beige socks and tried to contain my laughter. She was now in fact a vine leaf stuffed with grains of brown rice.

'What about UCL?'

'No.'

'Bristol? They have a whole module on the literary greats of the 1920s. You like that!'

'No, Miss.'

'Exeter? Holly reads English there.'

Holly was last year's Head Girl, whose great grandmother was the founder of Pipford. I remembered photos I'd seen of her on Facebook last year at Freshers' Week. She was huddled together with a group of middle-class girls in Ralph Lauren polo shirts of varying pastel colours. Each bore a frightening resemblance to the other with their aristocratic features; broad shoulders, straight noses and large horse-like teeth. Holly always pushed to the front of the pudding queue whenever it was spotted dick and custard. I shuddered at the thought of her.

'Definitely not Exeter, Miss.'

Miss Fielding puffed her flushed cheeks out and rolled her eyes. I edged back in my chair, sensing a stuffed vine leaf explosion was about to erupt. Grains of rice would scatter all over her office like hail.

'I just think you need somewhere better equipped at preparing a woman for the real world than Leeds.'

She had started as a pupil at the school and continued as a teacher for thirty-five years. I wasn't sure she knew what the 'real world' was.

'The universities you listed are breeding grounds for Oxbridge rejects, Miss. The thought of spending three years at one of them with pupils from boarding schools whose families do pheasant shooting every Boxing Day makes me want to cry.'

'Once again, you're being melodramatic. This is all very typical of you.'

'I'm serious, Miss. When those students graduate, they don't get real jobs. They trade in Barbour jackets for harem pants and go soul searching in Thailand. Surely that's not the future you want for me?'

She raised her eyebrows. I think I had left her speechless.

'Let's just hope that the English admissions department at Leeds favours sarcastic pupils with overly vivid imaginations, Verity.'

I arrived at Leeds thinking everyone would love me. I thought I would find my soulmates, my peers, my people. I would be the quirky girl from boarding school who everyone is thrilled to discover is normal, funny and 'just like them.' I couldn't have been more wrong.

I wanted to make friends – to learn, share and explore ideas – to release the shackles of my boarding school bubble and rebuild myself anew. Unfortunately, everything I thought would make me likeable just made me irritating. People in my halls were from humble, working-class northern backgrounds. They were politically active, advocated for the Labour Party and campaigned against austerity. I tried to get on board with their ideas, but I was disliked instantly. I vividly remember one girl named Mel. She told me that I tried too hard to hide my privilege, and that I would be more likeable if I just admitted that I was pro-Brexit rather than lied about it. She said I only sucked the dick of 'pompous, privileged Etonian knobs' who wore boat shoes and chinos. I cried for hours in my room. My background seemed to determine who I was before I had even figured that out for myself.

My friendship with Max was my saving grace, and without him, I would probably have dropped out. It didn't take me long to realise that Max was like home. He fills people up with a warm high and a sense of trust, even if they've only spoken to him for five minutes. It is a drug I call MDMA; the Max Dunn-Morgan Affect. I don't know how he does it, but he does, without thinking. Everyone always felt better having spent five minutes with him, including me – the boarding school brat that everyone hated.

'Don't worry, Verity,' he said, resting his hand on my shoulder. 'You can be my friend.'

Max was from Dubai, and had selected Leeds for the exact same reasons as I had. He too was trying to break out of some sort of bubble, and experience the big wide world for himself. Together, we became each other's three-year survival kit.

Of course, there had been 'Dazzling Derek' in final year. That was the nickname Max and I had given him, for his heartthrob boyband looks and short starring role in my life. He was heartbreakingly gorgeous. Tall, with sandy hair, deep brown eyes and a unique sense of style. Derek was from an elite group of third year guys who studied economics and brought their clothes from charity shops. I thought it was a joke when he had walked over to me in the library. He said he was nervous to ask, but would I go for a drink with him. I played it cool on purpose but couldn't keep it up for long. I succumbed to a drink with him and got sucked into a whirlwind.

'I can't wait to have sex with you,' he'd said to me on our third date. 'Just you wait. It's going to be amazing.'

Derek was, since birth, an overachiever. It was as if doing well at life and looking good whilst doing it was written in his DNA. Sex, therefore, would be something he wouldn't even need to try at – he'd be naturally extraordinary, just like he was at everything else, because he was Dazzling Derek. He thought sex would be as easy as learning the piano, getting an A* in his Mandarin exam and passing his driving test without a single minor. He would dive straight in, as if the mere touch of his penis was enough to make a woman orgasm.

The reality was that Derek and I could never find our flow. I could never get aroused because Derek went limp, and Derek went limp because I could never get aroused. Neither of us knew whose fault it was, so we played the blame game.

'I don't get it,' he laughed nervously, panting on top of me. 'Are you sure you don't have some sort of problem?'

'Why am I the one with the problem? You're the one that keeps losing your boner.'

He'd sigh, giving up. 'I've got a lot going on at the moment. It's the pressure from my parents, the stress of my dissertation...'

I usually spent the rest of the evening helping Derek with his 'chest pains,' which he later discovered were panic attacks. He was drinking Red Bull for breakfast, lunch and dinner for an extra burst of energy, which was wreaking havoc with his nervous system. I tried to help him wean off the drinks, but it just made everything worse. Having a girlfriend was distracting, Derek said, and he had to focus on finding a summer internship in a bank. We broke up a week later.

Max supported the Australia trip wholeheartedly after I called him and his boyfriend, Tom, that evening. I informed them that I had booked a one-way ticket and would be leaving next week.

'You should get a working visa and do a year out there.'

'But there's this job, Max. You know, the one at Stanley Solutions. I promised my parents I'd be back in time to start it next month.'

'The one with the hot interviewer?' chipped in Tom.

'Not hot, Tom. Arrogant. With an ego that inflates to the size of a giant parachute whenever he speaks.'

'Forget the job, Verity,' said Max, with his soothing, gentle wisdom. 'This is about your future! Play it by ear and see what happens. Naomi can help you figure everything out along the way.' I had somehow convinced my dad to get on board with the idea and give me a lift to the airport, on the condition that I was back in time to start the new job. (Which, of course, I wouldn't be, but he felt it necessary since my mother was best friends with the wife of the CEO.)

'Are you sure you've got everything?' he asked, going through his 'fool proof' travel checklist.

'Passport? Phone? Earplugs?'

'Yes,' I sighed, rolling my eyes like an embarrassed teenager. 'As if I'd forget those things.'

'Well, last time you ended up in a hospital with a brain concussion, so I have to be sure,' he smiled. 'Remember this is a holiday, not a lifelong trip. You promised your mother and I that you'd be back in time to start at Stanley's next month. I sincerely hope you meant that.'

'I did,' I lied. 'Just trust me, Dad. This is the last hurrah before I venture out into the big wide world of adulthood.'

He laughed, pulling me in close to his chest. 'I love you, sweetheart.'

'Love you too, Dad.'

* * *

I spent the entire plane journey lusting over my new life in Australia. I watched it like a film, starring the new Verity as the leading actress. I imagined the people she'd meet, the places she'd go; the bars she'd walk into, the clothes she'd wear, the tattoo she'd get. The love she'd find.

Twenty-one hours later, I was jetlagged and confused in a foreign airport, but happily enclosed in the familiar embrace of my best friend.

'It's so good to see you,' said Naomi, squeezing me. 'I've missed you so much.'

I breathed her in, realising she hadn't changed her perfume since we were fifteen.

'Let's go. I've got PG tips at my place.'

My eyes filled with tears. Even after all these years, she hadn't changed a bit. The most Taurusey of Tauruses. Loyal, devoted, and the sister I never had who knew me inside and out. 'No crying Vee! We're going to have the best time ever.'

Five days in, and we already were. I was resolute that I wasn't leaving Australia. In fact, I had drafted an email on my phone to send to Stanley's, informing them that I would be nourishing my soul with travel and experience as opposed to selling it to the depressing reality of the corporate world. Worded in more professional terms, of course.

Perth was everything I dreamt it would be and more. A large, suburban city on the west coast of Australia that infused beautiful open parks with skyscraper buildings and sandy beaches. Everything was fresh. The food, the people, the air. It was a warm, colourful, cosmopolitan paradise, where everyone says 'hey' at the end of every sentence and eats avocado on toast with pomegranate seeds on top. After a few long days of sunbathing, eating, and going out to bars with Naomi, I was convinced that I had found my spiritual home.

'I love it here,' I said, taking an enthusiastic bite of a 'cronut' at a nearby café outside Naomi's flat. 'I mean, a croissant and a donut in one? It's genius. Everything here is better than I imagined. Everyone is so...'

'Happy?'

'Yes! Happy. Everything and everyone just glows.'

'It's awesome, hey,' she smiled. Naomi had lived out here for two years on a partnership visa with her boyfriend, Ryan, who reminded me of a real-life cast member from *Neighbours*. He was an indigenous Aussie, who used expressions like 'barbie' for barbeque and 'doll' for babe. 'I'm staying out here forever,' laughed Naomi. 'As far away from my parents as I can possibly get.'

'What if it doesn't work out with Ryan?'

'Then I'll get a new boyfriend. Easy.'

I edged forward to her. 'What do I need to do to stay? I'm worried I'm gonna run out of money.'

'Can't you ask your dad?'

'Not this time. I'm serious about making it my own way.'

She paused. 'Staying here is really what you wanna do?'

'Come on, Naomi. People from where we're from don't end up in places like this. Look at how far you've come,' I continued. 'I mean, you totally wasted your education, but now you're halfway round the world with a place that serves croissants and donuts as one single pastry item on your doorstep.'

She laughed. 'I just know you have that grad job lined up, that's all.'

'A job I got because my mum is best friends with the wife of the CEO,' I sighed. 'I want to explore opportunities out here, with you. Imagine us living together again, somewhere other than boarding school. It'd be like Monica and Rachel in *Friends*.'

'It would be pretty cool,' she grinned. 'If you want, I can arrange for you to chat to Joe.'

'Who's Joe?'

'Ryan's friend. I call him the guru of Australia! He knows everything about this kind of stuff – visas, doing the move, the lot. He got his permanent residency last year.'

'Perfect!'

'I'll text Ryan now and arrange for us all to go to The Lucky Shag later this week.'

She saw me frown. 'A pub, Vee, not an orgy. Joe might be able to give you some advice on jobs and stuff.'

I smiled to myself. This was it – the magical, life changing transformative stuff. The glimmer of good things to come.

Hope.

* * *

'Crystals changed my life, and I've started fermenting vegetables.'

This was the first thing Joe said to me after I asked him to tell me something interesting about himself. He smiled as he spoke, watching me stare at the amethyst hanging on a piece of black string against his chest, which had definitely been waxed. I was sure of it.

Joe liked the interest I was taking in his necklace, as well as watching my brain attempt to decipher the link between rose quartz and fermented cucumbers. He was wearing flip flops, shorts and a white vest, which clung tightly to his small but muscular frame. An array of crystal bracelets and bands were loosely arranged on his forearm in sage, blue and pink. He looked as if he were about to host a yoga retreat and start handing out wheatgrass shots.

'I'm spiritual, you see.'

He elongated his sentences when he spoke, which was a deliberate attempt at masking his East-Anglian roots with a wannabe Aussie accent. I looked at him, wondering if he were a sort of crystal cult leader.

'I move through each day as if I'm travelling through honey, meandering through the lake of life in a seamless state of ease.'

'How did you become so enlightened?'

He shrugged. 'Books. Yoga retreats. Crystals. I cleanse them every day in saltwater to eliminate toxic energy and channel good vibes only.'

He held out his arm, revealing a small tattoo of the phrase etched on the back of his wrist in italic ink.

I stared at it carefully. 'Did you study the Romantics, by any chance?'

'No. Why?'

'You just quoted Wordsworth, that's all. Was wondering if you knew his work.' He didn't invite me to explain further, but I went ahead anyway.

'Wordsworth saw nature as God. He used to go and sit in forests and fields and lakes and see something of the spiritual in his landscape. Guess it boils down to nature being this unfixed, constant thing, and finding a sort of peace within that. As hectic as our lives get, trees will never stop being trees.'

Joe looked at me for a second, as if to check whether I was being serious, before throwing his head back and exploding into a fit of laughter.

'Where did you get this girl from, Naomi? Sounds as if she's walked straight out of an Austen novel.'

'Sorry,' I blushed, looking at the floor. 'I know I'm a geek.'

'You're fucking funny. Do you dye your hair?'

'No.'

'So it's naturally that colour?'

'Yep.'

He fiddled with a strand of it, pulling slightly. 'It looks like a caramelised chestnut.'

'Shut up Joe,' said Naomi, hitting his arm. 'You're freaking her out. I invited you along because Verity wants to explore the option of moving here. I thought you could give her some advice about jobs and stuff.'

Joe cast his eyes back over me. 'Jobs and stuff, huh? What sort of thing were you looking to do? Waitressing, like Naomi?'

'Actually, I was hoping to explore the publishing world.'

'The publishing world?' Joe smirked.

'I think it'd be perfect for me,' I said, with as much conviction as one could without really knowing what the publishing world entailed. I hadn't researched it properly, but I had an English degree, and I liked the idea of it. 'I'm open, of course. Journalism would also be great, or perhaps writing for a local newspaper. Australia's equivalent of the *Times*!'

He didn't say anything, which intensified my nerves. I began to overexplain.

'I have a copy of my CV at Naomi's place. It details all of my experience. Come to think of it, I should have just brought it along with me tonight.'

Joe was looking at me as if to say, who the fuck brings their CV to a double date? I looked to the floor, wondering the same thing. He broke into another fit of laughter. A deep, belly laugh this time.

'Jesus. You're fucking priceless.'

I felt like a comedian, who hadn't said anything funny other than present themselves on stage. I sensed Joe taking pity on me as the bar's evening entertainment, which was both unfunny and disappointing.

'It doesn't really work like that here, Verity,' chipped in Naomi. 'You can't just rock up to Australia and be a journalist. If you want to gain residency, then you need to find a job on the occupational skills list. Otherwise, you have to do farm work for a year.'

'Farm work?' I gasped. 'You mean, like, milk cows and stuff?'

'Don't stress, Vee,' laughed Ryan. 'It's fun. You meet people.'

'It's the only way to stay out here permanently,' said Joe. 'That, or a partnership visa, like Naomi's doing.' He paused for a second, looking at me, then at his watch. 'I should get going. I'm late for hot yoga.'

I giggled, remembering the time Max and I had tried it. We'd lasted two rounds of 'cat' and 'cow' positions, which had resulted in him mimicking Miley Cyrus twerking at the 2013 VMAs. I missed him suddenly, playing back the memory of his distinctive cackle.

'What's funny?'

'Nothing,' I blushed. 'I'm just terrible at yoga. I tried it once but couldn't take it seriously.' Joe's eyebrows frowned. He looked offended.

'Sorry,' I said, quickly. 'That was an ignorant comment.'

'Listen,' he said, cutting me off. 'Why don't we do brunch tomorrow and discuss the Australia residency thing some more? I can talk you through the process properly.'

'Brunch?' I asked, gobsmacked that he wanted to see me again. 'Sure, if you want.'

'Not if I want. I'm here to help you.'

Naomi and Ryan went silent, staring at the floor. I suddenly felt like their embarrassing child who they couldn't take anywhere in case they said something wildly inappropriate. Maybe they were thinking about getting me a special t-shirt to warn people of my socially awkward behaviour when we went out in public.

'I'll swing by your place tomorrow around noon.'

Joe lingered at the bar door for a brief moment, holding it ajar.

'Oh, and Verity?'

'Yes?'

'Make sure you bring your CV.'

* * *

When we got back later that evening, Naomi broke into a series of questions on the topic of Joe. She was querying me like a persistent news reporter, even though she had been at the bar the entire time. It was typical of her to interrogate me like this. She always became hyperactive and excitable whenever someone new with a penis entered the scene, even if it was just a semi-attractive DPD driver dropping off an ASOS parcel at the front door.

'Do you fancy him?' she asked, her mouth full with a toothbrush.

'No,' I snapped, pushing her shoulder, reaching for a makeup wipe. 'Of course not.'

'I think you do,' she jested.

'I do not, Naomi. Really, I hadn't thought about him like that.'

'I think he's sexy.'

I paused. 'Do you?'

'Yeah,' she said, spitting out toothpaste into the sink. 'He looks like a young Kurt Cobain.'

'Does he?'

'You can't deny that he's got a lil' summin summin,' she said, wiping her mouth with a towel. 'A mystical je ne sais quoi.'

A mystical je ne sais quoi. The comment stuck with me, as I snuggled into bed next to her that night. Despite my best efforts, I lay there, awake, unable to stop myself thinking about what brunch with Joe would be like.

* * *

'Where is he?'

I looked out of Naomi's window and restlessly tapped my fingers against the ledge. I hadn't slept well, and had been waiting for Joe to pick me up for twenty-five minutes. He had messaged Naomi earlier this morning asking for my number, which meant that I absolutely could not text him. Naomi assured me it was better this way round.

'Is it a date, Vee?'

'I don't know,' I said, walking over to fix my hair in the mirror again. 'Is it?'

'Not sure. That CV comment was weird, though, wasn't it?' she lay on the sofa, with a towel around her head. 'Wonder what he meant by that.'

'Well, he's just being professional, isn't he?' I said. 'He obviously takes me seriously as a woman, which is nice. Joe is clearly very mature.'

Naomi paused, looking at my reflection. 'What would you rate him out of ten?'

'Shut up, Naomi,' I snapped, feeling my cheeks burn. 'You asked me that last night. I told you that I can't rate someone I don't know.'

'You don't know Jake Gyllenhaal and you rated him ten out of ten.'

'Yes, well, celebrities don't count. What's with all these questions?'

She paused for a moment. 'I just want you to be careful, that's all. Joe is kind of... odd.'

'You were the one who recommended that I meet him! You said he could help me! Last night, you were encouraging me to-'

'I know, I know. He's just so deep into his crystals and stuff. He did a spiritual fast last year and didn't eat for four days.'

'Naomi, please. I'm going for coffee, not joining a cult.'

'I really love you. You know that, don't you?'

'Jesus, stop! I'm not going to get hurt. I'm going to get help. So we can do this Australia thing together, properly.'

We were interrupted by someone beeping their car horn loudly. We both looked at each other, startled, telepathically knowing it was Joe. Naomi rushed over in her dressing gown, peeping through her shutters.

'Fuck! It's him. Quick,' she threw me my sandals, acting as if we were thieves raiding a house and the home owners had just parked up outside.

'Ok,' I said, rummaging through my suitcase for my purse.

I unzipped it, staring at the polaroid photo of Max and I at a gig last year. I always carried it with me. It made me feel safe.

I felt guilty. I had hardly touched base with him since I'd arrived in Australia. We were overdue a catch up.

'Hurry up, Vee!'

I quickly misted on some perfume, grabbed my bag and hurried out the door.

'See you later. Love you.'

* * *

Joe was sitting in his car at the front of Naomi's apartment complex. His eyes were closed, even when I tapped the window.

'Sorry babe,' he yawned, opening them. 'I was meditating.'

'Meditating?'

'One hundred days of daily gratitude, innit.'

He scratched his head – his lateness unmentioned. 'Shit,' he said, looking down at his watch. 'I'm late, aren't I?'

'Yes, but it doesn't matter.'

It had mattered, of course. I had waited for him for

nearly half an hour. I paused, giving him an opportunity to apologise.

'I must've got distracted by the beauty of life, babe.'

I opened the door and sat myself comfortably in the front seat, deciding he was suitably excused as he had just said a line that sounded as if it were from a Shakespearian sonnet. I caught a waft of his smell, which was a pleasant concoction of sage, sweat and fresh laundry. His face brushed close to mine.

'You look nice.'

'Thanks,' I twitched, tucking my hair behind my ears. 'I brought my CV, by the way. It's in my bag – in a clear plastic wallet.'

A clear plastic wallet? Oh, god. The only thing worse than announcing you wish you'd brought your CV with you during a double date is actually bringing it with you to the second one.

'You did?'

'You told me to.'

His eyes glinted. 'What about if I told you to eat an entire cake in one sitting? Would you do that?'

'What…?'

'Or jump out of a plane, backwards, blindfolded…'

Joe watched me squirm. I could tell he was delighting in my discomfort. My heart started to beat fast.

'I'm joking, Verity. I don't need your fucking CV. I just wanted to see if you would actually bring it.'

'But why?'

'Dunno.' He shrugged. 'Funny, I guess.'

I looked away from Joe and out the window, staring at the sky. Australia suddenly felt vast, oppressive and humiliating. I wanted to run back home. Not inside to Naomi, but to my family home. Back to feeling loved and safe and understood.

'You're not crying, are you?'

'No,' I sniffed. 'It's just… homesickness.' I felt even more pathetic, like a kid wishing for their mum on the first night of summer camp with the Girl Scouts. There was no way I could cry properly in front of Joe. I barely knew him, and he was supposed to be helping me.

'Homesick?' His tone was stern. 'I thought you wanted my help to stay here.'

'I do.' I swallowed, feeling my throat thicken. 'Let's get going, Joe.'

We spent the rest of the journey in an odd silence, zooming along the highway. I was sure Joe was speeding, but I didn't say anything. I wanted to ask him questions about his day, his morning, his job, but I didn't trust anything that came out my mouth to not be irritating or the wrong thing.

We parked up outside a health café in the centre of town, taking a seat outside. It was gorgeously sunny, like every other day in Australia.

Joe slouched himself on the chair, menu in hand. 'What do you fancy? Matcha latte? Coconut water? Acai bowl?'

'Acai is a berry, right?'

Joe nodded. 'Originates in Brazil, babe. A superfood – great for your immunity. I think you'd like it.'

'Sounds delicious.' I smiled, handing the menu back to him. He got up and wandered inside to order.

I opened my bag and reached for my phone, deciding to message Max on WhatsApp.

Verity: Missing you.

He typed back instantly.

Max: I miss you too. How is it out there?

I thought about telling him I was in the company of a guy who was making me feel inexplicably strange, but I didn't. He'd worry unnecessarily and message Naomi. Joe was my golden ticket to Australia, and only he could help me get the life I'd always longed for. He's helping you, I told myself. Don't fuck this up.

Verity: It's great. Currently sat at one of those health café's about to eat my first ever acai bowl!

Max: You basic bitch. You on a hot date?

Verity: With Naomi. Why are you awake?

Max: Was having sex. I think I love Tom, you know.

I paused, watching Max type again.

Max: He's gone out to buy more condoms but I'm gonna tell him when he gets back.

I briefly recalled Max's twentieth birthday, when it had been me who had confessed my love to him. That tender feeling of an innocent love came to the surface, just as clear as it was back then. Still, I was happy for him.

Max: You ok?

Verity: Course! Better go. Good luck with dropping the 'L' bomb!

Joe wandered back, carrying two bowls of what looked like purple soup with single pieces of banana floating on top. I had seen pictures of acai bowls on Instagram before, regularly spoken about by an influencer named @hally-bondibabe. According to her, acai bowls are 'insane' and 'life' and 'perfect workout fuel,' and if you get one, then you will magically transform into her. When Joe placed the bowl of purple liquid down in front of me, it looked more like art than food. You could dip your paintbrush into it and splatter it on a canvas. 'Here you go, doll. Your first ever acai bowl.'

He plunged his spoon in and put it straight into his mouth. I copied him, instantly overblown by what tasted like black forest gateaux ice cream.

'I love it!'

'I'm glad,' he smiled, stirring his bowl. 'One of these a day and you'll never get ill again in your life.'

I decided that @hallybondibabe was right. I liked acai a lot.

'Let's take a look at this CV of yours, shall we?'

'You really want to?'

'Might be useful. Have you waitressed before?'

'No,' I said, reaching for my bag. 'But there's heaps of detail on there about other stuff I've done. I was head of debating society at Leeds, for example.'

I realised this wasn't a particularly sexy achievement. I placed the CV on the table. Joe picked it up, glanced over it and quickly turned the page. I suddenly had a flashback of Inflated Ego Interview Guy at Stanley's, and shuddered, remembering that I was supposed to be starting there in two and a half weeks.

'Yep,' said Joe, handing it back to me. 'Congratulations. You're hired.'

'Come on,' I laughed. 'You barely read it!'

'I don't need to. I already know that you're smart and talented.'

'Right.' I looked down, swirling my spoon in the purple pool. 'Look at what an idiot I've made of myself in front of you already.'

'I think you're cute.'

'Do you?'

'Yes. I mean, even the way you speak, it's…'

I looked up, hopeful. 'It's what?'

He sighed, looking into my eyes. 'It's just different. I couldn't stop thinking about the way you spoke about that Romantic guy – the one who likes trees.'

'Wordsworth?'

'That was it. You sounded so clever. It was hot. You're not like other girls.'

He edged closer to me, reaching for my hand. I felt my heart plummet and bounce.

'You're pregnant with brilliance, you know. And you don't even know it.'

I never really know how to receive compliments. It's a British habit – one that we've all adopted, collectively. That being, you are not British unless compliments turn you into a shrivelled, spluttering wreck.

Just then the waitress appeared. She was annoyingly enthusiastic, asking us about our acai bowls and whether we wanted to try a complimentary slice of gluten free banana loaf. Joe engaged in polite small talk with her, all the while ceasing to move his hand from mine. He began to stroke it, carefully with his thumb, tracing each one of my fingers until the waitress eventually disappeared back inside to get the bill. It was discreet, what he was doing – an act so small, yet simultaneously so explosive. A series of firsts, steadily erupting one after the other. The first taste of a new food. The first touch of a hand, igniting that very first hint of intimacy.

'Do you want to go to the beach?'

I looked at him briefly, noticing his small, boyish features. His freckly face and curly blonde hair; hazel eyes that were more green than they were brown. His face was somehow more attractive now than when we'd arrived at the café, all because of the way he'd touched my hand.

I smiled at him, feeling hit by an unfamiliar wave of confidence.

'I'd love to.'

* * *

Joe and I held hands the entire car journey with the car roof down. Every time we stopped at a traffic light, he looked at me, smiled, and did the hand-stroking-finger thing again. I watched his fingers feed through the gaps of mine like a mosaic.

'Where did you get your necklace from?'

'A Buddhist meditation retreat I went to in India last year. It was a gift to me from a monk in a temple.'

Joe watched me stare at him with religious reverence. He delved into a lengthy monologue about each different kind of crystal and what its properties were, and then said something about gut bacteria, kimchi and sauerkraut. It wasn't so much what he was saying, but more, how he said it. I couldn't take my eyes off him.

'How did you get into travelling in the first place?'

I asked the question as if he were a self-made Richard-Branson-like magnate, who had rocketed to success from the humblest of beginnings. Of course, none of this was true about Joe. He was, as it turned out, an English backpacker from Norwich who had secured residency in Australia through working on a construction site. In my eyes, this only made Joe even more appealing. He was someone with strength of character, who had worked hard to leave his boring English hometown for adventure and excitement. He had carved the very path that I had arrived in Australia to walk on. Joe was someone to aspire to.

'I left Norwich with just a rucksack and guitar. Minimalist living. It's a Japanese concept.'

'Is it?'

He nodded. 'You evaluate everything you own and eliminate accordingly based on whether it brings you beauty or spiritual purpose.'

I didn't really understand what that meant. To me, this philosophy eliminated practical household items, like a hairdryer, for example. Or a hoover. Still, I was careful not to say anything out loud.

'I made history, you know,' he continued. 'Me leaving that town was the most exciting thing that happened there since an eighty-year-old lady found a nineteenth century coin in her back garden.'

* * *

Joe parked his car a short walk from the beach and opened the boot. He pulled out a blanket, guitar, a crate of beers and a fancy camera.

'Let's go,' he said, taking hold of my hand and swinging his guitar over his shoulder.

We began walking through Cottesloe. It was a quaint, pretty town that had a large park filled with giant fir trees. The whole place was charmingly random; a fusion of quirky shops, abundant greenery and vast, azure shores ahead. I was surprised at how empty the beach was when we arrived. We practically had the entire place to ourselves.

'This'll do,' said Joe, stopping at a small space near some rocks. He rolled out the blanket and sat down, taking off his vest to expose his slender frame. He had a tattoo of a woman on his shoulder, with red wavy hair and large eyes. He caught me looking.

He pulled out a packet of cigarettes and a lighter from the pocket of his shorts, taking a long drag and closing his eyes.

'Want one?'

'No thanks.'

He tapped the ash onto the sand. 'Have you tried smoking before?'

I shook my head, laughing. 'I didn't realise that Buddhist retreats and smoking cigarettes were mutually exclusive.'

'Smoking relaxes you, actually,' he said, unimpressed by my sarcasm. 'It mellows you out, and being mellow is good for the brain.'

'Really?'

'Try it,' he said, handing me his cigarette. 'Just inhale. Allow it to pass through your lungs and flow through you.'

I did as instructed like an unblinking adult robot doll.

I had only ever practiced with a white candy stick on the school playground. I took a long toke, trying to mimic the sexiness of Olivia Newton-John in the final scene of *Grease*. It failed epically. I coughed, handing it back to him. Smoking tasted exactly how I had always imagined it would taste: an explosion of burnt pepper kernels and car fumes.

'I feel dizzy. I think I need to lie down.'

Joe laughed. 'How old are you, Verity?'

'Twenty-one.'

He paused for a second, looking at my legs. 'I like that birthmark on your thigh.'

I lay there, frozen, feeling his hand move up and down my skin as he studied the heart-shaped mole on the front of my leg. I always hated how it looked. It made me grateful for the ankle- length punishment skirts at Pipford in the summer. Joe watched me attempt to disguise the birthmark with the corner of the rug.

'You don't need to hide yourself from me,' he said, caressing my knee. 'I think you're beautiful.' He reached over, tickling my neck and pulling me into him, as I exploded into a fit of giggles like a child.

* * *

We stayed on the beach for hours, as I listened to Joe play songs on the acoustic guitar and share tales of his travels. Snorkelling in Bali. Sailing in Byron Bay. Stargazing whilst camping outside Margaret River. Diving into the Great Barrier Reef. It was like hearing him unravel a magical, mystery underworld, that I desperately wanted to be part of.

It was coming up to the evening. The sun was slowly turning in, when Joe asked me a strange question.

'Can you take a picture of me?'

'Sorry?'

'A picture,' he smiled, passing me his camera. 'For the gram.'

'Are you an influencer?'

'Well,' said Joe, rolling his eyes. 'Kind of.'

Influencers are to my generation what I imagine pop stars like Wham! were to the kids of the 80s. New, untouchable superstars. At least back then they were genuinely cool. Max says that influencers are overpaid marketing robots. He says their portrayal of a perfect life on social media is damaging, and a potentially contributing factor to the Gen Z mental health epidemic. I'm not sure what he would make of Joe. Then again, I'm not sure what Joe would make of Max.

Joe sat on the rug with his legs crossed, closing his eyes and holding his hands in a prayer position. I stood back for a moment and stared at him, wondering if this was another one of his attempts to make me feel like a brainless, dull-witted fool. I stared down at the technical piece of equipment clasped in my hands.

'How do I switch this thing on?'

'Here,' he said, wandering over to me. 'You just press this button, then this one to go back again. Oh – and can you stand back a bit? Want you to get the sunset in properly, that's all.'

He repositioned himself on the rug.

'And go at the angle from below.'

I edged back and began tapping away like a mum being bossed around by her teenage son. I felt ridiculous. An old man walked past and looked at us disconcertingly, but Joe didn't seem phased. He embraced the attention, adopting complex yoga positions – warrior, pigeon, cobra. The splits. I must have taken about twenty before I stopped.

'Here,' I said, handing the camera back to him. 'I'm sure they're great.' He looked through the pictures of himself, smiling.

'Your turn now.'

'Oh, god no,' I laughed. 'It's really not my thing, Joe. Sorry.'

'Well, that was the old Verity,' he said, dragging my arm towards the rug with the camera round his neck. 'This is the new you, who embraces the unfamiliar. Repeat it out loud, after me, like a mantra.' He took hold of my hands, closing his eyes. 'I embrace the unfamiliar.'

'Ok,' I said, feeling like a foolish virgin with a strong urge to impress this strange, influencer spiritualist. 'I embrace the unfamiliar.'

It looked as if we were reciting wedding vows.

'Just act natural and pretend I'm not there, baby.'

Baby. He'd just called me baby. I had always imagined a man calling me baby. It was a phrase I had fixated on obsessively in old Hollywood romance movies, as if it were a magical spell that would somehow turn me into Marilyn Monroe or Vivien Leigh. I would collapse helplessly into the arms of a suited, handsome man, who would kiss me passionately and ask me to run away with him. I hadn't imagined it would be with a male yogi influencer who cleansed crystals, fermented vegetables and made me recite mantras, but life has a way of surprising us.

I sat down on the rug, feeling awkward and embarrassed.

'Relax,' said Joe, rushing over to massage my shoulders. 'Don't be so... rigid. Drink some beer.' I quickly downed the rest of my bottle and took a deep breath. Joe stood back and began snapping away as I posed awkwardly.

'See, you can do it! Run your fingers through your hair and show me that beautiful laugh.'

I did as he said, looking away, then at the camera, then repeating it again. It didn't feel like me.

Joe grinned encouragingly like a French photographer on the set of Vogue. 'The caterpillar becomes the butterfly!'

I adjusted my pose, feeling myself loosen up. The alcohol was definitely helping.

'You look amazing, Verity.' Joe wiped the lens of his camera with his shorts and walked over, kneeling down to face me. 'There's something I want you to do for me, but I'm not sure you've got it in you.' He kissed me – slowly at first, but then passionately, with intention. I stopped for a moment, feeling the heat of his breath against my lips, then in my ear.

'Will you let me photograph you topless?'

'What? We're in public!'

'Hardly,' he said, looking around at the empty beach. 'It's art, Verity.'

I hesitated. I knew girls from back home who'd had naked images of themselves leaked on Facebook and social media sites by guys they thought they could trust. I couldn't allow that to be me. I would never live the humiliation down.

'Forget it,' he snapped dismissively. 'I didn't think you would.'

I paused, heart thudding. 'You wouldn't show them to anyone, would you?'

'No.' Joe's eyes glinted as he caressed his thumb against my cheek. 'I don't want anyone else to look at you, ever. I want you to be mine.'

Before I could think twice, I was unbuttoning my blouse, watching Joe stare at me as he lit up another cigarette. I unhooked my bra and nervously placed it down beside me, feeling new and foolish.

'Are you just going to stand there staring at me?'

'Yes.'

A warm sensation filled me inside. It was unfamiliar and deeply thrilling. Joe slowly lifted his camera to his eye and began tapping away for a few moments.

'Will you take your skirt off?'

'But then I'll be naked.'

'You can keep your panties on, silly.'

I did as I was told. Joe stared at me, edging back with his camera, looking deeply aroused. He was getting off on this – there was no doubt about it.

'Spread your legs open and look to the side.'

It carried on like this; Joe telling me to pose a certain way, to do a certain thing with my hand, my face, my mouth, and me, doing it, like some sort of human robot. After a while, I started to feel giddy from it all.

'Now I want you to try and seduce me.'

'Seduce you?' I giggled. 'I can't do that.'

'You already are.'

I adjusted myself onto my knees, lifting my arms behind my head, pretending to pose like a glamour model. I felt, for the first time in my entire life, sexy.

Joe stopped suddenly, putting his camera down. 'I need to fuck you.'

'What?'

'You heard me,' he said, walking over, loosening his shorts. 'I need to fuck you. And you're going to lay there, silent, whilst I do it, like a good girl.'

This, I knew, was the sort of 'dirty talk' that was supposed to turn a woman on. It was supposed to incite a feeling of arousal and danger. But it didn't. I went from feeling like an outrageous porn star to a frightened baby calf. Joe grabbed my face like a hungry animal, forcing his tongue aggressively inside my mouth.

'Stop,' I said, trying to pull him off me. 'Please.'

He ignored me. He tugged at my hair and raced his tongue furiously against my neck, then down my chest and stomach. I jolted, feeling his tongue flicker aggressively right between my legs. This was supposed to feel frantic, sexy and passionate, but it didn't. My body was cold and startled. This wasn't how it was supposed to feel.

'Please can we slow down?'

'No,' he snarled. 'Shut the fuck up, ok?'

I screamed out for help. No one came. No one was here. Joe placed his hand tightly over my mouth, pinning me down on the edge of the blanket. He hunched my legs up on either side of his shoulders. My eyes prickled as I felt the sharp force of him inside me. I felt the hard grains of sand graze against my skin as Joe moved up and down in furious, penetrative motions.

'Ouch,' I whimpered, feeling Joe immerse himself even deeper inside me. He put his fingers inside my mouth, suffocating me, gripping his other hand tightly around my neck.

'Stop. Fucking. Talking. Just let me do what I want.'

I lay there, silent, staring up at the black sky, desperately wanting it to be over.

He came quickly, forcing me onto my knees, inserting himself right into the back of my mouth. I chocked, gasping for breath, feeling his release skate down my throat like wet mud.

Neither of us said a word for several minutes. A hideous, unspoken horror lingered in the air for a moment. We both knew exactly what had just happened, but neither of us said it. The scene that had just taken place lay out in the open like a rotten, gutted fish.

It was Joe who spoke first, pulling his t-shirt on over his head.

'Don't go gossiping to Naomi about this, will you? I know what girls are like.'

He leaned in to kiss my forehead. I was trembling. He knew what he'd done, which was the most excruciating part of it all.

'This stays between me and you, ok?'

* * *

Naomi was still awake when I arrived back.

She leapt up in her dressing gown and came galloping towards me, wrapping her arounds around me tightly. It was like a melodramatic airport scene at the summit of a romantic movie.

'Thank God, Vee,' she said. 'You were gone for hours. I was starting to get worried.'

'Sorry,' I said, nuzzling into the safety of her warm embrace. 'I wasn't really on my phone.'

I wanted to pour out the truth of what had just happened. The way I had laid there in the damp sand feeling shaken, scared and breathless. But I didn't. I couldn't. Joe was the best friend of her boyfriend. He was the good guy helping me find a job. Admitting I had been raped would destroy the vision of my life in Australia. A life I still wanted for myself, desperately.

Besides, Naomi would thrive in the drama of it all. She would enjoy feeling like some sort of MI5 heroine that saves the day, fulfilling her duty as the trusty best friend. She would encourage me to call the police and report Joe. Maybe she would even tell Ryan, who would confront Joe, who as of today, possessed half naked photos of me on his camera. They were his to use against me now. It was decidedly easier to act like nothing had ever happened, even if it was the wrong thing to do.

'Vee?'

'Nothing happened, Naomi,' I swallowed. 'We just hung out. He's cool. I like him.' She looked at me suspiciously. 'Did he say anything about a job?'

I realised neither of us had so much as mentioned it since the café earlier that day – a scene which felt like a lifetime ago.

'He's going to speak to some of his friends at bars and restaurants.'

'Why is your hair covered in sand? And why are the backs of your arms all scratched and red?' I turned around to look in her wardrobe mirror, trying to act surprised at the sight of my skin which looked coarse and pink. 'We went swimming in the sea. Must just be my skin reacting to the cold, that's all.'

It felt so wrong lying to her like this. My sweet, sisterly best friend of nearly fifteen years. We told each other everything – all the tiny, insignificant details of our day. What we had for breakfast, our hair wash schedules, when our periods were late. Avoiding telling Naomi something as big as this felt like an act of self-incrimination.

'But you didn't bring a towel with you! Or your bikini. Were you naked? Was it skinny dipping?'

'No,' I snapped. 'I swam in my underwear. Anyway, I'm all sandy and gross. I'm going to have a shower.'

I wandered into the bathroom. She followed me in like security sniffer dog, peeping her nose over my shoulder to smell my hair.

'Were you smoking?'

'Yes.'

'But I thought you said smoking was expensive suicide for people who wanted to get lung disease whilst looking glamorous?'

'Well people change, Naomi.'

She paused. 'Did you have sex?'

'No.'

'Did you kiss?'

'Yes.'

'And?!'

'Nothing, really. He's a good kisser.'

Naomi giggled, then smirked. 'I knew he would be.'

* * *

I loved sharing a bed with Naomi. The gossiping, the sisterly bonding, the closeness. After what had happened today, I needed it to make me feel safe again.

'What's it like when you have sex with Ryan?'

'Passionate.'

'Really?'

'Yep. Sometimes I get him to leave on his orange overalls when he comes through the door. I pretend to be a damsel in distress who needs her boiler fixed, and then he grabs me and, well... you can imagine the rest. Let's just say things get pretty wild.'

'Does it ever get... aggressive?'

'Sometimes, but I like it a bit of rumble and tumble. I think it's sexy.'

'Does he ever, like... choke you?'

'Choke me?' Naomi sounded startled. 'What do you mean?'

'You know – hold his hands around your neck whilst he's having sex with you.'

Naomi shuddered. 'No way. I draw the line at a hair tug. Anything else is kind of rapey. Saying that, some women are really into BDSM...'

I suddenly felt my phone vibrate. It was Joe. I shot up, heart pounding.

'Hello?'

'You sound surprised.'

I rustled the covers and turned my back to Naomi. 'My phone made me jump. I wasn't expecting a call from you.'

'From who then?'

I began to stutter. 'Nobody Joe, I–'

'I forgot to mention it to you earlier. A good mate of mine called Stevo has a vacancy going at his bar. Tony's.

It's nothing special – shabby, rough around the edges. But they're gonna make it big this year, you know. Get a chef and some live music going. Anyway, they're willing to take you on for a trial shift on Saturday.'

'What?!' I screamed like an excitable finalist on *The X Factor* who had just made it through the first round of auditions. Naomi was prodding my back, desperate to know what was going on.

'They want you there at seven. Don't be late.'

'This is amazing!' I squealed.

'Are you going to say thanks?'

I paused, suddenly feeling the weight of Joe's hands round my neck again.

'Thank you, Joe. You're the best.'

* * *

By the time Saturday evening came round, I was terrified.

I had barely heard from Joe. He said he was busy on a meditation course, but had texted me the address of the bar earlier that afternoon. I told him that I had worked at a pub before, which was a big fat lie. I didn't know how to pull a pint or how many millilitres were in a shot. I knew nothing about different varieties of spirits, wines or how to make cocktails. Plus, I was clumsy. I tripped up, spilt things, smashed glasses on my way to reaching for a mug in the kitchen cupboard. There was absolutely no chance I could wing this, but I would have to try. My phone suddenly vibrated. It was a Facebook message from Lily Griffin, a girl from back home that I had met once at a netball tournament. I hadn't heard from her for years. She had, at the time, aggressively pushed me over and injured my shoulder, knocking me out of the way in an attempt to shoot a goal. She got disqualified and we had both ended up in the first aid tent, forced to bond against our own will. I had sat there with an ice pack on my shoulder, listening to her tell me all about how much she hated school and how she was going to move to LA to be a personal assistant to a celebrity. According to her, it's one of the few ways you get to experience fame whilst still living a normal life. From thereon, we formed an unlikely friendship, even though I know she had pushed me on purpose. She quickly became the main point of contact in our boarding school for alcohol, boys and parties. It was she who had introduced me to fetish Dom, which I had never really forgiven her for.

Lily: Vee! I'm looking to rent in London. You're still based there, right?

I ignored the message. If this shift went well, then I had absolutely no intention of going back to London ever again.

* * *

I arrived at the bar at 6.50 pm. I had located it eventually in a derelict, empty car park. It somehow resembled a shack in a Texas desert rather than a bar down a side alley just off the town centre. Tony's was clearly attempting to be quirky and anti-cosmopolitan. It was trying to look like a cute, purposefully rustic beach shack built from old white planks of wood with the paint chipping off. Really, it looked more like someone's shed in a back garden stuffed with useless electrical clutter that hadn't worked properly for years. The door was painted bright red, with a blue sign swinging on the front saying 'Tony's' in orange bubble writing. There were two shabby cars outside – both of which looked as if they were carrying a dead body in the boot. I wandered over to the bar, feeling my heart thud. There was country music playing inside, along with the faint cackle of two men laughing. I thought about turning round, but had a quick mental pep-talk with myself.

You are a smart, strong, independent woman. You are overqualified to be doing this job, but nevertheless, you are going to do it anyway. It is the start of your fabulous new life; the beginning of a whole new you.

I pushed the door open and stepped inside, proudly.

'Hello!' I beamed. 'I'm Verity.'

The first thing I noticed, aside from the sweaty man in a safari hat sat slumped on a bar stool, was the smell. The place positively stank. It was a festering concoction of urine, stale alcohol and Dettol – the vinegary type of smell that never bothers you when you're drunk, yet suffocates your nose when sober. Old photos of Hollywood pinup icons were wonkily placed on the walls, which were painted sherbet orange, the interior reflecting the horror of the seventies. This transpired to the carpet, too, which was a ghastly retro design of brown and magenta swirls. It was smelly, chaotic and confused. Frankly, it was quite an achievement that a place could be so drab yet simultaneously full of colour.

The man in the safari hat looked at me, sipping a pint.

'How's it goin' love? The name's Jonno.'

He looked like a St. Bernard dog. His eyes were sad, droopy and glinted whenever he stuck his tongue out, which was, rather revoltingly, a lot.

'Oi, Stevo!' he shouted, dribble escaping from his mouth. 'Quit bashing one out and get yer pansy ass out here.'

A tall, lanky man suddenly appeared, who by contrast, looked like an undernourished greyhound. He was significantly younger. Paler, too, wearing a t-shirt in a garish peach colour with the bar logo on the front in blue. He stared at me as if he had never seen a woman before. His eyes were dark, beady and hollow.

'You here for a pint or summin, doll?'

'Actually, I'm here to work. I'm a contact of Joe's. He recommended you both to me and said that I was to start at seven.' I glanced down at my watch. 'Which is around now, I guess.' Neither of them said anything. They both looked at each other silently for a second, and then burst out laughing.

'Good old Joey boy!' grinned Stevo. 'He's a mate of mine. You must be that chick he was telling me about. The one with nice tits who speaks like Jenny Austen.'

'Actually, I think you'll find it's Jane Austen.'

'Oooh! Did you hear that Jonno? We've got a sassy little smarty pants here.'

Stevo smirked. 'You think you're too clever for us, huh?'

They both stared at me, then at my boobs. I was covered modestly in a black summer dress, but it wasn't enough to detract from unwanted male glances. I longed for a way I could cover up somehow.

'Are you the one that's bonking Joey then?'

'Bonking?' I asked. 'What's bonking?'

'You know – screwing. Having a good old jiggety-jig of his jolly-wolly.'

Jonno spluttered into a fit of laughter. I watched the bags under his eyes jiggle. 'Are you shagging him, is what we mean, love. Is Joey tapping your ass.'

'Of course not,' I blushed. 'We're just… acquaintances.' They both paused for a second, staring at my boobs again.

'Uniform's out the back,' said Jonno. 'Pop it on and I'll walk you through the basics.'

Twenty minutes later, I was sandwiched between Jonno and Stevo behind the bar in matching t-shirts. We looked like three unenthusiastic charity volunteers stood outside in the rain at a cake sale waiting for people to purchase some stale jam tarts. I had tried to absorb everything they had shown me as best I could, but it was difficult. The different spirits were confusing, and the smell of the bar was getting worse due to Stevo's cheap aftershave and the stench of Jonno's body odour.

'Can you walk me through the till just once more, please?'

'Easy peasy,' said Jonno, hosing my ear down with sprinkles of his saliva. 'Key in the price of a shot, select the mixer, total, activate the chip and pin, boom. Onto the next.'

'You gotta be quick, here, lovely,' chipped in Stevo. 'No dithering, no chatting. Pour the drink and move on to the next customer. Got it?'

'Got it!'

One hour in, and I had definitely not 'got' it. As I discovered, Tony's was a bar which prized itself on selling niche, home-grown Aussie spirits, jumping on the modern bandwagon of supporting independent businesses. It was a place where people came to taste the best of alcohol as opposed to getting totally pissed off it. None of the bottle labels looked familiar to anything back home. I had made countless mistakes already, trying to serve three customers at once whilst attempting to distinguish one spirit from the other. I had muddled everything; confused gin with vodka, cider with ale, bourbon with Jägermeister. I had even poured out shots incorrectly, my hand so shaky that people had, to their joy, gained a double for the price of a single.

'This isn't gin, mate,' sneered an aggressive looking woman with dreadlocks and a septum piercing. 'It's vodka and soda water. I asked for gin, with tonic, ice, and a lemon wedge.' She slammed her glass down on the bar so loudly that I was surprised it hadn't smashed. 'Are you new as well as fucking stupid?'

'Sorry,' I mumbled. 'Everything looks the same here.'

I turned around to scan the spirits, but couldn't see gin anywhere. When I looked at Jonno, he was in deep conversation with an old regular at the bar. I peeped my head through the door out the back. I caught a glimpse of Stevo right at the end, sorting through a delivery box. I would have to abandon scary lemon-wedge lady and go and ask him.

'Stevo?'

He stopped what he was doing, glaring at me sinisterly.

'What?'

'Sorry to disturb you,' I said, shutting the door behind me. 'I can't see any bottles of gin. Have we run out?'

He held up a clear bottle from the box he was unpacking with a dark navy label. 'Four Pillars, babe. It's an Aussie brand.'

I walked over and knelt down to take a closer look. 'Mind if I take one? I've got an impatient customer out there.'

He took hold of my hand and pulled me into him. I froze, feeling his long fingers brush my hair aside and his hot breath tickle my ear.

'You know what will win you extra points here?' he mumbled. 'This.'

He placed my trembling hand firmly against his crotch. I shot it away instantly, horrified that he had a boner.

'What the fuck are you doing?'

'Don't act like you're not gagging for it,' he grinned. 'I've seen the pictures of you.'

My blood ran cold. Joe had promised me he wouldn't show the pictures to anyone. He had said they were for his eyes only. I wanted to run and cry; in which order, I didn't know. 'Don't look so scared,' he sniggered. 'You've got the best pair of tits I've ever seen.'

I had to get out. Not just from the bar, but from Joe. From Australia.

I leapt into the dingy office and grabbed my bag, feeling Stevo's beady eyes glare at me from the back of my head.

'Where do you think you're going, little miss smarty pants?'

I yanked off the hideous orange t-shirt from over my dress and chucked it at his face.

'I quit. You son of a bitch!'

* * *

I arrived back to Naomi's flat, but it was empty. The craving to see her was overwhelming. I missed her more now than I had done when I was in England. I looked down at the coffee table and saw she had left me a squiggly note in green felt tip. I had forgotten she said she was staying with Ryan tonight.

'Hope your shift went well. Be back in the morning and we'll go and get an acai bowl ☺ Love you! x'

I checked my phone which died instantly in my hand. I didn't know where I had put my charger; it was jumbled up somewhere in a heap of clothes on Naomi's bed. I hadn't heard from Joe since yesterday morning. I had tried ringing him on the way back to Naomi's flat, but his phone had gone straight to voicemail. None of my messages had delivered either. I knelt down on the floor and burst into tears, sobbing uncontrollably. Why was every man here such a creep? And why had Joe lied to me? Was he some sort of fraud? A monster, a sociopath? He had told me this job would be the start of everything, and that the pictures he had taken were just for him. It had all been frighteningly convincing – all too easy to believe. I jumped suddenly, hearing keys through the door.

'Vee!' Naomi burst in. She rushed over and cradled her arms round me, like a mother holding a baby in a war-torn country. 'I've just seen it on Facebook. I'm so sorry. What a bastard.'

Oh god. He'd done it. Leaked my pictures. My boobs were officially on the internet for the world and his dog to see. How could I have been so naive, so stupid? The humiliation made me cry even harder.

'It's ok, Vee,' hushed Naomi. 'We just need to figure out what we're going to do. He must have flown there yesterday. What a little rat.'

'Flown where?' My heart began to thud. Naomi knew something I didn't. 'What are you going on about?'

Naomi paused, looking guilty.

'Joe's in Bali. He's just been tagged in pictures on Facebook with another girl.'

'What?'

'I tried to text you but I assumed your phone had died. I walked in and thought that's why you were crying – because you'd just seen it all. I'm so sorry. I could tell how much you liked him.' Naomi unlocked her phone, getting up Joe's Facebook profile. Sure enough, she was right. Joe was stood grinning in the middle of a heart on the sand made out of shells, wearing his amethyst necklace and the same pair of trunks he had raped me in. His arm was swung round a tall brunette girl in a coral bikini whose name was tagged as Imogen Naper. The photo was uploaded with the caption:

'The best relationships are the ones where you can act like lovers and best friends at the same time. Reunited at last!'

They both looked incredibly happy. He was almost unrecognisable from the monster who had attacked me. My heart sunk. Not because it was broken, but because it was so deeply disturbed.

'Bali? How on earth–?'

'It's only a few hours away from here, Verity. It's like flying to Greece from England.'

I swallowed, feeling numb. 'Joe said he was doing a meditation course for a few days. He told me firmly not to text him. Now it all makes sense.'

'He's an arsehole,' said Naomi. 'I always knew there was something off about him – something sinister. This just confirms it.' She zoomed in on the photo, holding it up. 'She looks kinda old. You're far prettier, Verity.'

'Put it away,' I said, feeling my eyes prickle. 'I don't want to see it.'

'I think you should message her and ruin their holiday. She deserves to know what a total dick her boyfriend is.'

'I don't know if that's a good idea. What would I say?'

'You have her name,' said Naomi, like a sassy female detective in a crime documentary. 'Send her a private message and confront her with the truth. Tell her that Joe took you on a date to the beach and kissed you!'

It sounded ridiculous when Naomi said it out loud.

'There's no point in saying anything. I don't want contact with him, or Tony's, ever again.'

'What happened at the bar?'

'They were total creeps. I was out the back and one of them got all weird – he was so scary, so sleazy… he grabbed my hand when I went out the back, and…'

'And what?'

'He made me rub it against his boner. He told me he'd seen topless photos of me.'

'Photos?' Naomi looking shocked. 'What photos?'

'The ones Joe took of me at the beach. I was fooling around. He made me feel all sexy and said he wouldn't show them to anyone. That's why I was crying when you walked in. He'd gone and shown them to Stevo the greyhound.'

'You did a naked photoshoot? You saucy minx!'

'It's not funny, Naomi. Joe has all the evidence stored on his lame ass blogger camera. He can do god knows what with those pictures, with god knows who. Confronting him will be perfect ammunition for them to be used against me.'

'If he does, that's revenge porn, and we could get him

locked up. Which is what he should be, anyway. I'm going to get Ryan to beat him up.'

'Please don't,' I said, spotting a charger in the wall socket and plugging my phone in. 'I'm going to silently disappear. Tell Joe that a situation happened back in London and I had to go back.' I remembered Lily Griffin had messaged me. She was online when I opened Facebook. I tapped a quick reply to her.

Verity: How soon do you need to move?
   Lily: ASAP.

I felt, then, the death of a possible life. A life that never really was – just could've been. I knew I would never look back on this chapter, wondering what if, wishing I had stayed in case things turned out differently. This wasn't my path. I was abundantly ready to leave Australia behind. 'What are you gonna do, Vee?'

'I'm going back to London.'

Chapter 4 - Craig

Four months later
Soho, London

'Jägerbombs!' screamed Craig to the barman, practically bursting my ear drum. 'More Jägerbombs!'

'Jesus, Craig. No more Jägerbombs.'

'What about sambuca? It's the unsung hero of spirits – right mate?'

Craig winked at the barman, who just looked fed up. No one really liked Craig at the office. He was like David Brent with a glow up. He had the irritating enthusiasm of a games show host with the veneers of an MTV reality star. His passion for voice notes, along with his daily 'Pret flat white' Instagram selfies, didn't exactly help his case, either.

'Come on, Verity! Don't be a spoilsport.'

I had successfully passed my three-month probation period at Stanley's, and had been roped into a karaoke night at Retro Bar in Soho to celebrate. Apparently, it's company tradition whenever someone passes their probation. Craig's social intelligence wasn't particularly strong, but I think it was even obvious to him that I didn't want to be on this night out. Truthfully, part of me was still bitter. Bitter that life hadn't turned out the way I'd hoped. Bitter that I wasn't living my best life in Australia with Naomi. Bitter that through some cruel twist of fate, I had ended up back in London, doing the job I vowed I wouldn't be doing with someone I thought I'd never see again. You guessed it. Inflated Ego Interview Guy.

I give Craig a hard time, but I suppose he's not actually that bad. As thirty-year-old men in sales companies go, I suppose he is ok. More than ok, actually. Nice. Sweet. A good egg. He snapped his Achilles tendon last year, meaning that his left foot is still in a cast. Once it's off, he reckons it'll take him from a seven to an eight out of ten. I've shown his picture to Lily before, and we've both decided that he's a five (six, at a push.) Lily and I are harsh critics when it comes to rating men. I suppose that on some level, Craig deserves to be fancied. I just... don't.

Craig thrust a shot into my hand, clunking it against his Jägerbomb.

'Down this, then I want to see you slay the karaoke stand. Rumour has it you've got the vocal prowess of Dolly Parton.'

I felt my stomach churn. I had been mixing drinks for three hours, and it was starting to get the better of me.

'Sorry, Craig, but I need some air.'

I left my bag on the floor and sprinted out of the bar into the street, feeling the wind hit the back of my neck. I flopped to the ground against the wall, panting, numb and drunk, with my legs splayed out in front of me and my red hair hanging over my face. I must have resembled a sedated orangutan. I leaned over, feeling the blood rush to my head. I threw up, right there onto the pavement. How tragic. I hadn't been sick from alcohol since the first time I tried it when I was fifteen, when I raided my mother's liquor cabinet and mixed spirits together in an empty water bottle. The memory made me vomit all over again.

'Verity?'

I looked up. It was Toni, my closest friend at work, sparking a cigarette. I say 'close.' A more fitting term would perhaps be 'lunch buddy.' She had lent me an emergency tampon in the work toilets once, and we had wandered across the road to buy a panini together afterwards. Toni was on the marketing team. When I met her, I had approached with caution. Not only did she share the same name as that godawful bar in Perth, but she was slightly intimidating and witchy looking. A sassy Irish girl that you didn't want to get on the wrong side of.

'I'm fine,' I said, wiping my mouth with my sleeve. 'I promise.'

'You don't look fine. You should have seen the way you shot out of the bar. I wondered if it was Craig's fault. Was he hitting on you?'

Before I could answer her properly, I was throwing up all over again. She held my hair back, patting me on the shoulders. I think she had accidentally got ash in my hair, but I was too delirious to care. I just wanted to go home.

'You girls looking for a good time?'

Toni and I looked up at an old man with a missing tooth who was gawking at us up and down like a lech. I felt sorry for him. If he wasn't careful, Toni would knock him out. She was ruthless. It's what made her such an asset to the company, and simultaneously, a threat to men. 'Leave us alone,' she snarled. 'I'm helping my friend.'

'I know girls like you. You're one of the lippy ones. Too much attitude for your own good.'

'Don't speak to me like that you little fuckwit, or I'll kick you in the balls and stub my cigarette out in your left eye.'

'Toni! Verity! What's going on!'

Oh dear god. It was Craig running towards us in his cast, carrying my handbag like a camp astronaut. At least it did a good job at warding off the creepy man, who muttered some sexist remark beneath his breath and scurried off down the road.

'I'd better go, my love,' said Toni. 'Said I'd give Alex a blowjob in the toilets. You'll be alright with Craig, won't you?'

She wandered off back to the bar before I could respond, passing Craig on the way. He made his way over to me on the floor and put his shoulder against the lamppost, smiling.

'Don't look at me, Craig. I'm a mess.'

He reached for a tissue in his pocket and knelt down to wipe my face. 'Don't worry, babe. You're still an absolute rocket.'

He handed me back my bag. I knelt down onto the pavement and began rummaging for my phone. 'I think I'd better go home and forget this ever happened.'

'Home? Come on, don't be silly. Streatham is miles away. It'll cost you a fortune to get back, especially at this hour.'

I opened the Uber app to check the prices. £50 with a 1.7 surge. Craig was right. Still, I wasn't about to have a one-night stand with him. The guy was my manager.

'Stay round mine.'

'Nice try, but no.'

'I've just had my bathroom redone. You can test out the new shower.'

Craig watched me hesitate. I think he thought I was picturing the two of us having shower sex, which I was. Unfortunately, it wasn't an image that enticed me enough to take Craig up on his offer.

'It's not like that, Verity,' he laughed. 'I've got a spare room you can sleep in.'

Most men will try every trick in the book to get you to spend the night with them. Typically, they'll use lines that are purposefully easy to fall for. Examples include:

But we may as well share an Uber. But you look like you'd be the best little spoon ever. But you're not like other girls.

But I'm not like other guys.

This, however, was a slight exception. I looked as if I had just been dug up from a pond. There was precisely zero chance of this turning into a one-night stand, even if I wanted it to. I had been reckless with my salary this month, and couldn't justify £50 on an Uber. That was a week's shop, plus a meal out with Lily.

'Ok,' I smiled. 'Thanks, Craig.'

* * *

One hour later, I was sat at Craig's dinner table in a Spurs shirt with a towel wrapped round my head, about to tuck into a sushi platter for two. He had insisted we order food. He said it'd make me feel better. Really, it was just making me panic. I think Craig had lofty ideas about this being some sort of dinner date set up. He had dimmed the lights and was setting the table, about to light Jo Malone candles.

'I've been waiting for a special occasion to light these bad boys up.'

'Don't waste them on me, Craig. I'm your sad case of a colleague who just threw up.'

'It doesn't matter. As long as it's with you, then it's special.'

He began laying out boxes of sushi on the table: edamame beans, sashimi and an array of perfectly formed California rolls. My stomach rumbled. It all looked delicious. I suppose I ought to tuck in and be grateful.

'Bear with, Craig,' I chirped. 'I'm just going to pop to the loo.'

I wandered over to Craig's bathroom. As I removed the towel from my head and hung it up on the rail, I glanced in the mirror and realised that I was in desperate need of a hairbrush. I peered into Craig's cabinet in search of one, and to my relief found a large comb. I began working my way through the knots, until it got completely stuck half-way through the left side of my hair. Shit. I edged forward to the mirror, moving strands from a large clump, but it was getting worse. I tugged it some more; gently at first, but then frantically yanking it. Still, it didn't move. It was the most stubborn comb in the world. I was going to have to get creative. I tried jumping up and down, head banging like a heavy metal artist at a rock concert. The comb was trying to humiliate me on purpose. I was sure of it.

'Are you ok in there, Verity?'

Oh god. Maybe he thought I was on the toilet.

'Fine, thanks! Be out in a sec!'

I shook my head some more, this time swishing it from side to side like a model in a L'Oréal campaign. It was hope-less. This comb wasn't coming out for love nor money, and I couldn't stay in the bathroom any longer. I would have to go out and face Craig looking like this. He looked confused when he saw me arrive back at the table.

'Is that my comb in your hair?'

'Yes.'

'Right. Can I ask why?'

'I tried to brush my hair and it got stuck. I couldn't get it out,' I mumbled. 'Sorry, Craig. I didn't want to keep you waiting.'

'Here. Let me help you.'

He began tugging at the comb, desperately trying to remove it from my hair, but it hurt.

'Ouch!' I whimpered. 'You're pulling too hard.'

'That's what she said.'

'Stop being a dick. You're supposed to be helping.'

He began pulling again, which totally backfired. The comb snapped in half with one end in Craig's hand and the other matted into my hair. Brilliant.

'At least we saved fifty percent of it, eh?'

I rolled my eyes. Lily would have to help me with it tomorrow.

Craig sat down and began to eat. He took hold of his chopsticks, putting a large piece of wasabi straight into his mouth. I'm not sure if he was aware, but he had just consumed a tablespoon size of Japanese horseradish. His eyes began watering and his face turned bright red.

'I was wondering,' he choked, 'Whether I could take you to The Shard next week.'

The words came out as more of a spluttering sound. He leaned over to the side of the table and began gasping for breath. 'Jeez! This guacamole is fiery!'

I ran to his fridge and grabbed a large pint of milk, opening the lid, handing it to him. He was practically choking to death. He downed it at the speed of light, milk trickling all the way down his chest. I reached for some kitchen towel.

'It's wasabi, Craig! Not avocado!'

I felt like a doting Mum caring for her giant toddler, telling him off for climbing too high up the tree.

'Lesson learnt,' he gasped. 'Bloody hell.'

He sneezed out a large 'achoo!' as I wiped his nose. He coughed some more and I pat his back. Milk spluttered on his chin so I wiped his mouth. It was, by far, the least sexy scene I had ever witnessed – on both ends.

'I've cocked this one up, big time, haven't I?'

'I'm in no position to judge. I have half a comb stuck in my hair.'

'Guess we're even,' he laughed, helping himself to more sushi, inspecting it for any traces of wasabi.

'How about it then? You and I?'

He tried to wink, but his eyes were still watery.

'I just don't see you in that way, Craig. Sorry if that hurts you.'

'So you're saying I'm the nice guy?'

'Sort of. If it's any consolation, I'm the nice girl.'

'Can't we just be nice together?'

'Don't think it works like that. We have to go for the opposite. It's the rules of dating.'

'You're a cracking girl, Verity. Friends?'

'Always.'

Chapter 5 – Kyle

Two weeks later

Stanley Software Solutions Ltd.

Victoria, London

'I think we should make Hinge profiles.'

Toni swung her chair round to me, taking a bite out of her panini. It was midweek at the office, and we were thankfully not in earshot of anyone else. Toni was on an Alex Detox, finally admitting to herself that casual sex with a man who has deep rooted commitment issues is in fact, terrible for the female brain. She was two weeks clean of him. I was a proud colleague. But I wasn't getting roped into joining another dating app.

'Sorry, Toni, but I am not downloading Hinge.'

'Come on! Don't be boring.'

'You know about my track record with dating apps. Pablo was a car crash.'

She giggled, recounting the Spanish tapas bar, ice bucket, brain concussion story. Unfortunately, it wasn't a situation I had ever forgotten lightly.

'That was four years ago. You've evolved now. Besides, no one uses Tinder anymore. It's full of divorced dads and strange middle-aged men posing as Abercrombie models who send you heartfelt sonnets promising you the world.'

'What makes you think Hinge will be any different? You do realise that it's still a stranger behind a screen, don't you?'

'It's less dodgy, for a start. You answer questions about

yourself on your profile so the person can 'get to know you' before you meet. It's actually a more human way of connecting.'

'Name me a single success story.'

'My housemate. She's having the time of her life with a guy she met on it a few weeks ago.'

'And by that, you mean he's taking her on a tour of all London's hotspot date venues just so he can sleep with her?'

'Wrong. He told her he's looking for something serious.'

Toni wasn't particularly skilled in picking up on the sales pitch every man gives in an effort to sleep with you. I wasn't much better, but still, I was learning. 'Never trust anything a man says until he has cum' was a new motto that Lily had taught me.

'Hinge is full of men,' pleaded Toni. 'Proper, adult men. Stable, emotionally mature and ready to commit.'

Perhaps I needed to swallow my pride and 'get with the times,' as much as it pained me to admit. Toni was right – I had come on leaps and bounds since the Pablo days. Besides, Max had met Tom on a dating app, and they had been together for almost two years.

'Fine. We can make Hinge profiles.'

'Yay!'

Twenty minutes later, Toni and I had morphed into two children distracted by their exciting new toy on Christmas morning. We sat in silence, browsing images of strangers listed as potential lovers or boyfriends. Hinge granted you access to an ocean of single men at the tip of your finger, for no cost at all. Lawyers, bankers, actors, doctors, surgeons, fitness instructors. It was like online shopping for a soulmate – but with an arcade of limitless possibilities, where you could be as choosy as you want, because you have all the money in the world.

'Do you think pineapple belongs on pizza?'

'Absolutely not,' said Toni. 'Why?'

'At least one in three men in London disagree with us. I'm discounting them for lack of originality.'

Toni shuffled her chair towards mine. 'What d'ya think of this guy?'

She held up her screen to show me a picture of a man named Seb, aged twenty-six, tensing his biceps next to a drugged-up tiger in Thailand.

'Isn't he gorgeous?'

I took a closer look at his profile. All I got from it, was: 'Hi. Here are photos of me of abroad so I can show off about how well-travelled (and ripped) I am. I'll also include a video of me playing with my niece, to convince you that I'm sensitive. I am in fact, a colossal fuck boy, but you'll find this out after I sleep with you and then ghost you.'

Toni looked like a happy pixie. I felt bad bursting her bubble.

'We just matched,' she grinned. 'We're going for drinks this weekend.'

'That was quick. He only courted you for six minutes.'

'What can I say?' she sighed, tilting back on her chair. 'They don't call me top-seller Toni at this place for nothing.'

I paused, struck by the next person I saw on my screen. His name was Kyle, aged twenty-five. Damn. He was HOT. He had a bright smile with brown, curly hair. I looked at the picture of him on a beach in Cornwall, clutching a surf-board, windswept and grinning.

I liked the sound of his answers, too.

This year, I really want to: Increase people's awareness into the importance of men's mental health.

The hallmark of a good relationship is: Ordering two mains and going 50/50 on both.

I take pride in: Keeping my house plants alive.

I swiped right instantly. It felt like the equivalent of clicking 'add to cart' when shopping on ASOS.

Later that evening I was sat on the sofa with Lily, continuing this new-found Hinge hype over a glass of sauvignon blanc. It was a highly enjoyable combination, even if Lily wasn't participating.

'You're gonna get arthritis on your thumb.'

'Leave it out, Lils. This app is a fucking revelation.'

'I don't need Hinge. I'm already on Raya.'

'What's Raya?'

'A dating app for celebrities.'

'But you're not a celebrity.'

'Well I manage one. It came with the job.' Lily was the day-to-day manager of a recording artist named Tash who was rumoured to be the next Rita Ora.

'I matched with a member of One Direction last week,' she said proudly. 'And got talking to actor who was an extra on *You*.'

'Wow.'

'Pretty cool, eh? Except he asked me to promise that I'm not going to fall in love with him. That's the trouble with dating famous men. They come with an ego the size of a solar system.' My phone suddenly pinged with a Hinge notification. I jumped up on the sofa, spilling half my wine in Lily's hair, screaming.

'What is it?' Lily practically jumped out of her skin. 'Is it a spider?!'

'I just matched with Surfer Guy!'

'Oh,' she said, repositioning herself on the sofa. 'House Plant Guy?'

'Kyle. Surfer Guy. I think it's more fitting.'

Lily and I had an abundance of nicknames for all our male conquests – none of which related to any of their actual birth names. Joe was 'Psycho Guy.' Pablo was 'Bilingual Boy.' Craig was 'Inflated Ego Interview Guy.' Lily was currently dating a man named Toby who had a passion for driving Lamborghini's round Knightsbridge. His name, therefore, was 'Car Guy.'

'Shall I message him first?'

'No way. The egg does not travel to the sperm.'

My phone vibrated again. It was Kyle, who had responded to a picture of me in Australia.

Kyle: Hi, Verity! Nice to (virtually) meet you ☺ I love Australia. When did you go?

I looked happy in the photo – beaming and full of life. I had captioned it 'take me back.' I didn't want to go back, of course. The photo felt as if it were taken from a different life, where I existed as a shadow of the woman I was now. Still, travel always sparked conversation.

I glanced over at Lily, who was deeply immersed in an episode of *Sex and the City*. I knew she'd tell me to 'play hard to get.' That was her usual strategy. Sometimes it worked. Mostly, it just made men scared.

Verity: I visited Perth last year. My best friend moved out there. Best place ever!

I could definitely think of better places than Perth. From my experience, it was full of creepy men who make you do weird things like grope their crotch and pose naked on the beach.

I looked through Kyle's profile again. He was laughing with his friends at Glastonbury, smiling with his family on a hike in the Lake District and speaking in a suit at a business conference. He was impressively multifaceted; funny, wholesome, kind and driven. The whole image of him was perfect.

Verity: I'm glad we matched.

I decided to follow my message with a heart eye emoji. Kyle typed back almost instantly.

Kyle: You're gorgeous. Where are you based?

Verity: Streatham. Moved here a few months ago. What about you?

Kyle: Tooting Bec. Cornwall, originally.

Verity: Love Cornwall. Used to go all the time as a child. It's one of my favourite places!

I had only visited Cornwall once, but Kyle didn't have to know this. I quickly realised that this was the beauty of dating apps. You are meeting someone for the first time. The past 'you' doesn't exist. There is only the present 'you,' the brand spanking new 'you'. It paves the way for an upgrade, for a rebirth. How you recreate that version of yourself is entirely up to you. If Kyle was seemingly every man, then I had to be every woman. Independent but not too independent. Feminine but not too girly. Caring, but not a pushover. Sexy, but not slutty. Ten minutes later, Kyle and I exchanged numbers and continued chatting over WhatsApp.

I told Kyle that I was expecting a promotion at work, but was always the first one on the dancefloor (career driven but fun). I told him I went to spinning classes, but was still on the hunt for the best pizza in London (healthy but not boring). I changed my WhatsApp photo to a picture of me dressed glamorously for a night out, and told Kyle that I make the best spaghetti Bolognese he's ever tasted. (Sexy but nurturing.) Half an hour later, he asked me on a date.

I was giddy with excitement. This was my perfect opportunity to re-carve myself as a brand-new woman to a brand new man. I was going to be smart, confident, sexy and independent; someone my nineteen-year-old self deeply envisioned but never had the confidence to become, thinking she was too out of reach. There was no doubt about it: I was going to blow Kyle Cunningham from Tooting Bec away.

'Lily!' I burst into her room excitedly, sitting on the end of her bed. 'Guess what?' She looked up from me, nestled in her duvet like a burrito wrapped in cotton wool.

'Psycho Joe has been rightfully sectioned?'

'No,' I said. 'Surfer Guy asked me on a date!'

'That was quick. Where? And when?'

'Madison's, I think. Tomorrow evening.'

She shuffled up to me. 'Let me guess. He's a business consultant for PWC, or something?'

'Deloitte, actually.'

Lily was used to wild dates with tour managers and music producers in members clubs and hotel lobbies. She had even blagged her way into obtaining a Soho house membership, meaning she rarely interacted with 'normal men' at mainstream venues. In my opinion, she was lucky to have me as her sweet humbling friend amidst the chaos of her semi-famous life. It worked for me, because I got to tag along to everything with her. I opened her wardrobe, casting my eyes over her vast selection of clothes. The best thing about living with a female friend is that both your closets merge together to form one giant communal wardrobe. Lily had accumulated hundreds of one-off pieces from upcoming designers. They originally sent their pieces to Tash to promote on photoshoots, but she never wore them, which meant they were Lily's to take home at the end of the day. It made deciding what outfit to wear a fun but overwhelming task. I wanted to leave my clumsy, spluttering self behind and re-create myself entirely. I wanted to be Verity 2.0.

'Give me the brief,' said Lily. 'What vibe are we going for?'

'Smart, sexy but also wife material.'

'Right.'

'I'm going to slap on some tan in a moment so it looks like I've maintained an eight-month glow from my travelling days last year.'

'But you don't have travelling days, Vee.'

'I don't, but you have.'

Lily frowned. 'You're going to lie to him and say you went travelling round South-East Asia?'

'Yep!' I smiled. 'And you're going to help me.'

'What if he catches on?'

'He won't. Just educate me on a few places you went to so I can impress him. It's like fancy dress, except this time, I'm keeping the outfit. Verity new and improved. You can help me invent her.'

Lily looked at me, thinking. She could never resist an outrageous idea – how big or small didn't matter. Ever since we were fifteen and she'd snuck me out of boarding school to attend a party with her on a field, she got a buzz from rebelling against the ordinary.

'Kyle visited twelve different countries in a year and built an orphanage in Tanzania. I need to be on an equal playing ground with him.'

Lily began shuffling tops around, eventually pulling out a black lace bodysuit with a plunged neckline. It looked like BDSM-style lingerie.

'What about this?'

'It's a date, Lily, not a brothel interview.'

She looked offended. 'It was a gift from Michael, thank you very much.'

Michael was Lily's sugar daddy from LA. He sent her clothes and designer bags in exchange for 'weekly intellectual conversation' on FaceTime. Initially, he had wanted Lily's old underwear, but she had negotiated it to just talking only. Lily's argument was that she needed expensive items to keep up appearances and be taken seriously in her industry. Having the latest bag would impress people and therefore advance her career. As long as she never had to meet or touch Michael, she didn't mind.

'This is expensive shit, Verity. It's from Agent Provocateur.' She watched me look at it hesitantly.

'Dress it with a blazer and some jeans. Remove the blazer ten minutes into your conversation.' I wondered if I should be taking notes.

'Talk about something serious first, like work or travelling, to show you're smart. Undo the blazer, and BOOM! You are not only a well-travelled career woman, but a saucy little minx, too. You start to tick boxes in his brain.'

I nodded like an enthusiastic bobblehead car toy.

When I got into bed that night, I started lusting over the new woman I was about to become. The prospect was exciting. The potential of this Verity was infinite.

* * *

It was a warm spring evening when I met Kyle. We had both arrived early.

He was easy to spot, even among the busy crowd of city workers, for he looked exactly how I'd expected him to look. Nothing about his face was surprising. I hadn't been catfished. Phew. It must've been a minute or so that I hovered by the tube exit like a creep, watching Kyle wait for me. I wanted to remain a stranger for just a moment, before I breathed life onto the version of him, of us, that I had envisioned so precisely in my head. I had gone as far as ten years into the future, imagining which shade of curtain fabric we would be selecting together from The White Company in our new flat. I'd say cream. He would say duck-egg blue. Perhaps we would embellish the curtain rails with small golden trinkets as a sentimental reminder of our honeymoon resort in Bali. I made my way over, feeling the familiar thud of that first date heartbeat. I didn't realise how much I'd missed it.

* * *

Kyle possessed a steady charm which made me feel as if I were a close friend rather than a stranger. Conversation rippled as we sipped on endless gin and tonics, which just kept appearing in my hand. They were starting to get the better of me, so that when the conversation of travelling came up, I was too cocky for my own good.

'I can't believe how much travelling you've done,' smiled Kyle. 'What stood out to you the most about Thailand?'

I had remembered everything about Bali and the Philippines, but nothing about Thailand. All I knew was that mango and sticky rice tasted really nice together, and that was something I had learned through ordering a take-away last week when I couldn't be bothered to cook.

Elephant story. Use the elephant story.

It came back to me, just in the nick of time. 'Swimming with elephants in Chang Mai.'

'Wow! You did that?'

'Yep.' I decided that now would be the right time to carefully remove my jacket and reveal Lily's brothel outfit. 'I stayed in an elephant sanctuary for three days and fed them bananas.' Kyle looked both impressed and turned on. Win!

'The main elephant was called Rosa. She had been rescued from a circus, so was used to performing tricks. You know – picking us up with her trunk and everything. The baby elephants were untamed, running around sweetly in mud puddles. It was adorable.'

Kyle looked at me earnestly. I sounded frighteningly convincing. I was starting to believe it all myself.

'We had to research the hell out the sanctuary, though. I wanted to ensure that none of the elephants were abused.'

'Good.' Kyle looked serious. 'I feel strongly about preserving animal welfare in tourist attractions.'

'Oh god, me too. It's a real passion of mine. A calling, some might say. Protect the elephants!'

Kyle smiled. 'I'm so happy to have met someone who feels the same. I would've probably got emotional, seeing all the animals in their natural habitat.'

'I have to admit, Kyle, I did shed a tear. It's something I'll never forget. The only downside was getting bitten to death in the sanctuary overnight by mosquitos.'

In hindsight, I probably could have left that detail out.

I had never been to Thailand before. I had never seen a baby elephant in my life, and I didn't like mud either.

'The thing about me, Kyle, is that I just love adventures. I struggle being in one place for too long.'

This was another lie. After Australia and Joe, the idea of heading blindly into the unknown freaked me out enormously. Country, job – the situation didn't matter. I didn't like adventures. I just wanted to be the type of woman who said she did.

'Tell me about you,' I said, resting my hand on Kyle's for the first time. 'Consultancy, right? I know how competitive those firms are.'

Kyle sighed. 'To tell you the truth, I hate it. My heart's in teaching, but I can't admit that to anyone. Especially my parents. I blend in here, right? Sat in this suit, in this bar, with you. Sure, the money in consultancy is great. The power, the lifestyle, the scope for success. You can get a real adrenaline rush from it, especially when you secure a massive deal…'

'But?'

'I feel empty inside. I go to bed at night, and none of it matters.'

I was taken aback by Kyle's sudden burst of vulnerability. He looked at me hopefully, waiting for me to say something comforting. Either that, or he wanted me to share something deep and meaningful about myself. In the words of Carrie Bradshaw, I had been emotionally slutty with men before – given too much of myself away too soon. I wasn't about to let it happen again. I remained self-contained.

'If teaching is what you really want to do, then you should go for it.'

'I'm from a strict family. It just doesn't work like that.'

There was a hint of sadness in Kyle's eyes that part of me yearned to tend to. I wanted to open up and connect with him on some deeper, human level, but I couldn't. I was afraid.

Old Verity would have poured her heart out to him without thinking twice. She would have told Kyle to quit his job and start a PGCE. She would have given some heartfelt speech about screwing what everyone else thinks and trusting your gut. She would have gone home and sent him links with courses to look at. She was the nice, sweet girl, who I didn't want to be anymore. Truly, I think Joe had killed her off.

'Stick at your job,' I said. 'You never know where it could lead.'

Kyle kissed me when we said goodbye at the station. It felt sweet and teenage-like.

'I've had a great time with you tonight,' he said, running his fingers through my hair.

I lingered for a moment, feeling the warmth of his breath on my lips, wishing I hadn't lied to him at the bar. His fingers curled around mine.

Leave now. Make him want you more.

'When can I see you again?'

I pulled away, hearing my tube arrive.

'Soon.'

* * *

I collapsed on Lily's bed as soon as I got home, feeling mixed up and strange.

'He believed everything I said to him.'

'See,' she winked. 'You've got him wrapped round your finger.'

I looked at Lily, then down at the lace leotard clinging to me tightly. I was angry at it. At Lily, at myself, at Rosa – the performing elephant from Thailand. I ripped open my jeans and yanked the leotard off over my head, throwing it on Lily's bed. She stared at it, as if it were a dead bird that had just shot through the window and landed on the duvet. I sat on the bed naked, as tears streamed furiously down my face.

'What is it, Vee?'

'I'm ashamed of myself for lying like that,' I sobbed. 'Why am I so fucked up? Why couldn't I just show him the real me?'

She didn't move to comfort me further. Instead, she muttered something sharp and true from beneath her breathe.

'This is all because of Joe.'

I drank in what she said like hot, burning liquid.

This is all because of Joe.

The words sunk to the pit of my stomach and dug in like knives. Lily had a way with words. They were frightening and precise. Not always what you wanted to hear, but always true. Just then, my phone vibrated. It was a text from Kyle.

'So happy I've met you. Sweet dreams. x'

I slept in Lily's bed that night.

'Are you ever afraid to be seen, Lily? Afraid to be seen by someone and feel your heart shatter into a million pieces?'

I watched her pause for a long time. Eventually, she said: 'No. I wear my heart on my sleeve without thinking twice. It's superglued. It won't come off.'

'I've always envied how brave you are, you know.'

'I'm not brave,' she laughed. 'You survived a rape. You're the bravest person I know.'

She turned to face me. 'Remember the first time I met you at the at the netball tournament when we were fifteen?

I kicked you out the way so I could shoot a goal. I injured your shoulder. I'm sorry I did that.'

'That was years ago. It doesn't matter anymore.'

She squeezed my hand beneath the sheets. 'I don't want what happened to make you scared. Of life, or yourself.' She paused. 'I love you, you know. You're my best friend.'

'And you're mine. Now until the end.'

* * *

I saw Kyle again the following week for a second date. We spoke some more about travelling. I hadn't wanted to lie again, but worryingly, it happened without thinking. When he asked about what I did in Australia, I told him all about my fully fledged career as a cocktail waitress. 'It was probably the most fun experience of my travelling days. Pouring shots, dancing on tables, partying whilst working. I'd do it all again in a heartbeat.'

Kyle invited me back to his house after. It was then that we slept together. It had been the first time I'd been underneath a man since Joe, and frustratingly, he was all I could think about.

'Relax,' hushed Kyle, kneeling above me. 'You flinch when I touch you.'

I shuffled beneath him, unsure on what to say. I knew I was making this uncomfortable for the both of us.

'Is it your first time? It's ok if it is.'

'Of course not.'

Kyle paused for a long moment with flushed cheeks, hesitating to say the thing he wanted to say. It slipped out eventually.

'Did someone hurt you?'

I wondered what he would do if I said yes. How he might react if I poured the entire rape story out and let my mouth run wild, naked in bed together for the first time. I couldn't bring myself to tell him the truth. It was the wrong conversation to have and the wrong time to have it. I wondered if there would ever be a right time. Not just with Kyle, but with any man. When would the outrage of what Joe did to me ever not be real and messy and ugly? Kyle could never find out. No man ever could.

'I like you Verity.' He pushed my hair to the side and kissed me deeply. 'I like you a hell of a lot.'

That night, I learned that Kyle's best quality of all was patience. I was eased into sex again without needing to tell Kyle what had put me off it so much in the first place. Gradually, our bodies melted into each other, and with each stroke, each glide, the memory of Joe forced between my legs faded away. Kyle pulled me into him after, warm and close.

'Stay for the weekend.'

By some romantic accident, I stayed for six. Every weekend for the rest of that month and a half was spent with Kyle, lazy, long and lovely. On Sunday's we didn't wake up until noon, and I lived in his t-shirt for the rest of the day feeling as if I were floating on a cloud. I took joy from getting to know his quirks – like how he was incredibly particular at chopping vegetables (they all have to be even in length and shape) and took precisely twelve minutes in the shower. He was passionate about recycling and never forgot to take his own bag to the supermarket. In fact, Kyle would have rather done the ten-minute journey home and back again than pay 15p for a new one. He treated his houseplants like babies and watered them down in his bath tub every Sunday morning. It was then that I texted Naomi describing him as husband material.

The more I got to know Kyle, the more I liked him. He responded to my observations about life with a certain degree of inquisitiveness that is not often found in men nowadays (I'm not actually sure if it ever was). He was kind, curious and empathetic, and made my brain feel as if it was the brightest, most sparkly thing in the whole world. Kyle was raised so that in any situation, anywhere in the world, no matter the circumstances, he could walk into a group of people and feel at ease, furthermore making them feel at ease, too. Be it an African tribe, a cabinet meeting, a riot or a war zone – Kyle possessed the charm and manners of a man who knew exactly how to handle it. It's what made him so trusted by his friends. It's what made him good at his job. It's what made any woman feel lucky to have met him, and even luckier to be with him. I wanted to show him off to everyone – this new found person of mine. I was certain he was the one.

It was the last Sunday of March and Kyle and I were on the sofa eating spaghetti. 'Redbone' by Childish Gambino was playing soothingly in the background. I knew I had to go home soon, but I was dragging it out for as long as possible. Kyle yawned, putting his bowl down on the table, stretching his arms out. I decided to bring up the topic of me leaving. Not because I wanted to go, but because I wanted to take a selfish joy from watching him beg me to stay.

'I should get going. I have a bunch of stuff to sort for tomorrow.'

'Stay for the week.'

'None of my clothes are here, Kyle. I'd have to go home first and then come back.'

'Do that, then stay forever.'

He pulled me in tightly to his chest, locking his arms around me. It felt like coming home. I had never experienced anything like it before in my entire life.

'Be my girlfriend.'

'What?' I pulled away, unable to believe what I had just heard. 'Are you joking? I mean, are you sure?'

'Yes,' he laughed. 'Unless you'd rather I was joking?'

'I'm just taken aback, that's all. It hasn't been that long.'

'Two dates and six weekends. Every time you leave I feel empty.'

I paused. This was really happening.

'I'm following the feeling,' he said. 'And this feels right, doesn't it?'

Splinters of warmth shot through my body. I felt lit up, hit by something alien but lovely. The room turned fuzzy.

'Yes,' I said. 'Right is exactly what it feels like.'

I couldn't sleep when I got home that night. I had a boyfriend. I had a boyfriend. I HAAAAAD A BOOOOOYFRIEND!

* * *

It rained every day for the next two and a half weeks. Everyone in the office was miserable, except me. The lovesick, floaty feeling never left, and I was never tired, either. Always awake but ever so slightly adrift since the evening Kyle had asked me to be his girlfriend. I jolted as I heard my work phone ring at my desk. It was Craig's line.

'You were supposed to send me that report by two. It's three.'

'On it now.'

He turned his chair round to look at me directly through his office window.

'You also haven't made fun of me for two weeks.'

I sighed, peeping over to him through the glass. 'You called to tell me that?'

'I suspect there's a fella on the scene.'

'I don't know how to answer that to you.'

'You can tell me anything.'

'Fine,' I said. 'I, Verity Ellis, have a boyfriend, which

means that flirty work banter with Mr. Craig Maguire must cease. Taking effect from now.'

'A boyfriend, eh?' Craig turned his back to me on the chair. 'Are you happy?'

'I think so.'

I watched him fiddle with his tie. 'Well then I'm chuffed for you, Verity. Everyone deserves to feel happy.'

There was no denying that Kyle Cunningham was sudden. He seemed to have erupted from out of nowhere. Online dates are always supposed to surprise you somehow. Sometimes they are bad – the disappointing kind. Usually, they are just ok – the normal kind. Occasionally they are nice – the hopeful kind. Rarely are they good – the exciting kind; and almost hardly ever are they amazing – the unicorn kind. This, however, was something else entirely. It was transformative.

Kyle was a natural romantic. He was never cheesy or gushy – but somehow knew exactly what I wanted to hear when I needed to hear it. Every morning I woke up to a simple 'Hello beautiful...' text from him – without fail. Every lunchtime it was, 'thinking of you', and every evening, after an hour of talking on the phone, he'd text me to say: 'I can't believe you're mine.' He said it was his job to make me feel special, and I quickly became used to it. Booking midweek activities for us to do together was an example of how he went about it, and this evening, we were going for drinks at a fancy bar.

'How's it going with Kyle?' asked Toni.

'Heavenly. I'm seeing him tonight, and I think he's going to say it.'

'Say what?'

'The L word.'

Toni looked startled. 'Well... shit.'

'Yeah. I know.'

* * *

When I met Kyle that evening outside St Paul's Cathedral, there was something different about him. I picked up on it instantly.

'What's wrong? You're being vacant.'

Kyle laughed. 'Vacant?'

'A little distant, that's all.'

'I'm stood right next to you.'

He was being stubborn. I hadn't seen this side of him before.

'Talk to me,' I said gently pulling his arm. 'What is it?'

'Long day. Struggling to close a deal, that's all.'

I knew he was lying. When we arrived to the bar, Kyle's quietness was making me tetchy. By the time we had sat down with our drinks, I was met with the strong sense that he would rather be elsewhere.

'We don't have to do this, you know.'

'Do what?'

'Drinks. I don't mind if you want to go back to the office and finish some work.'

I briefly looked out the window. The London views were spectacular, but neither of us cared. My eyes were now fixed intently at Kyle, whose were fixed even more intently on his double gin and tonic.

Eventually he spoke.

'I lied to you.'

My heart thudded. I felt hot and began to panic. 'Lied to me…? What do you mean you lied to me?'

'Earlier, when you asked what was wrong. I told you I was struggling to close a deal. That wasn't true.'

'So everything's ok at work?'

'Never been better.'

I waited for Kyle to say something horrid and earth-shattering that definitely wasn't going to be I love you. He chose instead to say nothing, which in turn, made me angry.

'Stop playing mind games.'

'I'm not.'

I couldn't stand his petulance. I took a sip of my drink and slammed it hard on the table, which made Kyle jump.

'Well, whatever this weird melancholic silence thing is that you're doing, just stop it.'

Kyle looked down into his lap, guilty. I sensed he wanted to say something difficult but was struggling. Maybe there really was something bothering him. I used my straw to scrape a large ice cube up from the side of the glass and straight into my mouth.

'Whatever it is, Kyle, you can tell me.'

The ice made me sound as if I were having a stroke. It was the coldest ice cube in the world.

It was making me look stupid on purpose, just like Craig's comb that time.

'Jesus, Verity,' he sighed, running his hands through his hair. 'I didn't want you to freak out like this. I mean, it's nothing bad, it's just—'

'Just fucking tell me!'

The ice cube shot out of my mouth and straight onto the table, covered in my saliva. We both stared at it for a moment.

'See what you made me do?'

I began scooping it up with my napkin, wiping the table down. A middle-aged businesswoman on the table next to us stared. The barman looked over too, raising his eyebrows, wiping a glass.

Kyle leaned forward, placing his hand on mine.

'I want to have a threesome.'

'Sorry?'

'A threesome.' He lowered his tone. 'Me, you and another girl.'

It wasn't what I thought he was going to say. It wasn't the end. It was, perhaps, a glitch. A small, salvageable glitch. My instinct was to approach it like a problem, to which I ought to respond as calmly and as gently as possible.

'So what you're saying is that I dissatisfy you?'

'Not at all. The sex is great.'

'… But it bores you.'

'No. It's great, like I said.'

'So you want to sleep with other women?'

'No. Well… no. I don't think so. Not really.'

'Not really?' I said. 'What do you mean not really?'

'Err… well, I…'

'You're hesitating. Why are you hesitating?'

'Would you just calm down, please? You're acting crazy.'

'Crazy?' I took a large sip of my drink, with a strong urge to hurl it straight at Kyle's face. 'I'm crazy? You're my boy-friend who has just admitted he would like to fuck another woman. You're crazy.'

'It's a turn on seeing you get so fired up like this, I must say. Maybe another woman will drive you crazy.'

'Stop trying to be clever,' I snapped. 'I'm straight.'

'I thought you said you kissed a girl when you went to Thailand?'

I paused, heart pounding. I recalled the baby elephant story in Chang Mai that I had told Kyle on our first date. I had also told him that I'd got drunk and kissed a random girl staying in the sanctuary. It was a foolish thing to have done, but I couldn't admit to him now that I'd made it all up. I don't even know why I'd said it. Besides, we'd come too far. We were now in a fully- fledged relationship.

'Many straight women still find that they enjoy sexual experiences with other women,' he said. 'It can be sensual.'

'Well mine wasn't. It was a stupid drunken kiss, and I barely remember it. Why are you fixating on it so much?'

'Why do you think?' laughed Kyle. 'It's fucking sexy, that's why. I thought you'd be down for us spicing things up.'

'Spicing things up doesn't apply to us, Kyle. It's reserved for fifty-something-year-old couples trying to save their marriage.'

'You loved it when we went down on each other at the same time last week. In fact, that was your idea.'

'That was different. Threesomes aren't experimenting. They're consensual cheating.'

He took hold of my hands. 'I've never had one before, Verity. It'll be new for me too. You're the one I want to try it with. Don't you want us to have adventures together?'

'Sure,' I muttered. 'Just not the type that involve me watching you sleep with someone else.'

'Talk to your girls. Research it, maybe. All I'm asking is that you at least think about it and keep an open mind. Would you do that for me?'

I looked deep into Kyle's eyes, searching for something. I didn't know what. They always made me feel warm and safe, but right now, I was getting nothing. I thought Kyle was going to tell me he loved me. Not ask for a goddamn threesome.

I looked down at the table, feeling sad and dispirited. The sweet, drifty feeling I had become so accustomed to since meeting him evaporated like smoke.

It felt like the beginning of the end.

* * *

The following evening, I grabbed a bottle of white wine from the fridge and took two glasses from the cupboard. I walked over to Lily's room and kicked the door open without knocking.

'We're having a porn party.'

Lily laughed, closing down her laptop. 'I thought you'd never ask.'

I unscrewed the bottle, pouring each one of us a glass. 'Know any good sites? I'm a total novice.'

'A porn party? I was kidding, Verity. Although apparently you're not.'

I took a very necessary large gulp of wine. 'I'm about to tell you something Lily, and I would appreciate it if you could respond as least judgmentally as possible.'

'I have a sugar daddy who sends me designer bags every week. Judging isn't my style.'

'And on that note, Kyle and I are thinking about having a threesome.'

Lily froze, dumbfounded. 'What?'

'I said thinking about. Not going to. You just said you wouldn't judge me.'

'I'm not judging,' she said. 'I'm just shocked, that's all. I didn't think you were into that type of thing.'

'Well, are you?'

'What? With you?'

'No,' I said. 'I'm asking if it's something you've ever thought about, that's all. Going there with a girl.'

Lily took a sip of wine and shook her head. 'I don't like the idea of involving a third party. I'm like a territorial tiger – If I saw some girl sucking my man's dick then I'd break her neck.'

One hour and a bottle of wine later, Lily and I were watching our second threesome on the internet. I never really got off on watching porn. I found it staged, showy and slightly uncomfortable. That said, the dynamics were eye-opening. I gawked at the man on Lily's laptop screen, shiny and orange. He was in his element with two blondes; one on her knees, the other kissing his neck.

'This is misogynistic as hell. It's driven entirely by him. Why does porn rarely centre around female desire?'

'Tell me about it,' said Lily. 'You can literally see his ego inflating like a balloon as she's giving him head.'

'This isn't turning me on in the slightest.'

'What about two girls?'

'Ok, but nothing hardcore.'

Lily typed in, 'Girls kissing' and found a short, ten-minute clip which showed just that. Two girls kissing each other, removing their clothes, fondling. It was slower, more intimate than the other clips. They were normal girls, just like Lily and I. They were totally lost in pleasure, in another realm entirely.

'This is hot.'

I caught Lily's eyes for a second, briefly imagining what her lips might feel like on mine. She caught me staring and burst out laughing.

'Don't even think about it.'

'Yeah. Too weird.'

* * *

It was twelve minutes past noon. The office was quiet and becoming predictably empty as people scurried off to their usual lunchtime habits. It always began around now. Stephanie, the older lady I sat next to, had gone to heat her soup in the microwave. She would call her soon to be ex-husband at the same time, desperately trying to work through their messy divorce settlement. Craig was shuffling around, getting ready to leave for his physio appointment. Toni's manager was out of sight, which meant she had given up on pretending to work entirely. She was spinning round on her chair like a child on a teacup ride, scrolling Instagram, nibbling on a panini.

I had come to learn all the intricacies of Toni's routine. I had watched her do the same thing for three days like clockwork, contemplating going over to her but backing out at the last minute. I was too scared to say the thing I wanted to say; the thing that Kyle wanted me to say. He had nagged me every night when we spoke on the phone. I'd had to make up a lie that Toni and I had both been too busy to talk about it. The truth is that I was terrified.

I shuffled my chair a few metres over, dragging the thud of my heart along with me like a dog on a lead.

'Hey,' I mumbled. 'I need to ask you something.'

'Go for it.'

She didn't look up from her phone. I turned around to double check that we weren't in earshot of anyone senior or professional. I whispered in Toni's ear, shakily.

'Have you ever had a threesome?'

She tilted her head back and laughed loudly. 'Of course!'

She said it as if threesomes were as normal of an activity as eating out at a restaurant. Maybe they were. What did I know?

'Why are you asking?'

She stared at me blankly. I felt incredibly seen. It was as if she were a witch who had just made all my clothes disappear, rendering me stark naked on the chair. The idea that she might see me naked, on a chair or bed, made me feel hot and fidgety – in a good or bad way I did not know.

'Kyle wants to experiment. Neither of us have tried it before.'

She nodded, taking an enthusiastic bite of her panini. 'And what about you?'

I blushed, uncomfortable. 'What about me?'

'Well, is it something you want to do?'

'No. Yes. Maybe. Can you keep your voice down?'

'Sorry,' she giggled. 'Have you come over here to ask me?'

'Yes.'

She looked at me for a moment, as if she were undressing me with her eyes, imagining it all. I had done it to her, of course, although not publicly. Kyle said he thought Toni was sexy when I showed her to him on Instagram, and I elbowed him in the ribs. Secretly, I kind of agreed with him. I had looked at pictures of Toni on my own when Kyle was asleep, dimming my phone light right down. Toni was incredibly attractive, although not in the classic sense of the word. She looked like a wolfish pixie. She was both thinner and taller than me, dark and willowy, with small, sharp features: blue eyes, a small nose and a short black bob. She could pass for a woman a lot older than her twenty-five years, although in spirit she was young and zesty.

'When were you thinking?'

'Kyle's place this Saturday. We can have some drinks and stuff when we're there to break the ice.'

'Ice breaking isn't really my style,' said Toni, eyes sparkling. 'I prefer mass destruction, you know. Hurtling in like a bullet through butter.'

Her words made me feel cold.

'You've got nothing to worry about,' said Toni, touching my arm. 'This is going to be fun.'

* * *

'What time did you say she was coming again?'

For a man who negotiates million-pound business deals with the Chinese and Russians, I had never seen Kyle look so nervous. I watched him pace the kitchen, reopening the window he had decided to close two minutes ago. It was raining outside. Droplets thudded violently against the glass and the wind howled. The whole night was angry.

'That's the third time you've asked me,' I snapped, getting up to close the window. 'Eight. She'll be here at eight.' I looked down at my phone to check the time. 'Which is any minute now.'

I sat back down at the table, pouring myself more wine.

'I just offered you more and you said no.'

'And?'

'It's just a bit of a waste, that's all. You never finish drinks.'

'You never finish putting away dry laundry.'

'And?'

'It's just an observation. You leave dry clothes out on the rail longer than necessary because you can't be bothered to put them away.'

Kyle sighed, slowly walking over to me. He began massaging my shoulders, resting his chin on the top of my head. 'I appreciate you going through with this.'

'Frankly, Kyle, I'm not sure you do.'

Kyle sighed. 'For God's sake, Verity! I gave you a choice with all this. The idea was never forced onto you. I thought it'd be something you'd enjoy.'

'Enjoy? Right, yes, sure. Sorry – my bad. I will just sit back and enjoy watching you cheat on me with my colleague.'

'You're the one who bloody set it up!'

'Because you asked me to!'

Truthfully, I was confused. I felt an odd mixture of curiosity and fear that I didn't want to admit to Kyle any more than I wanted to admit it to myself. I didn't know what these new, scary emotions meant for me; let alone our relationship. Really, I should never have lied to Kyle about being such an adventurous girl in the first place. If I hadn't made up that story about me in Thailand, then we wouldn't even be in this position. I had sold him a false version of who I was since the night we met. Everything had been a lie – from what I said, to the clothes I wore. He had been led to believe that things like threesomes were all part of the package deal of dating a girl like me, and that was my fault.

'Don't think that after tonight threesomes are going to be some sort of weekly occurrence, because they won't be.'

'What if you like it?'

'What if I don't?'

I stood up, reshuffling the organised line of spirits and wines Kyle had laid out. It looked as if we were about to host a cocktail making class.

'I have a feeling you'll be pleasantly surprised.'

'What are you Kyle, a mind reader?' I snapped. 'Stop trying to predict how I feel.' Suddenly, the doorbell rang. Kyle's eyes lit up like a kid in a candy shop.

'I'll get it!' he squealed.

'It's just a doorbell,' I snapped. 'You don't need to look so fucking happy about it.'

I walked to the bathroom and decided to call Max. I had told him about the threesome plan yesterday. He said I could call him in case of an emergency, and it felt like this was. He answered on the second ring.

'Everything ok?'

'No,' I said. 'She's just arrived. Kyle's gone down to let her in.' I paused, fiddling with the head of Kyle's toothbrush. 'I'm so scared. I don't think I can go through with it, Max.'

'Then don't. No one's forcing you.'

'I mean, what if I like it? Does that make me bisexual?'

'Not necessarily. And if you are, then who cares?'

My mind was frantic. It was impossible for Max to have a reasonable conversation with me. 'But then, what if I hate it? Kyle will break up with me if I do. He'll find another girlfriend.' My heart ached at the thought.

'No he won't. He loves you.'

'He hasn't said so yet. And if he does, then he loves who he thinks I am. Not the Verity who gets combs stuck in her hair.'

'I miss that bitch.'

I suddenly heard the door open. Toni was in the building.

'I've gotta go, Max. Talk soon.'

I hung up the phone and looked in the mirror. I barely recognised the girl staring back me. Since meeting Kyle, I had rebelled against everything I was. I had made up adventures in Thailand. I had told lies about things I'd done in Australia. I had even begun straightening my red hair, shoulder length since the comb incident. It was meant to be frizzy and wild. My Mum always told me she liked it unruly. She told me it stood out. We hadn't spoken properly for ages since I'd moved in with Lily. We argued a lot, but I was filled with a rare urge to cuddle her. I crouched down to the floor and tilted my head against the bottom of the bathroom basin, closing my eyes. I could hear faint muttering in the kitchen and the sound of Toni's stilettos cluttering against the floor.

Why was she wearing stilettos? I wasn't wearing stilettos. Was she trying to have one up on me?

She had never met Kyle before, let alone stepped foot in his apartment. Still, this wasn't the type of thing that would have fazed Toni. She was the type of person to make herself overly familiar and well acquainted with any new person or place she came into contact with. 'Verity!' I heard her coo my name excitedly along the hallway. 'I've got bubbles!'

I remained on the ground, observing the metal bars of Kyle's towel rail. I didn't want to move from where I was.

'Verity? Are you in there?'

Eventually, I stood up and opened the door. Toni was standing there in a black fur coat, her lipstick bright red. She grinned beneath the harsh, white light of the bathroom. I had never seen her in non-work clothes before. Her appearance was striking and powerful. She looked like a prostitute from Manhattan in the 1920s. A very confident

95

prostitute. She wrapped her arms around me tightly, as if it had been months since she'd seen me, as opposed to yesterday at work. She had drenched herself in perfume that smelt like roses and candy floss.

'Come on,' she said, grabbing my hand. 'Kyle's getting out champagne flutes!' It was as if I was the guest, not her, and Kyle was her boyfriend, not mine.

Kyle stood there, bottle in hand, pouring sparkling wine into three new glasses. He stared at me, whilst I stared at Toni staring at him. I hated the way she was looking at him, slouched against the counter, smiling.

'Do you fancy Kyle, Toni?'

Both of them froze, staring at me. I wondered if they'd perhaps had a private conversation by themselves on their way up the stairs, negotiating who would be doing what, where, and in what position. Kyle looked furious, as if I were ruining his masterplan.

'It was an innocent question,' I said, helping myself to a glass from the table. 'But you can admit it, Toni. We're all friends here.'

'Sure,' she said, removing her coat. She sounded a lot more Irish than usual. She was often told by men that it was a sexy accent, and as a result, she never betrayed it. 'Kyle is a good-looking guy.'

'Well, that's convenient, because Kyle already said that he finds you pretty.' I walked over to him, stroking his back. 'Isn't that right, babe?'

'Christ, Verity,' he muttered beneath his breathe. 'What's gotten into you?'

'How about I put on some music?' said Toni, breaking the strange atmosphere. 'Can I connect to your speaker, Kyle?'

I stood back, watching the two of them fiddle around with Toni's phone. Standing together, shoulder to shoulder, they formed a beguiling image. I didn't know if it aroused me or made me jealous. I was always mesmerised by Kyle's looks. Lily often described him as 'genetically privileged,' and she was right. He was dashingly handsome – like some sort of Disney character; even more so paired against Toni's delicate frame. I imagined them deep in a sphere of lust, rubbing their bodies on top of each other. They would look sexy doing it. People would pay to watch it. The smooth, seductive rhythm of 'Redbone' by Childish Gambino filled out the room. It was the same song that had been playing in the background when Kyle had asked me to be his girl-friend. This was obviously not a detail he had placed any sentimental value on which was disappointing, given that he'd made a Spotify playlist specifically for this night.

'Shall we?'

Toni and I followed Kyle in to the living room, sitting ourselves down on the sofa like anxious porn star audition-ees. Everything was still, except the wind, the rain and the music. Nobody knew what to say, where to look or what to do.

Do we talk? Do we drink? Do we dive straight in?

Kyle dimmed the lights and sat down on the carpet. He looked like an expectant dog waiting for some sort of treat. He stared at me and Toni, eyeing up the two girls who were about to fulfil his wildest dreams. It was Toni who incited the first movement. With him.

She got up from the sofa and crouched down like a black, shiny panther on all fours. I watched her spine curve as she began slowly kissing his neck like a black cobra. She was going to eat my boyfriend. Kyle looked startled at first, but then leaned back, pulling Toni on top of him. The two of them wrestled slightly with each other, making out on the carpet. She was crazy for him, and he was loving every second. My eyes were cemented to the image of them; my boyfriend and work colleague. On paper, it felt like an impossible scenario, yet here it was, happening. Bright, raw and filthy; half dream, half nightmare. There was no time to feel. I could only watch. The two of them were moving like wildfire. Toni held out her thin hand towards me, meeting my eyes with cold, frosty desire. She had red lipstick smeared around her mouth which made her look like a vampire.

'Get involved,' she said hungrily.

I knelt on the carpet, looked down at Kyle's crotch. I could see he was hard. Toni stroked it whilst looking at me seductively. It didn't arouse me. It hurt me. Suddenly, she clasped my neck and began to kiss my lips. She swirled her tongue in long, slow circles around my mouth. It felt like diving into the sea for the first time. I pulled away, gasping. Kyle was stunned. 'That was so fucking hot.'

Toni leaned into kiss me again. I moved my tongue in her mouth. She tasted like red fruit sweets mixed with tobacco. I tried to relax, but I couldn't. The sound of Kyle's hard, heavy breathing paired with the wet sensation of Toni's tongue in my mouth dissolved into an odd, frightening blur.

'Touch Toni's boobs, Verity. Play with her nipples.'

'Shut up,' I sneered, pulling away from Toni. 'You're a business consultant, not a porn director.'

Toni giggled with lipstick-stained teeth. 'It's ok. I don't mind you touching my boobs.'

She brushed my hair to the side and began kissing my neck. I rolled my head back and looked over at Kyle. He was watching us obsessively, unbuttoning his trousers. Toni groped my left breast, wimping out fake moans. She was putting it on, I could tell. It was utterly weird and cringe-worthy. Kyle pulled down his boxers and began playing with himself. The scene that was once intriguing was now just wholly unsettling.

'I can't do this,' I said, pushing Toni off me. 'Sorry.'

Toni looked like a shocked child who had just had her dummy yanked out of her mouth. I shot out of the room, as if she really were about to eat me like a six-foot python. I grabbed my phone and bag from the kitchen island and sprinted down the stairs of Kyle's building, tripping over half of them, bruising my leg. I was too numb to care. I stepped out into the cool, wet air, feeling droplets of rain spit on my face. It felt refreshingly real.

The wait time for the Uber was seven minutes. I waited for what felt like seventy, expecting Kyle to come running after me.

He never did.

* * *

Everything was strange on Monday at work. Craig's cast had been removed. Stephanie had finally come to an agreement with her ex-husband. Lo and behold, Toni was genuinely working. She was even wearing glasses, which was something entirely new, and her eyes hadn't left her computer screen for approximately three hours. It was coming up to lunchtime. She would have to leave soon to get her usual panini. She always liked to go early to avoid the queue. Either way, she would have to walk past my desk. Maybe then she'd look at me. She hadn't contacted me all weekend. I had thought about texting first to resolve it, but it didn't feel like my responsibility. I don't know whose it was. Kyle's perhaps, but I hadn't heard from him either. I was still wounded that he'd left me outside in the rain and hadn't come running after me. By the time I had arrived back home and sobbed to Lily about what had happened, I'd assumed our relationship was over. If he had slept with Toni, then it definitely was.

The silence from both of them was suspicious. Toni had

potentially betrayed me through sleeping with Kyle, who had broken the trust of our relationship through hooking up with my colleague. Of course, I didn't know if any of this was true. It was just a feeling. A gut feeling. And as every girl knows, gut feelings never lie.

If it was true, then Kyle would try to justify it. So would Toni. They were both good with words. Good at convincing people. They both possessed the natural charm of sales people, charismatic enough to make the wrong thing seem like the right thing and a bad idea seem like a good one. It's an art. Manipulation, perhaps. It is undoubtedly what drew me to the two of them as people in the first place.

Kyle would deny that it was cheating. He would say it was a threesome, and threesomes aren't cheating. He would do an excellent job of making me believe him. For a second, I probably would; then I would shout at him that there were only two parties involved after I'd left, and whichever way he wanted to look at it, it was betrayal. Maybe I would tell him that I regretted ever meeting him. He would cry, and beg for my forgiveness. I would laugh at him. Maybe then he'd tell me he loves me. He would then tell me he was sorry, meaning anything but. Maybe I'd punch him in the balls. Maybe I'd go for his neck. Maybe I'd drop to the ground, heartbroken. I had played out every possible scenario in my head like a trailer to the sequel of some gripping thriller. Each one seemed just as twisted as the other. Perhaps I had lost someone I loved, or thought I loved. Perhaps Kyle loved me. Perhaps Toni loved me. Perhaps they loved each other, which was the ugliest and most frightening scenario of all to contend with.

The idea that they had spent the rest of Saturday night rechristening all the secret places in Kyle's flat where he and I had made love was heart-breaking. On the coffee table. Against the washing machine. Sat on the window ledge with the curtains half open. Kyle got off on the risk of the neighbours seeing us. All the random places, back in the early days of my relationship with Kyle, where everything was lustful and exciting. If they had done it, then Toni would leave a trail of her black hairs around Kyle's flat. His white towels would be stained with makeup. The heels of her stilettos would leave black marks on his wooden floor boards. These were the types of annoying female habits I knew drove Kyle mad, but for Toni he'd let them slip. He'd do anything for her, his adventurous Irish vampire.

My work phone was ringing. It was Craig's line again.

'How's the new leg?'

'I just looked over that report you sent. There's a ton of mistakes, Verity.'

'Sorry. I'll get on it right now.'

'You're slacking. It's out of character.'

'Sorry. I've had a lot on my mind lately, with Kyle and–'

'I don't care. Just fix the report.'

He slammed the phone down. He had never snapped at me like that before. What was with this office today? I stood up and looked around the room. Everything and everyone seemed pissed off at me. Even the light above my desk started flickering.

'Jeez,' I said, looking up at it.

'What's your problem?' Stephanie frowned. 'Are you talking to the light?'

'Yep. One of those days.'

'You ought to call maintenance, you know. Get it looked at.'

Sorry Stephanie, but I have the repercussions of a failed threesome with my boyfriend and our marketing coordinator to deal with.

She had a tendency to nag. It was usually something that I blamed on her middle age, but today it was making

101

me want to push her spinning chair across the office and straight into the door.

I looked round the room to find Toni. She wasn't at her desk. That was odd. I could've sworn she'd been there a few minutes ago.

Maybe she really was a witch.

I looked ahead through the double doors. It was then that I saw the flicker of her shiny black bob. She was taking the fire exit downstairs to exit the building. I grabbed my bag to follow her.

'Maintenance are closed today, Verity, but you could try calling them later.'

'Thanks, but this is maintenance of my own.'

* * *

I was on a witch hunt. I hurried down the stairs in the same frantic pace as Saturday night, feeling the throb of my bruise from when I had tripped over. It hurt like hell. I pushed open the fire exit and turned left. Toni was standing by the traffic lights a few metres away, waiting to cross the road. I ran over to her, clinging onto my bag. The closer I got, the further my heart sunk. By the time I had caught up with her, it had plummeted right to the bottom of my stomach.

'Toni! Wait up!'

She didn't turn around. I knew she could hear me. I was terrified to look into her eyes again, but I knew the moment was imminent.

'Hey!' I grabbed her arm as we stepped onto the street corner. 'We need to talk.'

She finally turned to face me. She looked a whole lot different without red lipstick smeared round her mouth. Her face was chalk-white and tired. I stared into her small, yellow irises, transfixed on a mother and baby outside the coffee shop from across the road. Toni's eyes harboured guilt, and an odd vulnerability I'd never seen before. The remaining contents of Saturday night unfolded without Toni even needing speak. Her eyes told me everything I needed to know. Toni had reddened the landscape of my fairy-tale relationship. She had blood on her hands. She had gone at Kyle like a thirsty mosquito. She had slept with my boyfriend.

Chapter 6 – Caleb

Three months later
L'antico Pizzeria, Fulham Road

When I told my parents that I was starting a new job at a PR firm, they were crestfallen. 'Public relations? She'll be eaten alive like a lamb to a pack of wolves,' sobbed my mother into her napkin. 'Tell her, Charles!'

She hadn't met with my father for seven years. As soon as she had found out from Simon, the CEO, that I was leaving Stanley's, she had sent my father a panic-stricken email demanding we all meet for dinner to talk through my quarter-life crisis. So here we were, clustered together in a small Italian restaurant just off the Fulham Road. I wanted to get it over with as quickly as possible. I had a night out with Lily planned to celebrate my new job, which I was starting next week. There was absolutely nothing that either of them could do to stop me, although lord knows they were trying.

'Your mother's right, Verity. Perhaps you're disillusioned as to what the industry is really like.'

'Tell me, then, Dad. As an experienced banker of twenty-eight years. What is PR really like?'

'A colossal waste of your education, for one. I imagine you'll be flirting with businessman over long lunches to get their latest gadget featured in the Argos catalogue.'

'Fucking hell, Dad. No one reads the Argos catalogue anymore.'

I quickly remembered my mother's disdain for swear words – they set her off like a firework. 'What does one do nowadays when browsing for a new television, then, if not sift through the Argos catalogue?'

'Ever heard of the internet?'

'Are you just going to ignore the potty mouth on our daughter, Charles? Brixton has rendered her utterly corrupt!'

'Streatham, Mum. I live in Streatham.'

We were the only people in the restaurant. The family who owned it seemed grateful for the business, but equally, were watching us as if we were totally nuts. This was confirmed when my mother's tears began to literally plop onto her pizza. The manager looked at us disconcertingly, whispering something into the waiter's ear. Once my mother cried, she couldn't stop. It was a sickness. Like most men, my dad never did well with a crying woman. They made him scared and confused, especially when it was Karen. She was the scariest of them all. Her tendency to breakdown over something as small as a speck of dust on the lamp and blame him for it was a key factor in the dissolution of their marriage. My dad often just sat back and told her to calm down, which was worst thing he could have said of all. Unfortunately, this was not something he ever really learned from.

'Calm down, Karen, and eat your pizza. The dough is good here. Some trendy business called aged sourdough, if you've ever heard of that.'

'Never mind the bloody pizza dough, Charles! Our daughter is effing and blinding like there's no tomorrow. Although who can blame her these days, living in Brixton…'

'Streatham, Mum! Streatham.'

'It's the same thing,' she snapped. 'A dodgy area heaving with bongos and criminals selling incense on stalls. I'm disappointed you allowed that to happen to our daughter,

Charles. She had a decent roof over her head living with you.'

She looked up, sniffing her nose into the napkin. It was already sodden. The waiter walked over to give her a new one. I mouthed the word 'sorry' to him, feeling responsible for my mother's sporadic outburst of hysteria.

'I can't help but feel this change in your temperament is down to that Lily Griffin. She was always a terrible influence on you Verity, what with that peculiar heritage of hers…'

'Don't, Mum. Please, just don't.'

'I can't help it, Verity. You know how I feel about her. A loud girl from a loud family. Her mother used to arrive at those netball tournaments with a portable radio playing Turkish music! I'd have to take a couple of aspirins when I got home from the headache of it all.'

I looked at her with disgust, reminding myself of why we barely had a relationship anymore. Her backward opinions on the world had caused a rift between us ever since I was a teenager. We had only grown further apart as the years had passed. My mother had me later on in life, and therefore, fell into a slightly older generation of high society women in London, whose opinions on the world were shaped by those of their forebears; children of The Blitz, who still regard Britain as an empire. As a result, my mother had a tendency to stare that little bit longer at two men holding hands in public, and was that little bit more distrusting of the Indian family who dry-cleaned all of her expensive coats. My friendships with Lily and Max were deemed wildly inap- propriate compared to someone like Naomi, for example, who my mother always described as a 'nice and unassuming young woman.'

'Personally, Karen, I wave a flag for all nations. I've just hired a cleaner from Lithuania, would you believe. Those Eastern Europeans are marvellously skilled at what they do.

That said, I am swinging towards stringent border control and a free market, what with Brexit on the horizon…'

I listened to my Dad drift down a long, painful sermon on the pros and cons of Britain's EU membership. It was about the only topic he could discuss with my mother which didn't lead back to their messy divorce and whose fault it really was. Both my parents thought I had left Stanley's because I was bored, and the work had become uninspiring. This was true – my role no longer challenged me the way it used to. However, the deeper reason was that Toni and Kyle had entered into a relationship a mere two weeks after the threesome incident. Everything in the office was a reminder of the fact it had happened, and their relationship was some nightmarish by-product of it. The constant gifts he was sending to her desk every week didn't help, and frankly, it was all becoming too much to bear witness to. Hampers, chocolates, cupcake deliveries. My eyes prickled, as I remembered the note Kyle had left Toni accompanying the flowers on her desk one lunchtime. No one was around, and I had snuck over to read it when Toni had popped out to get her panini. Kyle had sent her a bouquet of roses, with a filthily handwritten message etched on a small white card that had made my stomach curdle. It read:

By the time you receive these, my cock will be six hours away from being deep inside your tight little pussy. May each fuck with you be even better than the last, if that is even possible. Kyle x

It was disturbing for me to read, and even more disturbing for the delivery man, who'd had to drop the bouquet off at reception addressed to 'The Sexy Irish Minx' on the fourth floor. The most disturbing part of all, though, was that Toni had left the envelope on her desk, half opened, as if she wanted me to read what was inside. I had burst into tears after I'd seen it. I had to go to the bathroom to call Lily.

'He's just delivered a bloody bouquet of roses to her desk. Roses. With a handwritten note. What is he, Shakespeare all of a sudden?'

'Long stem or short?'

'Does it matter?'

'Yep. Short are cheaper than long, which proves he isn't shit.'

Moments later, Toni flounced back to her desk smiling as sweet as a Georgian peach. She sat back down and bit into her panini. I hadn't seen her so hungry for something since she'd slithered over to Kyle's neck with the appetite of a snake. She took one of the roses and brought it lazily up to her nose, inhaling deeply. It had the longest stem I'd ever seen.

I cried myself to sleep for a week.

'What does Kyle think about you leaving Stanley's, Verity? I imagine he's in agreement with your father and I. Career stability is very important in life, especially at your age. It doesn't do well to flounce from job to job as and when one pleases.'

'Kyle and I aren't together anymore, Mum.'

'Crumbs! Why ever not?'

'We broke up last month. He had… other commitments.'

'What a shame. I was ever so fond of him. A charming young man, he was, from a nice well to-do Surrey family. I had strong hopes for you two settling down together. You could have had the upper floor of Rebecca's house.'

Rebecca was a cousin of mine, who had recently renovated a large townhouse in Wimbledon with her husband and their two small daughters. They had built an apartment style annex on the top floor and were looking to rent it out to 'a young, fun couple.' To me, it sounded like the premise of another bizarre sexual arrangement, although perhaps I was cynical.

'Kyle has a new girlfriend now,' I snapped. 'She's called Toni. Perhaps you could recommend them both to Rebecca, seeing as you like him so much.'

My mother didn't say anything – just raised her eyebrows and sipped on her Shirley Temple, staring at the little black dots on the crust of her pizza as if they were live ants. I was starting to get bored and tetchy. I wanted to leave. I stretched my arms and yawned – the first signal of an early departure at a meal you don't really want to be at but sort of have to be.

'I'm afraid I'll be making a move soon. I would say this conversation has been productive, but I'd be lying. I'll be taking the job regardless, and start next week. The office is in Clerkenwell.'

'Verity Rose Ellis, you shall do no such thing! Sit back down!'

'Enough, Karen. Verity is almost twenty-four. It's about time we trusted her to make her own decisions. I trust she knows what's best for her.'

I smiled at him gratefully. My dad always had the final word, and as the ever so slightly grounded parent, I was glad of it. Even in the ten years that had passed since the three of us had sat round a table together, this was not a dynamic that had changed, nor was it one my mother had forgotten. She didn't try to further prevent me from leaving.

'Just know you can always change your mind, Verity. I can contact Simon again to get you your job back at Stanley's in a heartbeat.'

'No need,' I smiled. 'Lily has already reserved a sugar daddy for me, you know. Just in case. Which reminds me – I'm late to meet her.'

A look of terror returned to my mother's sour face. The waiter dutifully returned with more napkins. My mother wept into five.

'Calm down, Karen. I'll order you a tiramisu.'

I pecked my dad goodbye on the cheek, feeling guilty for abandoning him with my mother.

'We'll talk soon, Dad.'

'See you, darling. Say hello to Lily for me.'

* * *

I gave Lily an extra tight hug when I saw her. She was waiting for me outside Embargo on the Kings Road, wearing an oversized jacket that had 'dreams so wet' written on the back in red paint. Lily had found it left behind at a recording studio in Brixton once by a famous rapper. We later discovered it was worth £4000 from a random Argentinian brand in Dover Street Market.

'You are literally 2018 Rihanna.'

'And you are literally 2018 minutes late. How did the intervention go?'

'How do you think?'

She frowned sympathetically. 'Tears and tantrums?'

'On Mum's end, not mine. She sobbed onto her pizza, literally, and said that PR is going to eat me alive.'

Lily laughed. She knew the extent to which I despaired over my mother better than anyone.

'Kill & Kontent sent you a welcome hamper, by the way. I left it in your room.'

'Nice. What was in it?'

'A bottle of prosecco, five free classes at Barry's Bootcamp and half a box of Guylian shells.'

'What happened to the other half?'

'I ate them. Duh.'

Sometimes when Lily and I went out together, we made up fake identities. Lily had started this game last year, when she had taken up a new hobby of phoning estate agents across South West London disguised as a wealthy socialite named Lilian. She would leave our Streatham flat in one of Tash's wigs and the latest Prada bag that Michael had sent, just so she could mooch around expensive properties in Mayfair. She said that the pain of walking past them in the street without knowing what they looked like on the inside was keeping her up at night. I remember one time I had accompanied Lily to a five-storey townhouse in South Kensington. She dressed me in sunglasses and a trench coat with a black Chanel bag, and told me to pretend my name was Vivian. Under no circumstances was I allowed to speak, just in case I giggled. When the estate agent had asked me what I thought of the bathroom, Lilian had answered for me.

'Sadly Vivian can't talk. She's still mourning the loss of her Shih Tzu Pomeranian.' I stared at the ground, trying not to laugh.

'Good heavens,' said the estate agent. 'I'm so sorry.'

'Winston was the light of Vivian's life,' said Lily, patting my shoulder. 'She's been wearing sunglasses for two weeks to hide the puffiness of her eyes. They've shrivelled to the size of two burnt raisins.'

Tonight, Lilian and Vivian were at it again, blagging their way to the front of the queue. This time, we were two successful influencers for fashion brands.

'Wear this,' said Lily, handing me her jacket. She knelt over and hoisted up her bra to fill out her cleavage. 'I'm going to get us free entry and a VIP table. Watch and learn, my darling.' Whoever said that men are the head of the household and women are the neck turning it were right. What they forgot to add, was that the same logic applies to bar owners, for Lily Griffin could manipulate them down a fine art. When Dex, the manager, appeared, Lily said we were two influencers who would promote his bar on

Instagram in exchange for a VIP table and free champagne. He was lucky, she said, as usually it costs to hire girls like us. Dex fell for it like a dopey love-struck fool.

'We've been screaming out for girls like you,' said Dex. He was old, ugly and bald, wearing a white shirt with half the buttons undone. I wasn't really sure if he knew what the term influencer meant. He was probably told by his marketing team that it is something he should care about to make his nightclub more successful. 'All that Insty-meme stuff is excellent marketing for us.'

'Instagram, Dex.' Lily smiled, touching his arm. 'Don't worry. I can teach you everything you need to know.'

He was eating out the palm of her hand. It was best I kept mouth shut. I stared down at the floor pretending I was Vivian again, mourning the loss of my Shih Tzu Pomeranian. Really, I don't think it would have made a difference if I spoke or not. Dex was too distracted by Lily's cleavage and sweet talk to question anything. Whether this was because he was too gullible of a man, or Lily was too manipulative of a woman, was hard to tell.

'Don't suppose I could get your number, Lily? You're a bit of me, you are. Would love to take you out properly in Chelsea sometime.'

Lily always knew that enamouring bar owners came at a cost. If we liked the place and wanted to go back, Lily knew she would have to text them once a week to keep the relationship alive; like their Instagram photos, go for dinner, pretend she was interested.

'Pass me your phone, then.'

Dex looked like the cat who got the cream. I couldn't help but feel sorry for him. If Lily was remotely unimpressed with the place, then chances were he would never see her again.

There were three guys on a table across from us dressed

head to toe in designer clothing. Everything was branded – from their caps, to their jackets, to their man-bags. Even their phone cases were designer.

'Do you think they're footballers?' I asked. 'Influencers, I reckon. Or local Chelsea boys.'

'Maybe they're both.'

I knew how Lily's brain was working. Designer meant rich, and rich meant relevant. Relevant meant connections, and connections meant moving up in the world. She was trying to play it cool on purpose in case they came over to us. I didn't want to break it to her that this seemed unlikely. They hadn't looked up from their phone screens from the second we had walked in. I studied them all individually. None were particularly drop-dead gorgeous – they just looked incredibly cool. I stared at the one in the middle. He was probably the flashiest of all three, dressed in Gucci trousers, a white t-shirt and a chain necklace. He looked expensive and unavailable. I found myself slightly bothered by the fact I was bothered by him. Designer brands were never something that fazed me, yet here I was, fazed by him. Ugh.

'I bet they're stinking rich,' gushed Lily. 'They've practically raided Selfridges.'

Lily would know. She spent a lot of time in Selfridges – particularly on the first floor, wandering around the menswear section. She said that's where you find all the 'niche, hot guys.' That's where she had met Liam – the first official love of her life. He had just touched down in London and was shopping for clothes because he'd lost his suitcase. Liam was a tour manager to a famous DJ, staying at the London Edition Hotel. After just one date, he had given Lily a key to his room and they embarked on a five day whirlwind. Lily and I went to a couple of free gigs, featuring Tash as the guest star. After a pushy conversation about her management situation, Lily had landed her dream job as a celebrity assistant, and from thereon, her career was born.

'His outfit alone is worth £5k.' She was referring to Gucci guy. 'Dibs.'

He was frowning whilst typing fast. He seemed incredibly busy, as if he had better places to be. This, I think, is what made him so attractive. He was slick, cutting-edge and entirely out of reach. I sipped on my glass of champagne, waiting for something to happen. The second Lily went to order us shots, it did.

'Nice jacket. You've got style, girl.'

Gucci guy was stood in front of me, grinning. I felt my eyes gravitate towards the chain round his neck, then to the hair on his chest, then up to the dark pools of his eyes.

'Oh,' I stuttered. 'Thanks.'

'Casablanca, right? Limited edition?'

'Actually, this jacket isn't mine. It belongs to my friend—'

'Lily! Nice to meet you.'

'Caleb.'

Lily handed me a shot and told me to down it. She kissed Caleb on either cheek, who then leaned in to kiss me. I brushed my cheek against his, catching his rich smell of oud. Caleb was the obvious leader of the pack. As soon as the other two saw him at our table, they followed like sheep. One was in a Balenciaga cap, the other in a Givenchy t-shirt. These items of clothing were the only way I could tell them apart. Stood together, they looked exactly the same. 'We're brothers,' said the one in the cap. 'I'm Harry, this is Anthony.'

'Verity.'

'Not seen you here before, Verity.'

'Probably because I've never been here before, Harry.'

He looked at me suspiciously. 'How did you end up in VIP then?'

I knew guys like him. The Chelsea Guy. They sat themselves a tier above everyone else and thought that the Kings Road was named after them. I refused to allow myself to be intimidated by his undeserved cocky aura.

'I'm well connected, actually.'

I smiled, feeling smug that I had successfully shut him up. And damn right, I thought. These Chelsea guys need putting in their place every now and then.

That night was a very good night to be twenty-three. Lily and I got very tipsy very quickly. It never took much for either of us, especially when we were together. The magic of friendship often contributed to our drunkenness. We ditched Caleb and his designer posse in favour of our own fun. We danced and sang and squabbled and laughed and danced and laughed again. The bar was like our chessboard – every man in the room our chess piece. We had a lot of nerve. We flirted with men we had no intention of kissing, and kissed men we had no intention of going home with. If a guy did ask us on a date, we kindly thanked them for expressing their interest and said we'd get back to them later, running away, cackling, just for the hell of it. Lily looped her arm through mine as we headed out of the bar, preparing to hail a cab home. I loved the feeling of our arms linked together. It made me feel invincible.

'Even if a guy were to take me to Paris for twenty-four hours, it wouldn't come close to the fun of being with you, Vee. Not even by a long mile.'

'That'd be the longest first date ever. And the dreamiest, too.'

'You'd fall in love and never come home.'

'That's not true,' I said. 'I'd come back home to you, with a present.'

'What would you bring me?'

'A box of Ladurée macarons. A really big box – the biggest

one they had, filled with a macaron in every shade of pastel.'

Lily and I were two young women painting the good old days of our twenties with mad, magical splendour. We swept our brush across every single colour in the paint palette of life – each shade a new bar, a new man, a new experience – without a care in the world for the mess we made on the canvas. We were carving out the tales we'd one day live to tell, that in fifty years from now, would form the most beautiful mosaic that we'd step back from and admire as two old ladies with chipped teeth and a glint in their eye.

Like a child, Lily wailed:

'I'm hungry. I want dessert.' Caleb appeared, as if by magic.

'The boys and I are heading to Novikov,' he said. 'You girls wanna join?'

'Novikov? The last time we went there, Lily lied to the waiters and told them it was my birthday.'

'It's true,' she said. 'We went five months later, just because we felt like free cake and attention.'

Caleb laughed. 'You girls are trouble.'

'It was worth it,' I giggled. 'They brought me out a chocolate cake with caramel inside that poured out like a stream of golden lava when I stabbed my spoon into it.'

'Golden lava?' grinned Caleb. 'Now that, I have to try.'

'Verity's starting at a PR firm next week,' boasted Lily. 'Give her six months and she'll be on the front page of *Forbes* magazine.'

'Six years, perhaps,' I blushed.

'Well,' said Caleb. 'I bet it'll be the prettiest front cover they've ever done.'

Caleb, Lily and I clambered into the back of a cab, along with Harry and the other one of Caleb's friends whose name I kept forgetting. Anthony, I think – the one in the Givenchy t- shirt. He barely said a word, and was taking nonstop selfies with the light flashing brightly on his phone. He was one of those irritating people who felt the need to produce a lengthy documentary of his night out compromising of twenty-five Instagram stories.

'I want you to take us to that place with all the fancy desserts,' slurred Lily to the driver.

'Where every table has a button which says press for champagne.'

The driver looked fed-up by her drunken behaviour already.

'Bob Bob Ricard, mate,' said Caleb. 'Upper James Street, Soho.'

The boys didn't seem to mind that Lily had redirected us to another venue. They just seemed grateful to be in our company, even if that did involve following us to restaurants at midnight just to eat dessert.

'Seems as if you know London like the back of your hand,' I said to Caleb.

'I'm a man about town.' He moved a strand of my hair from my face. For some reason, I always liked it when a guy did that. 'I guess your mate Lily wasn't joking. We really are going out just for dessert.'

'We once went out to three different restaurants in one night; one for starter, one for main, and one for pudding.'

'You missed out a fourth and fifth for appetisers and coffee.'

'Guess we couldn't think of enough venues.'

Caleb grinned. 'That's cos you hadn't met me yet.'

When we arrived to Bob Bob Ricard, the waiter said they were closing in fifteen minutes. Lily despaired at the news, exploding into a mini tantrum in the foyer.

'But I want your strawberries and cream soufflé with icing sugar on top!'

'And I want your chocolate fondant that melts when you put your spoon in!'

Lily and I were still tipsy enough to find ourselves utterly hilarious, even if nobody else did. The waiter, whose name was Antonio, couldn't have been less amused if he tried.

'Sorry girls, but there's simply nothing I can do.'

It was then that the door swung open. Caleb strutted in with the two other boys. They looked like a small army of designer minions.

'We're with these girls,' he said. 'Table for five, please.'

The waiter looked at Caleb's Gucci trousers, then at his Rolex, changing his mind.

'Certainly, sir.'

Lily was in the silliest mood she'd ever been in. All airs and graces she'd assumed at the beginning of the evening to impress these boys had gone entirely out the window. She was pushing the press for champagne button a hundred times over, screaming for the waiter at the top of her voice.

'Bring me champagne! Antoniooo! I want my champagne!'

She had been doing this nonstop for about ten minutes. The boys found it hysterical, but it was starting to infuriate the waiter. He didn't take kindly to being called by his first name. 'Please respect the rules and stop pressing the button,' he sneered. 'This is a fine dining experience, which you are ruining for other customers.'

Lily looked up at him with puppy dog eyes, slouching her head on the table.

'Or else what... Antonio?'

'Or else I am well within my rights to demand that you leave.'

'You can't ask me to leave,' slurred Lily. 'You haven't brought me my strawberry milkshake yet.'

The waiter looked panicked, questioning whether he had misheard our original order. He reached in his pocket for his notepad.

'You requested the soufflé, madam,' he snapped. 'I have it written here.'

'That's odd. I could have sworn I asked for a strawberry milkshake.'

'Soufflé,' he said. 'You said soufflé! See!'

He waved the page in front of Lily's eyes. It was like watching an exhausted parent reason with the naughtiest kid in the playground.

'Your soufflé is on the way. In the meantime, all of you troublemakers – shhh!'

He walked off and turned around halfway to look at us, pretending to zip his mouth shut. We all laughed. Our desserts soon appeared: soufflé, fondant, and, lo and behold, a strawberry milkshake which looked as if it had arrived straight from a 50s diner. I rolled my eyes and told the boys that this was typical of Lily. It was classic her to get two of something for the price of one – men, desserts – all aspects of life, really.

I shared my chocolate fondant with Caleb. He admired the lava-like dessert, which led me to begin sharing pointless facts about volcanoes. I was explaining how they are actually very important to the earth and help regulate its natural temperature, when he interrupted me. 'What are you doing on Monday?'

'Huh?'

'I want to take you on a date. Outside somewhere, if the sunshine holds out.' The others all stared, waiting for me to say something.

'Only if you want to, of course. I mean, you don't have to.' I opened my mouth to speak, but Lily was doing it for me.

'Verity's starting her new job on Monday, so I'm afraid that won't work.'

'How about Thursday?'

'Thursday would be great,' I smiled, before Lily could interject again.

She began telling a story of the time she had dog-sat the chihuahua of a very famous celebrity one time in LA, who had invited her to a lavish house party to say thank you. It was a story I knew well. I had heard it a million times on countless occasions with different groups of new people. Still, I pretended that every time was the first.

'Don't tell them, Vee!' said Lily. 'Let them guess.'

I zipped my mouth again to copy the waiter from earlier. The boys began firing out random suggestions.

'Kanye West? Justin Bieber? Mike Tyson?'

'Mike Tyson?' snapped Lily. 'Do you seriously think Mike Tyson would own a chihuahua?' Lily was fantastically good at telling stories. When she recounted her celebrity experiences, it never came across as bragging. It was a talent she had; to share tales of her lifestyle in a way that made people feel engaged rather than irritated. There was never a need for her to say you had to be there, because people felt as if they truly had been, and were experiencing it for the first time through the lens of Lily's own humble eyes. 'He's really normal,' she'd said once about a famous actor, 'except for the fact I saw him put milk in his tea before he took the teabag out.'

'She's nice,' about a famous singer, 'except I caught her eating Weetabix with a fork on the back of a tour bus.' As a result, Lily left people with the strong sense that she was an incredibly down to earth person, despite the circles she mixed in.

Caleb took hold of my hand coyly beneath the table. At first, I thought it was because he found Lily ostentatious. That was until he interlocked his fingers through mine and brushed his thumb against my finger. He knew what he was doing; igniting that first gleam of desire between us. It gave me butterflies. I smiled across the table at Lily, trying to convince her that I was engaged in her story, when all I think about was what Caleb was doing to my hand.

Lily leaned across the table and clicked her fingers at my face.

'You're staring into space, Vee. Why are you grinning like that?'

Caleb moved his hand down to my thigh, caressing it up and down. Shit.

'Nothing,' I said, sitting up. 'I was just daydreaming.'

This didn't encourage Caleb to stop. It was like a blazing private firework display between his hand and my leg that I couldn't withdraw my mind from. Lily rolled her eyes and started talking about how TikTok was going to be the next big thing. Frankly, she could have been talking about a zombie apocalypse, a pot of gold at the end of a rainbow or a trip to the moon – it wouldn't have mattered. Nothing could distract me from how my body was reacting to what Caleb was doing.

We soon left the restaurant and said goodbye to the boys. Caleb and I exchanged numbers and he wished me luck for Monday. On the tube back home, Lily and I began to speculate about my impending date with him.

'Perhaps he'll take you on a private yacht in the Thames. Or on a spin through London in a convertible Ferrari.'

'A Ferrari?'

'Well, he has a Rolex, doesn't he? And for every guy with a Rolex there's a Ferrari to go with it.'

I laughed. 'Is there clear evidence to back that up?'

'Sure there is,' said Lily. 'Car Guy had one Rolex per Ferrari. It was a 10:10 ratio.'

'Ten?'

'Yep.'

'Jeez.'

'I know.'

* * *

Every first day of a new job for a twenty-something year old woman keen to make her mark in London is the same. She arrives starry-eyed with a takeaway coffee in hand, thinking she has arrived at the summit of a mountain, yet leaves feeling as if she has been pulled through a tornado backwards. I arrived at the Kill & Kontent office in Clerkenwell ten minutes early, thinking I was Andy Sachs from *The Devil Wears Prada* post glow-up. I had even dressed to match my favourite outfit of hers – pearls, a cream coat and a Ruslan Baginskiy hat.

'Good morning!' I beamed. 'I'm here to see Kristen Kill.'

The girl at the reception desk glared at me coldly through her glasses. They were Chanel, of course, just as Lily and I had predicted. She sniffed disapprovingly and typed something on her computer. It was as if she took satisfaction from the clickety-clack sound of her fingers against the keys. She picked up the telephone and stared at me with a sorry look in her eyes. Lily told me to expect the girl on reception to be a colossal bitch. She said all women on front desks at swanky office buildings are, and have names like 'Bianca' or 'Melissa.' Apparently it comes with the job description. You cannot get hired unless you are a bitch in a tight bun with a name that makes you sound like a playground bully. The woman's hair was scraped back into the tightest top knot I'd ever seen. It pulled her face back so much that it looked as if her features were withstanding a wind speed of 100 mph.

'Name, please?'

'Verity! What's yours?'

'Jennifer. Not Jen, or Jenny. Just Jennifer.'

'I can see how that would be annoying,' I smiled. 'Sometimes, I think I prefer being called Verity, but trouble is, I'm so used to Vee now...'

'Take a seat. Kristen will be with you shortly.'

I'd had my fair share of interviews in the run up of this job to know that 'shortly' meant anywhere between ten minutes to an hour. Never less, sometimes more. I decided to avoid making further conversation with Jennifer, even though she had taken to buffering her nails and didn't look particularly busy. The building was vast, white and gleaming, with tall open windows and a glass spiral staircase in the middle that was long enough to reach a floor for every department of the company. I had been placed in tech, but there was also retail and leisure, energy and industrial, food, FMCG and crisis and issues. I stared at the bouquet of white roses in front of me, perfectly arranged in a giant fish bowl. I revisited the memory of Toni smelling one of the roses from Kyle. It still made my stomach curdle. No matter how tough this job is, or however much is expected of me, I had to remind myself that I had made the right decision. I had to get out of that job at Stanley's. There was no looking back; only forwards.

'Verity?'

I looked up and saw a tall, glamorous woman in her early fifties standing in front of me. She was wearing long cream trousers and an elegant chiffon blouse. It was the woman who had interviewed me on Skype. It had felt more like chatting to an old friend than a CEO. It was Kristen Kill.

I shot up to shake her hand, but she laughed and embraced me tightly instead. She smelt of gardenia flowers. I could feel eyes burning in the back of my head. I didn't need to turn around to know that Jennifer was staring.

'Look at you. You're even more adorable and doe-eyed in person.'

'And you're every bit as elegant and classy as I imagined.'

Kristen smiled. During the interview, she said that I reminded her of herself when she was my age. Not just in appearance, for both our hair was the exact same shade of flame like red, but in ambition, too. She thought London would be the city where she found love; instead, she found her career. When I told her that my expectations of London were the same, she had looked at me tentatively. She was glancing at me now in the same, warm way.

She had long, tousled curls that fell loosely to her shoulders like velvet stage curtains. For some middle-aged women, this hair length is ageing, but for Kristen, it seemed to take years off her. Her features were delicate and her skin was tight and porcelain. Whether this was down to Botox or eight hours sleep a night was hard to tell, although apparently in PR you're lucky to get five.

'Follow me. I'm going to give you a tour and introduce you to the team at tech.' She looked down at my shoes. 'You happy to take the stairs in heels?'

'Sure,' I said. 'I can run a whole mile in heels, maybe two.'

'And that's why I hired you.'

Kill & Kontent clearly hadn't been stingy on the office furnishing like Stanley's had. Everything here was new and inspired by 1920s art deco. Every floor until the seventh contained chandeliers, pendant lights and velvet emerald sofas.

As we passed each level, I noticed city by-passers stare through the windows. I couldn't blame them, for this was clearly a company where image was everything, no matter which department you worked on. Kristen greeted everyone we passed with the same warmth she had greeted me, and equally, they were just as stylish as she was.

'This is where you'll be based,' said Kristen, as we arrived on the fifth floor. 'There's a coffee bar on every level which is open to you every day. It's all free – get as many flat whites as you want.'

Kristen led me into a large room, full of people sat at

desks with Apple computers. It was noisy, and had the chaos of an uncaged zoo, swarming with people all doing different things in different positions. Some were up, some were down. Some were neither up nor down, kneeling on their chair with a stressed looking on their face trying to get someone's attention from across the room. There was no obvious system to the style in which people were working. One man in glasses was sweating profusely, frothing swear words to a client down the phone. 'What do you mean Sony don't want to be included anymore? The magazine has gone to print as we fucking speak! AS-WE-FUCKING-SPEAK!' By contrast, two other men were gossiping behind him and about him, sipping on cappuccinos and nibbling on pastries without a care in the world. One woman was staring at her screen as if she was trying to solve the enigma code. She frowned suddenly, as if a deal had just fallen through that had cost the company billions. She started crying.

'Tears are all very normal here, Verity. PR is a ruthless game.'

'So I've been told.'

'It's cut-throat, but just about the only industry where a woman can express her femininity and power all at once without society making her feel bad about it.'

I looked around the room, overwhelmed by the pandemonium.

'How do you juggle everything, Kristen? Do you have kids?'

She shook her head. 'I chose my career. Articles these days will convince you that you can have both, but the women that do aren't having sex with their husbands.'

Kristen looked like a regal empress watching over her land of wild and riotous civilians. I stared around the room, noticing that the K&K company logo was printed onto all of the windows in long, swirly writing.

'I am passionate about success – but above else, success in women. Kids weren't for me. The only dummies I deal with are men.'

I laughed.

'Your role here will be heavily relationship focused – meeting clients, building connections, and above all else – getting people what they want. It makes PR the perfect job for a woman. Men are easy to manage,' continued Kristen. 'You can wrap them round your finger in any way you want to.'

I giggled. 'And the women?'

'Less so. They already know your game, because they're out there playing it too.'

Kristen walked me over to my desk and introduced me to Hayley, the senior account executive, and Daniel, the account manager. They seemed nice, but so had Toni back on my first day at Stanley's. These days, I didn't trust anyone.

'I'll leave you with these two,' smiled Kristen. 'The gems of my company.'

'She says that about everyone,' laughed Daniel. 'I try not to get a big head.'

'We'll throw you in at the far end of the sea, but equally, don't be afraid to ask for help if you find the water too deep.'

I nodded, trying my best to process this contradictory advice.

* * *

The rest of the day was a blur. When Kristen had mentioned throwing me in at the far end of the sea, I hadn't realised she had meant it so literally. I felt as if I were trying to breathe underwater with lungs when everyone else had gills. Even Hayley, who was only a year older than me, seemed incredibly confident in what she was doing. I was set up on the computer and assigned three clients that I would share with her: JBL, Livewire and Hotpoint. I was told that it would be my job to gain as much exposure for the latest tech as possible and meet with journalists in order to convince them to publish the products of my clients. This, according to Daniel, was the most important aspect of the role, and as long as I could do it, and do it well, then I would succeed.

'A lot of the industry professionals in tech are thirty to fifty-year-old men,' said Hayley. 'And they're a sleazy lot. It's like they were the geeky guys at school who have all this pent-up testosterone from the years they never got laid. Now they're successful, they feel they're owed it.'

'The trick,' she continued, 'is to flirt with them enough so that they feel inclined to give you what you want, without you feeling like the only way to get it is to suck their dick. That'll be tough for a pretty young thing like you.'

'Why?' I walked over to Hayley, whispering in her ear. 'I'm not a slut you know.'

She burst out laughing. 'No honey, but you're a cute red-head who would probably believe me if I told you I had seven husbands.'

'You don't, do you?'

'See! Pretty, red and gullible. Most people who are ginger are angry that they are. You're not. You're like... a unicorn. If I was a horny married man, you'd be my prime target. You'll just have to try that little bit harder to get taken seriously by the male journalists,' she said. 'I had to learn the hard way.'

I didn't ask how she had acquired her wisdom. I wasn't sure I wanted to know. It might dissuade me from PR altogether.

'Most men in the tech world are married,' said Daniel. 'But not happily. They'll still cheat on their wives.'

'Really?'

'Of course,' Daniel laughed. 'And not just the men. When I started out in Retail and Leisure, a female journalist asked if I fancied a quickie with her in the bathroom. She was in disbelief when I told her I was gay. Her response was: you're not gay, you're queer. And queer men still sleep with women, right?'

'That's awful! Did you report her?'

He shook his head. 'This is PR, darling. The to-do list never ends, and reporting a thirst-trapped menopausal woman asking for sex in a restaurant toilet is hardly at the top.'

* * *

By the time Thursday had arrived, I had almost forgotten about my date with Caleb.

'Are you joining for work drinks tonight?' asked Hayley. 'The office runs an open bar every Thursday downstairs. We rinse it dry and get absolutely sloshed.'

I widened my eyes in amazement. The combination of a sassy PR company of 300 people combined with an open bar seemed lethal. I couldn't go, of course, because tonight was my date with Caleb. I hadn't spoken to him since Tuesday, when he had asked what my favourite foods were. Apparently, it was vital information that he needed to know for our date this evening.

'I'm meeting a guy tonight.'

'Get you! Who is he?'

'He's called Caleb. I met him last weekend.'

'Where's he taking you?'

'Not sure. Lily suspected a yacht on the Thames.' I lowered my tone. 'We also think he owns a Ferrari.'

Hayley laughed. 'If he owns a Ferrari, then he'll almost definitely own a Rolex.'

She winked at me on my way out, muttering 'Don't do anything I wouldn't do,' in a way that suggested there probably wasn't a hell of a lot.

* * *

Caleb had asked me to meet him at Primrose Hill. When I arrived, he was waiting for me with a Fortnum & Mason picnic hamper and a Burberry blanket.

'I'm taking you for a picnic,' he beamed. 'I treated us to a hamper and brought an extra blanket in case you get cold.'

We began walking through the pathways, heading to the summit of the hill. Caleb looked like a handsome distraction, and I quickly forgot about work. The guy had style, that was for sure. He had restyled baggy suit trousers, rolled up at the ankles with Gucci trainers and a black t-shirt. He was wearing Tom Ford sunglasses, too – not that it was particularly sunny, but warm enough to not need a jacket.

'You smell good,' he smiled.

'Scent is important, you know. It leaves a memory.'

He laughed. 'You don't need perfume for that. You of all people, baby girl.'

Unlike Lily, I don't find pet names cringeworthy or annoying. I love it. I lap it up. I enjoy the fuss and attention. Depending on who's saying it, it is an aphrodisiac, which makes me feel desired and safe, all at once. I had always longed to be someone's baby. Someone who genuinely meant it, unlike Psycho Joe. I wondered if Caleb's charm worked on all the girls he dated. There was something about the smile he gave afterwards which suggested that it did. Perhaps the drinks had got the better of me on Saturday to let the dimples on either one of Caleb's cheeks go unnoticed. They gave him a sweet, boyish cheekiness against the slickness of his style. He was an incredibly suave and put-together guy.

'I like your red hair,' he said. 'It's what drew me to you last time.'

Caleb caught me looking at the Rolex clinging to his wrist, shiny and thick.

'I went for the blue face tonight,' he said, holding it up against the sun. 'Not bad, eh?'

'It sure is lovely. You must've worked hard for it.'

I was desperate to know more about Caleb and his job. Frankly, it was all very vague. When Lily had asked Caleb's designer minions on Saturday, they'd said that the three of them were all 'freelance traders.'

'You trade, right?'

'Yeah. It was Dex who got me into it.'

'Dex? As in, the manager of Embargo?'

Caleb nodded. I giggled, remembering how he had asked for Lily's number thinking it was the start of some epic romance.

'Dex is like an uncle to me. We go way back.'

Caleb's tone was blunt. I sensed he didn't want to go into further detail, and this was probably the best I was going to get from him. For now, his riches would have to remain a mystery. 'How do you like Chelsea?' I asked.

Caleb shrugged. 'I prefer Mayfair, to be honest. Box. Sexy Fish. Amazonico. Better vibe.'

I remembered when Lily and I had gone to Box with Liam. We were in a booth with a few other famous singers and some random YouTube star. Lily had kissed him on purpose, trying to make Liam jealous after we discovered a lipstick mark on one of the wine glasses in his hotel room at the London Edition. It was a bizarre array of events, just like every night out was with Lily. It could never just be normal. But we didn't want normal. In fact, if nothing out of the ordinary had occurred, then it wasn't a good night at all.

'Where do you live?'

'West.'

Again, this was something I sensed he didn't want to go into. He didn't ask where Lily and I lived. He just changed the subject.

'Saturday sure was eventful,' laughed Caleb. 'You girls know how to have a good time, I'll give you that.'

'I try to live life to the full and say yes to everything,' I said. 'And that's all down to Lily's influence. As you probably guessed, she's my partner in crime.'

'I can tell you girls have a great friendship,' smiled Caleb. 'You should hang onto that. It's rare.' He paused, gently removing a strand of hair from my face again, holding my gaze for a fleeting moment. 'I say we pitch up here.'

I held the hamper as Caleb rolled out the blanket on a flat section of grass. It was a perfect spot. We had privacy, and a spectacular view of London in all its springtime glory. Combined with the splinters of pink in the sky, it was something to behold. Caleb brought out two glasses from the hamper, pouring me a glass of champagne.

'Cheers to our first date.'

'Cheers to that.'

I have always thought the end of spring to be a flirtatious time of year. Come early evening, the season teases you with the hope of later sunsets and the faint tickle of lukewarm air on your skin. Summer is nigh; you can feel it coming, and the bounds of never-ending days that lie ahead wait patiently on the horizon like a sleepy tiger awaiting its nap.

'How about your love life, then?'

I always dread this question on dates. It's the same as when the guy you're seeing has the audacity to ask how many sexual partners you've had. It is unnecessary, overly personal and irrelevant. It frees up room for judgement that doesn't need to be there. For me, at least, the answer is rarely straightforward, and the Kyle and Toni saga couldn't have been less of a conventional breakup story if it tried. Caleb and I were having a perfect evening together. I didn't want to ruin it by recounting the threesome scenario, which unfortunately, was firmly etched in my memory.

'I've only ever been serious with one person.'

'What happened?'

I shrugged. 'Life happened.'

'Are you still in touch?'

'No.'

'Whose fault was it?'

'Not mine.'

'Everyone says that.'

'Yes, but really. It wasn't mine.'

'So you had your heart broken?'

I paused. 'What are you, a dating detective?'

'Everyone gets their heart broken,' said Caleb. 'It's the price we pay for breaking someone else's.'

I paused for a moment, wondering if I had ever broken someone's heart. Max broke mine, through no fault of his own. Same with Dazzling Derek. Then there was Joe, and Kyle, who had etched away at the loose fragments of my heart in a slower, deeper kind of way. The type that chips rather than shatters, painfully, and keeps on chipping away like a woodpecker goes at tree bark. It's the harder type to get over, because sometimes the chipping carries on for weeks – maybe months. Sometimes years. It is the indefinite kind. I'd rather get my heart shattered into a million pieces once, and only once, than have the kind of heartbreak that chips. The only thing Pablo had given me was a brain concussion, and the only thing that had broken with Craig was his comb.

'You're cold, aren't you?'

Caleb took a sip of his drink and reached for the other

blanket, wrapping it around my shoulders. He was close to me now. I smelt the sweet fragrance of the champagne on his breath, just for a moment. I leant forward and pressed my lips gently against his. He pulled me in closer, moving his tongue in my mouth like the first tear of a rugged wave after a calm swell. Everything stayed perfect for a good twenty minutes – him, me, the park and the sky.

* * *

Caleb offered to give me a ride home. I said yes in a heartbeat and we walked over to his car. It wasn't a Ferrari. It was the shiniest black Jeep Wrangler I had ever seen.

'This is yours?'

'Sure is.'

Caleb smiled, reaching for his keys in his pocket in the sexiest, most effortless fashion that made me want to squeal and run away behind the nearest tree to do an excitable girlish twirl. I love dates like this. Dates that give you a tingling rush of excitement and make you feel like a teenager again. He opened the door for me, smooth as oil on a marble floor. The seats were still warm from the bask of evening sun. It wreaked of leather and expensive cologne. In the back of my mind, I had pressing questions about this fancy vehicle. I couldn't fathom how it had come into his possession along with a Rolex collection, a suspected Ferrari and maybe even a yacht in Monaco. I had an inkling Caleb would be vague if I asked, the same as when I had asked about his job and where he lived. It was all suspicious, but I didn't want to think about it now. I'd think about it tomorrow, with Lily.

'Where is it you live again?' he said, revving the engine.

'Streatham,' I blushed, fastening my seatbelt. 'No judging though, please. I'm sure your place is far fancier than mine.'

There are probably a few things more exhilarating than the thrill of riding in a car with the guy you fancy and holding his hand whilst he drives, but I haven't discovered what they are yet. Add music and early summer to the mix, then I'm convinced there is nothing that could even come close.

As soon as Caleb turned on the radio, 'Livin' On A Prayer' by Bon Jovi began playing. It was one of my favourite songs. Caleb turned it up to full volume and we sang at the top of our lungs with the windows down. We sped along the road like a foolish pair of reckless teens, wild and happy, as if time and death were miles ahead of us.

'Slow down!' I shrieked, feeling rollercoaster-like adrenaline. 'You're gonna have an accident.' He gripped onto my hand tighter, singing to all the words. He didn't miss a single one. As we approached a traffic light, he slowed down, interlocked his fingers through mine and said: 'This is the only song in the world that I know word for word. I've heard it a hundred times.'

'We can change it if you want.'

I attempted to switch the radio station, as if it were not his car, but ours.

'Keep it on,' he smiled. 'With you, it feels like I'm hearing it for the first time.'

When we eventually parked up outside my flat, Caleb kissed me repeatedly. Every time we stopped, and I reached for the door, he pulled me in to do it all over again. It was turning into a comical never-ending cycle, not that I minded.

'This time, I've really gotta go. Busy day tomorrow.'

'Sure,' he said. 'I'll call you.'

'I'm busy this weekend, but I'm free next…'

'I'll call you.'

I got out of the car and watched Caleb drive off with James-Bond-like suave.

As soon as I knew he was gone, I stood on my doorway and squealed, doing the twirl dance that I had been waiting to do all night long.

* * *

Why do guys never call when they say they're gonna call?

If they say they're gonna call you at six, it'll never be at six, will it? It'll be at 6.16, or 6.46, or 666 days later.

It was coming to the end of another stressful week at work, and another round of Caleb's mixed signals. He had texted me after our date, thanking me for a 'perfect evening,' saying he would be in touch to make plans for us to see each other again. Fourteen days had gone by, and not once had he called to suggest a second. Texts? Sometimes. He would message occasionally, checking in, telling me useless facts about his day and making small talk about mine. Sometimes, he would reply to my Instagram stories with emojis, but it never went further. The little interaction that existed between us seemed to revolve around everything except a second date, and I couldn't understand it.

'You could always be the one to suggest meeting up again,' said Hayley. 'It's 2018. It doesn't always have to be the guy.'

'Well, Lily always says that if a guy wanted to make it happen, then he would.'

Hayley rolled her eyes. She had never met Lily, but for some reason, she never liked it when I spoke about her. 'Your mate Lily doesn't know everything, you know.'

Before I could respond, Daniel was charging into the office. He was carrying a leaking coffee cup and looked incredibly stressed. Despite never writing on paper, he always had a pen behind his ear, the end of which was now in his mouth.

'Go on Daniel,' I laughed. 'Tell me what I've done wrong.'

'Change of plan, Verity. I've got the timings of the event wrong. You need to get there for two.'

'I thought you said three?'

'Two. It's two. I said two, didn't I?'

I began to browse my inbox. 'No, actually, I think you said—'

'It doesn't matter, darling. Just go now.'

This was my first time going to a network event. I felt nervous. Craig used to go to them occasionally to sell our employee engagement software. Now it was me going, to discuss products with journalists and represent Kill & Kontent. I felt prestigious.

'Chop, chop!' said Daniel, snapping his fingers. 'What the fuck are you waiting for, a solar eclipse?'

Everyone in PR swears. To manage their frustration, or sound sassy, I'm not sure. I think it's both.

'Get a cab. You absolutely cannot afford to be late.'

He was late for everything.

'Oh, and make sure you do network. Don't just… stand there.'

'Speak to the tech journalists, get a sense of their publications,' he continued. 'Make connections. Make them sick of the sound of your voice. Yap away – you'll get remembered.'

'Sure,' I said, putting my jacket on. 'Anything else?'

'Fix your hair,' said Hayley. 'You could do with a spruce up.'

* * *

When I got home that night, I decided to call Naomi.

'Babe! Sorry, it's difficult to talk at the moment.'

I could hear screaming kids in the background. 'You haven't had a baby already, have you?'

'I'm just nannying. What's the latest with the guy who took you on that picnic date?'

'He replies heart eye emojis to my Instagram stories. That's about as good as it gets.'

'Did he seem keen when you saw him?'

'Yes! The guy brought an extra blanket in case I got cold, Naomi. And then there was the way he kissed me...'

'Kisses can be deceiving. The quality of a man's kiss doesn't necessarily reflect the quality of their interest in you. Remember that.'

Naomi was incredibly wise for someone of her age. She had always been that way, ever since we were young. It was in her nature to be maternal. I don't know where it had come from, really. It was just who she was.

'How's things with Gabe?'

Naomi and Ryan had split up shortly after I left Australia. When I had asked why, she told me it was because Ryan's drinking had become a problem and he had declined help. As soon as I knew they had split up for good, I came clean about the rape. Naomi had burst into tears when I told her, saying she wished that we had reported Joe. In hindsight, I wished we had too. It pained me to know that Pyscho Joe was still out there, loose in the world.

'Gabe's good. I've never been happier.'

'Do you miss Ryan?'

Naomi paused. 'No. When you realise that the person you were with can be replaced, your whole view of them changes.'

I suddenly heard Lily's keys turn through the door.

'Better go, Naomi. I'll text you later.'

Lily charged upstairs and came straight into my room without knocking.

'You're back early for a Friday! How was it at the studio?'

I tried my best to sound bright, hoping an optimistic

tone would detract from the fact I was fed up having not heard from Caleb.

'Cut the bullshit, Vee. You're in one of your weird moods.'

I sighed. 'Fifteen days, Lily. Fifteen days of pure confusion. Caleb hasn't asked to meet up again but still sends emoji responses to my Instagram stories. I mean really – what is a girl supposed to do with the stupid yellow heart-eyed face?'

Lily sighed. 'The lowest form of courtship is men who respond to your Instagram stories with the number 100, a flame, or a heart-eye emoji. It is the bare minimum. It is poor flirting. It is, frankly, pathetic.'

'I still don't know where he lives or what he actually does for a living. He just said he's a "trader" and lives somewhere in the West.'

'Has he been active on social media today?'

I nodded. One of the liberations that the twenty-first century grants a modern woman is access to a man's every waking move. Providing they are social media friendly, which Caleb was, then you can see where they are, who they're with and when they were last online. Never has it been easier for a woman to develop her detective skills, and Lily was the best in the game. She once tracked down a guy on Facebook who her friend had kissed at a bar, just from his first name and university. If that doesn't qualify for a job at the MI5 then I don't know what does.

'When was he last seen on WhatsApp?'

'18.34. An hour ago.'

'Instagram?'

'Twenty minutes ago.'

'Facebook chat?'

'I don't have him on Facebook.'

Lily paused in thoughtful contemplation. 'Maybe he's hiding something.'

I watched her frown. 'You don't think he's got a girl-friend, do you? I can't take another guy leading a double life. It was bad enough with Joe.'

She shook her head. I watched Lily think again, conspiring. Every theory she came up with was announced with utmost conviction, as if it were clear, factual knowledge.

'Maybe he's got a physiological problem that he's embarrassed about. Something to do with his penis.'

'That's obscene.'

'I'm serious! It would make perfect sense as to why he hasn't suggested another date. The more he sees you, the closer he'll be in having to admit it.'

'Like what? Two sets of balls?'

'Yeah. Or an extra dick.'

'That's possible?'

'Yep. It's called diphallia. It affects one-in-five-million men.'

'Which makes the chance of it being Caleb practically zero.'

Lily shrugged. 'You never know.'

I laughed. 'So what you're saying, is that the reason Caleb hasn't texted me is because he was born with not one, but two dicks?'

'Yep,' smiled Lily. 'Two dick Caleb.'

'Imagine having to deal with two dicks in the bedroom. You'd have to do everything, twice.'

'One could be for a blowjob, the other could be for sex.'

'How would you know which is which?' Lily and I spluttered into a fit of giggles.

'Wait a minute,' I said. 'It's Friday. Why the hell aren't we out?'

* * *

When in doubt on a Friday night, go to Mayfair.

Lily and I decided to go to Box – half in the hope of bumping into Caleb, half in the hope of bumping into an upgraded version. We selected each other's outfits – me in a little black dress, Lily in a red slip. We took a shot of vodka and called an Uber, heading out into the warm embrace of an early summer's evening.

Box is filled with unconventional people talking about unconventional things. The people that go are alluring, beautiful creatives, who live freely having escaped the death trap of a 9-5. As a result, they relate to the world more fluidly. Box is not the type of place you would just stumble across on a casual stroll around the city. You have to know a particular type of person who knows a particular type of London. If you don't look the part, or at least put up a good enough show of acting like it, then you are denied entry. When Lily and I went last time, we got talking to a bunch of sixty-year-old millionaires, who were so enthralled by our riveting conversation about life in an English boarding school that they invited us back to a member's club with them. Had I not talked Lily out of it, she would have gone and woken up in Vegas.

I stood at the bar, glancing round the room.

'We'll never find him in here, Lily.'

'Just wait,' she said, handing me a porn star martini. 'The world is smaller than you think.' Sure enough, Lily was right. By the time I had finished my third cocktail, I had spotted Caleb. He was a few metres away in a small group of guys who looked like clones of the minions who had accompanied him last time. Caleb was wearing the Gucci trousers again, looking every bit as stylish as I had remembered.

'That's him,' I muttered with a pounding heart. 'He is literally over there.'

'Told you he'd be here,' smiled Lily. 'You gonna go over there?'

'Absolutely not. What the hell would I say? Hi Caleb, just wondering why you haven't arranged another date since our first one fifteen days ago. Wait – let me guess. It's because you have two dicks and are embarrassed to tell me!'

Lily rolled her eyes. 'You don't need to make it all dramatic, Vee. I'll come with you.'

Before I could say no, Lily was grabbing my arm, dragging me over to their group. As soon as Caleb caught us walking over, his face lit up. I suppose it was a good sign that he looked pleased to see us.

'Verity! Lily!'

He greeted us with a kiss on either cheek. He seemed genuinely delighted at the coincidence.

'What are you both doing here?'

'You know,' I said. 'Out and about. Living our best lives, as always. It was spur of the moment that we ended up here.'

'It's great to see you,' he beamed. 'Really, I'm made up.'

Then why have you given me fuckboy vibes and shown mixed signals for fifteen days?

'These are my boys from back home.' They looked up and gave a wry smile before glancing down again to continue phone scrolling – every millennial's favourite activity in a social setting. I caught one of them messaging someone on Instagram with a blue tick.

'And where exactly is home for all of you?' smiled Lily. 'Where do you all live?' I kicked her with my shoe. I could have killed her.

'West.'

'Yes, but where in the West?'

Before Lily could say anything else, I interjected.

'Lily and I are just going to pop to the ladies' room. We'll be back in a moment.' Now it was my turn to drag Lily away.

'You can't interrogate him like that,' I hushed. 'You'll make us look crazy.'

'I thought you wanted answers,' she snapped. 'I was trying to help you.'

We topped up our lipgloss and sparked friendly conversation with the lady selling lollipops. Convinced she had found a lifelong friend, Lily carried on talking. As soon as I swung the door open to head back out to the bar, I was face to face with Caleb. I could tell he had come to find me on purpose.

'You look gorgeous.'

'Thanks,' I said. 'Just something I threw on.'

I didn't know what to say – how to confront him about our first date, or address the lack of the second.

'I should have called you. I said I would.'

I did my best to dodge past him. He laughed, stopping me. 'Don't be like that, baby girl.'

'Baby girl now, am I? And there's me thinking I'd been ghosted.'

'I haven't ghosted you. I've been busy. Work's been…'

'Manic?'

Caleb paused, looking uncomfortable. I felt awkward, too. Embarrassed that I was overreacting, given that we had only been on one date. He didn't actually owe me anything – I just couldn't stand any more pathetic Instagram emoji replies.

'I can handle the truth, Caleb. I thought we had a good date together, but if you're not interested, just say.'

Suddenly, Lily appeared, grinning. Great. Just what this situation needed – a drunk Lily. A drunk, grinning Lily. The girl was up to something; I could see it in her eyes. I had no idea what was about to come out her mouth, but I knew it would make the situation with Caleb a hundred times more awkward that it already was.

'What we're really wondering, is if you give out mixed signals because you have diphallia.' Caleb was baffled, and I couldn't blame him. Lily is too unfiltered for her own good sometimes. Involve alcohol, and you would be wise to just cellotape her mouth shut.

'Huh?'

'It's a rare condition, you see.'

Lily sounded like a medical professional with a clipboard and a lab coat, specialising in the male anatomy. 'It means you are born with not one dick, but two. We wondered if that's why you'd been playing hot and cold with Verity – because you were embarrassed.'

'What on earth makes you think I have two dicks?' He looked down at his crotch. 'I mean, should I be flattered?'

Lily's eyes moved to the bar. I noticed she was staring at a much older man in a faux fur coat. 'You guys!' she squealed. 'It's Ben Thompson! The Ben Thompson, at the bar! In the same room as me. I can't breathe!'

I had never seen Lily lose her cool over a famous person in my life. She referred to Ben Thompson a lot. A 'big dog' music producer, apparently – and notoriously difficult to track down. He had a thick beard that made him look like an ancient Viking.

'I've been trying to hunt him down forever. I thought he was in LA. In his last Instagram story, he was in LA! Can you believe the chances?'

She placed her hands together in a prayer motion, whispering 'thank you' to the universe and scurried off announcing she had an empire to build.

Caleb and I were left standing opposite each other in an uncomfortable silence. I could feel the tension between us – whether it was awkward or sexual was hard to decipher. Suddenly, he grabbed my arm and thrust me against the wall, kissing me passionately. It had the intensity of an action film romance scene between the hero and his muse.

'And then you go and kiss me like that and it just makes it even more confusing.'

Caleb moved his mouth toward my ear. My stomach flipped, thinking he was going to kiss my neck, but instead, he whispered: 'Let's get out of here, baby.'

I squirmed with delight, feeling like a Bond girl.

I told Caleb I had to go and say goodbye to Lily first. When I went over to her, she was deeply engrossed in conversation with Ben. She would kill me if I messed this up for her, but what I had to say couldn't wait.

'Sorry to interrupt. I just came to say goodbye to my friend.'

'Please do,' grinned the strange musical Viking guy.

I knelt down, whispering into Lily's ear. 'What is shared between one female brain and another is not something that should be discussed with men, ever. Especially if it involves accusing the guy your best friend likes of having two dicks.'

'Yeah. Sorry about that.'

'I'm going back to Caleb's place. I'll text you later.'

'Report back,' winked Lily. 'With details.'

* * *

Caleb was tense when we drove to his house, and I couldn't understand why. His confident charm which had enticed me in the first place had evaporated entirely. He was a nervous, uptight wreck. I was starting to wonder if perhaps he did have an underlying health condition – a neurological one.

'You seem on edge. Is everything ok?'

'Of course I'm ok.'

His voice was strained. He was definitely not ok.

'You're all shaky, and your eye keeps twitching. Is there something in it?'

'No,' he said, rubbing it. 'Just tired, that's all.'

'Sorry about Lily's comment earlier. You have to take her with a pinch of salt. Or a tablespoon. Or a bucket.'

I was trying to lighten the mood, but Caleb didn't say anything.

'She was joking. It's a funny story, actually. We were conspiring reasons as to why you hadn't...'

I quickly realised the story wasn't funny at all. It wasn't even one of those, you had to be there moments. All it did was paint Lily and I as two irrational nutcases who deserved an Olympic medal in jumping to conclusions. It was best I changed the subject.

'How far to your place?'

'Half an hour, roughly. We'll be driving for a while yet.'

'If I ask where you live this time, will you tell me?'

I was careful to keep the tone light-hearted. Maybe it would relax Caleb, although his shaking seemed to have worsened. Was I about to get abducted? I suddenly got a flash back to four years ago – baby Verity in Spain before her first ever Tinder date with Pablo. At the time, I'd felt as if I were about dive into a deep, dark sea of the unknown and sink to the bottom. A similar wave of uncertainty hit me now. Maybe this was really it. Maybe I was going to die. Suddenly, Caleb blurted defensively:

'I live in Uxbridge, ok?'

'Uxbridge?'

Caleb nodded. 'West London.'

Yes. In a suburban town on the end of the Metropolitan line, in Zone bloody 6.

Uxbridge is so far out, that it is barely even in London. I remember visiting it several times with my grandmother as a child. From what I can recall, it is not a place where people walk around in Gucci trousers and drive Jeep Wranglers. They push buggies instead, soothe their wailing toddlers with a Greggs sausage roll and browse the aisles of Poundland. I was shocked, to say the least. Caleb owned a Rolex collection, designer clothes and a suspected yacht in the south of France. I couldn't reconcile this image of him in… Uxbridge. It was the biggest plot twist of all.

'Are you judging me?'

'No!' I said, unconvincingly. 'It's just a little far out. When you said West, I assumed you meant Kensington, or something.'

I tried to reassure Caleb that I didn't mind, that where he lived didn't matter, that he should have just been honest from the start. The more I tried, the more awkward it became. The rest of the journey ensued in a long, uncomfortable silence. We both knew he had distorted reality. Something told me there was more to come – and I was right. Caleb's house was semi-detached, located on the corner of a suburban road overlooking an off-licence. It was crusty and derelict; the grass was unruly but mostly dead, and the paint was flaking off the front of the walls. I had to dodge round the bins just to get to the front door.

'Be quiet when you come in,' he whispered, turning his key. 'My Nan will be asleep.'

… And the plot thickens.

Had Caleb been honest from the start, I would have found this type of situation endearing. A sweet, humble guy, living with his elderly Nan. How lovely. How wholesome. It was the fact he wore Gucci trousers and pranced around Mayfair with an army of designer minions in matching Rolex watches that was so very puzzling. I couldn't put the two images together. Who was this guy? And more importantly – how on earth did he afford his lavish lifestyle? The house was even shabbier on the inside. I was hoping for evidence; clues for it to all make sense somehow, but all it did was riddle me further. Why had he bent the truth so much? But then again, why had I back on my first date with Kyle?

Every room was carpeted – including the kitchen. It was a stale, mushy pea shade of green, even worse than Miss

Fielding's favourite colour from Pipford Hall. Caleb's sink was stacked high with dirty pots and pans, which looked as if they had been neglected for weeks on end. There was a stench coming from an overflowing rubbish bin which lingered across the entire corridor. It was a wonder Caleb hadn't contracted the smell himself. If he were any younger, and I was a local neighbour popping in, then I would have alerted the social services.

'Sorry,' he whispered, guiding me up the stairs. 'Kitchen needs a clean.' I smiled politely through gritted teeth.

'Don't suppose you'd mind taking your shoes off, would you? Nan's fussy.'

She must be blind, too. Perhaps Caleb is her carer? But then – how would he have time to be a trader? It was becoming increasingly apparent that this was perhaps not his job, but I couldn't say anything. Not yet. There still wasn't enough evidence. As I removed the straps of my heels, I glanced down the hall to catch a glimpse of the living room. All I could see was a turmeric-coloured velvet chair with an ashtray resting on the arm. Behind it were double sliding windows overlooking a small garden with grass and brambles a metre tall. There was a swing out the back, too. Did he have a child? I tiptoed up the stairs, following Caleb to his bedroom. It was small and dingy, and had obviously been his since childhood. He had a single bed with posters of footballers on the wall. Above it was a picture of him grinning from ear to ear in a football kit. He must have been around ten years old when it was taken. There was a man wrapping his arms around Caleb's shoulders. It was 'Uncle Dex,' the nightclub owner.

'I know it's small,' muttered Caleb, embarrassed. 'I'm saving for a better place. Viewing properties in Notting Hill next week, actually.'

Somehow, I didn't believe him. I perched on Caleb's

bed. It was the only place I could be without feeling as if I was in the way. There was just about enough room for his wardrobe.

I suddenly felt my phone vibrate.

Lily: Did you mean to share your location? It says you're in Uxbridge.

Verity: Caleb's place. I'm safe. Will explain tomorrow.

I put my phone down and looked up at Caleb. He was no longer Gucci Trousers Guy. He would now have to be known as Uxbridge Guy, or maybe even Zone 6 Guy.

'You looked beautiful tonight.'

He placed his hands gently on my face and began kissing me. Before I could think, I was beneath him, kissing him back. There were questions I wanted to ask; answers that I needed; but for now, it would have to wait.

* * *

Having sex in a single bed is like trying to wade through a muddy swamp: difficult, uncomfortable, and hazardous. It will probably involve falling over, twice. Even with me on top, sex was utterly impossible. Caleb kept moaning that the springs in his bed were squeaking too loudly.

'Shhh! You'll wake up my Nan!'

We had to give up eventually. There was simply not enough room, and I was too concerned with making noise. Truthfully, I think the moment had passed. I think it had passed a very long time ago. My stomach suddenly grumbled loudly. I clutched it, terrified it was going to wake up Caleb's grandmother.

'You're hungry,' he whispered. 'Want to order pizza?'

'Sure.'

Caleb opened Uber Eats on his phone and began browsing toppings.

'What do you like? I'm a pepperoni man.'

'Pepperoni it is.'

We lay squashed in his bed together whilst we waited for it. He began fiddling with my hair, stroking my shoulder. I stared up at the ceiling, trying to piece together this bizarre jigsaw puzzle.

'I know you're not a trader, Caleb. Just be honest with me. What do you really do for work?' I felt his heart thud beneath his chest. I wasn't trying to embarrass him on purpose. I hated that he felt the need to hide the truth from me, but equally, I felt entitled to know it.

'I'm a male escort to older women.'

I shot up, dumbfounded.

'A toy-boy?'

'This is why I didn't tell you. I was afraid you'd judge me, and now you are.'

I went quiet. 'Your circumstances are none of my business, Caleb.'

'I shouldn't have lied. I wanted to wait for the right time to tell you.'

'Is that why you blew so hot and cold with me? Because you were worried about showing me the truth of who you are?'

He nodded. 'I like you. I was afraid.'

'Do you do it to... help with your family?'

He shook his head. 'I do it to pay for stuff, for me. A two-week fling with a married woman from Italy got me this.' He held up his Rolex, grinning.

'She was married?'

'Most of them are. They have a fetish for younger men. It means you end up doing exceptionally well in the industry when you're my age.'

I couldn't believe what I was hearing.

'How much older are they?'

Caleb shrugged. 'Varies between forty to sixty.'

Suddenly we heard a car pull up. Caleb threw on a dressing gown, Versace slides and walked down to get the pizza before the doorbell rang.

I sat there, speechless. A male escort? I was judging, but I couldn't help it. I knew about escorting. It was easy money, and it paid well. Very well. Lily and I had read up on it before. We agreed that whilst it would be adventurous, it was too demeaning for either of us to actually go through with. Somehow, the relationship Lily had with Michael felt different to this. It was just talking – there wasn't a sexual element involved. Besides, Lily was transparent in a way that Caleb wasn't. Sleeping with older women to pay for designer items in order to carve out a false version of yourself was on another level. Suddenly, it all made sense. Hanging around in Mayfair was obviously how Caleb had built up his clientele. Perhaps if he was doing it for a more ethical reason, such as helping his family, then my outlook would have been different. If he had the money, why hadn't he got his Nan a nicer home than this? What did that say about who he was, as a person? This was not some suave millionaire from Chelsea with a yacht in the South of France. This was a toy-boy from Uxbridge who lived with his Nan and slept in a single bed beneath posters of football players. All I could think about was Caleb in a leather thong and a bow-tie, strip teasing for a woman old enough to be his mum. I heard him walk upstairs. I began putting on my clothes, checking the cost of an Uber back to Streatham. It was expensive, but desperate times call for desperate measures.

'You're leaving already?'

'I think it's for the best. Don't you?'

To my relief, Caleb didn't seem too bothered.

'I've called a cab,' I said, adjusting my bra. 'It'll be here any minute.'

I grabbed my bag and began walking down the stairs. This time, I didn't care about tiptoeing. Caleb followed, showing me to the door. I was hurt he hadn't offered to pay for my Uber, but then again – what did I expect?

'Verity?' He said as I walked out.

'Yes?'

'Can you transfer me £9.12 for half the pizza, please? I'll text you my bank details.' Two words: The audacity.

For every guy with a Rolex, there's a story behind it. And it isn't always pretty.

Chapter 7 – Abel

Three months later
Kill & Kontent PR, Clerkenwell

I had lost half a stone since starting at Kill & Kontent.

It wasn't intentional. It was down to the relentlessness of my PR lifestyle. The days were as long as the to-do lists, and the to-do lists were as never-ending as the caffeine intake (or in Daniel's case – cocaine). As I settled into my role, six o'clock finishes quickly became a thing of the past. It was frowned upon to leave the office until everything was completed. Sometimes, this meant staying until half past ten at night, speaking with clients over an evening meal of Diet Coke and fruit pastels.

'You sound delirious Verity,' wailed my mother on the phone one evening. 'Do you have any idea how worried I am?'

I couldn't put off calling her any more than I already had. She had left me dozens of voicemail messages over the last few weeks, asking whether I was eating, sleeping, and if I still remembered her. (No, no, and unfortunately, yes.)

'Your father's been in touch. He says you've hardly spoken to him. We're both very concerned…'

'I'm fine. I promise.'

'You know I loathe the word "fine." Where are you now? It sounds terribly noisy.'

'I'm leaving work, Mum. As for the noise – I'm in central London.'

'You're leaving work? At this hour? Good heavens!' She paused. Her voice had turned coarse. Tears were imminent. 'Don't tell me things like this, Verity. It upsets me so.'

'Long hours are part of the PR industry, Mum – an industry I am now very much in.'

'What will you eat for dinner this evening, then?'

'Dunno. I'll heat up some shepherd's pie or something.'

'Oh! well I am pleased. If I did anything right as a mother, it was to teach my daughter how to make shepherd's pie. It's a skill that serves a woman for a lifetime.'

This was a lie I had to say in order to cease her nagging. Really, my free time wasn't spent buying ingredients to prepare wholesome meals. It was spent arm in arm with Lily in Mayfair, sipping on cocktails and kissing random men at bars. On Sundays we were either snooping round properties as Lilian and Vivian or binge watching *Absolutely Fabulous* on the sofa. Truthfully, I don't think either of us knew how our oven even worked.

Despite going to an all-girls boarding school, I had never bothered too much about my weight. It was surprising, given that Pipford was fraught with girls suffering from every eating disorder imaginable, which seemed to mutate in a single sex environment. Lunchtimes were supervised, and the process was like going through airport security. You formed a single line outside the dining hall, and were inspected with military precision as you walked in. If your plate looked suspiciously unfinished, you were summoned into the boarding mistress's office, put on a pair of scales and interrogated with questions. I was once called in for leaving half a portion of hotpot on my plate for two Thursdays in a row, just because I disliked undissolved gravy granules. For two weeks, I had to tick off my lunchtime attendance on a clipboard. It was barbaric.

'You've lost weight,' said Hayley one afternoon at work. 'Are you on a diet?'

'Nope,' I said, signing an email. 'I just haven't cooked a meal for months.'

She nibbled on the end of her pen, twirling a strand of her hair. 'What's your deal then?'

'What deal?'

'Well, what are you on? Laxatives? Cigarettes? Pills?'

'Pills? God, no!'

'So you purge, then?'

I couldn't believe how casually she was talking about eating disorders, but then again – I could. This was a hot topic in my sixth form common room, and one I knew all too well. It felt like being back at school again.

'Hayley,' I whispered. 'I don't have an eating disorder. It's probably just the stress of working here.'

'I'm desensitised,' she sighed. 'Been bulimic since I was fifteen, haven't I?'

I felt uncomfortable. Apart from men, Hayley and I rarely spoke about anything personal. I had blurred that line with Toni, and it had been disastrous. Now that Hayley had admitted it, it all made sense. Hayley went to the toilet on a suspiciously frequent basis and sucked obsessively on mints. I should have been more receptive – confronted her gently, given her a safe space to open up.

'I can recommend you some support groups if you like,' I said. 'I used to accompany my friend to them. There's loads in London…'

'Thanks, Verity, but I survive. I survive just fine.'

Daniel suddenly burst through the doors, striding to my desk with the fierceness of a runway model.

'Kristen wants you. Now. Like, right now.'

'I thought you said two?'

'I said one. It was one, wasn't it?'

I didn't bother checking my emails to prove myself right and Daniel wrong. I was getting used to his appalling timekeeping.

'Go, go go!' he said, clapping his hands in my face. 'What are you waiting for – Gwen Stefani?' Kristen was in the middle of an intense phone call when I arrived at her office. I paused, watching her speak through the glass. Somehow, she was even more beautiful when she was stressed. She paced the room, waving her arms in frustration which made her gold bangles sound like wind chimes. Eventually, she ended the phone call and buried her forehead into her hands. It was clearly an unsuccessful conversation. Despite being the CEO, Kristen's presence made me feel more at ease than anyone else in the company. She smiled at me to come in, and I took a seat immediately.

'Tough client?'

'Just a miscommunication,' she dismissed. 'How are you, sweetheart?'

'I'm well. Did Daniel tell you about–'

'About your work with Livewire,' she beamed. 'Which is why I've called you in today. I've discussed it with Daniel, and we want you to represent the company at the ATC next month.' The ATC was a big deal. It stood for the Annual Tech Conference – a large-scale event hosted every summer for everyone in the industry. It was the perfect opportunity to scout new clients for Kill & Kontent. Hayley told me it was Daniel's job to go, although this year, she was hoping it would be her. I couldn't believe Kristen had asked me. She read the shocked look on my face.

'No ifs or buts, Verity.'

'But I–'

'It's not a question of company hierarchy. It's a question of charm; who is most able to retain clients and attract new ones.'

'Hayley's face lights up when she talks about the ATC. Plus, she seemed jealous when I went to that networking event last month…'

'Enough. I've got to a to-do list the length of my arm, and it doesn't include listening to tales of your imposter syndrome.'

'Sorry, it's just Hayley–'

'Is good behind a screen but lacks charisma in person. You're going, and I've already confirmed your attendance. Case closed.'

I suddenly imagined Hayley's disappointment when she realised that I would be going to the ATC rather than her.

'Please lose those sorry little puppy eyes. You deserve this opportunity.' Kristen reached for her purse, leaving a £20 note on her desk. 'Go and buy a sandwich from that new deli across the road. You're in desperate need of something calorific and beige.'

I didn't know whether to be offended or not, but as I reminded myself: this was PR.

* * *

'What can I get you?'

Shit. He's hot. Very hot. Pin me up against the wall and kiss my neck right now kind of hot. Think, Verity, think. What do you want? Tell him what you want! I cast my eyes up at the menu, but all the words blurred into meaningless squiggles. They looked more like hieroglyphics as opposed to sandwich fillings. My heart was doing dubstep. I think it was the combination of having had four coffees before noon and being around a man who looked like a sculpture that had just come to life in a museum.

'Can I have a BLT, please?' I blurted. 'With no tomato or lettuce. Or mayo.'

I was talking far too quickly. I seriously needed a restraining order against caffeine.

'Well then it's not a BLT, is it?' said the guy. 'It's a bacon sandwich.'

He leaned forward, flexing his arms. He was watching me watch them. He grinned knowingly, sensing the effect he was having on me.

'Fine,' I mumbled, reaching for my purse. 'Well then I'll take a non-BLT, BLT.'

Why am I so awkward?

'Anything to drink?'

'An orange juice, please. I need to load up on the vitamins.'

'Well in that case I'll add a ginger shot.'

He winked at me and I smiled back. We were flirting, I think. I gazed at him preparing my order, fantasising about being enveloped in his strong, muscular arms...

Just then, a customer walked in. I took it as my prompt to grab my sandwich and head back to the office.

'Take a loyalty card if you like,' said deli guy, handing me my order. 'They're just by the front.'

I had an overwhelming urge to step out my comfort zone and do something spontaneous. I was going to do a Lily; seize my destiny and grab it by the balls. I scribbled my name and number down on the back of a loyalty card and left it on the counter. I hurried out the door quickly, waiting for fate to work its magic, feeling like the baddest bitch in the world.

* * *

I was impressed with my move at the coffee shop that afternoon, and decided that the world needed to hear about it. By the world, I meant Lily.

'Guess what happened today?'

'You got a promotion?'

'No, but I did get asked to attend the Annual Tech Conference this July.'

'See!' she said, reaching for a bottle of wine from the

fridge. 'I knew from the second you came in tonight that you'd made a killer career move.'

'And a bad bitch move. I met a guy at a coffee shop and gave him my number.'

'You did not!'

'I absolutely did.'

'Iconic. You a year ago would never have done that.'

Lily was right. This time a last year, I was entangled in a Kyle whirlwind; lost in an all-consuming haze of brand-new romance. When our relationship had puttered to a stop, I'd spent countless nights in my bed wondering if I would ever feel the same about someone else again. After the Caleb situation, I had grown cynical.

'Has he messaged you yet?'

I nodded. 'Earlier this afternoon. His name is Abel. He wants to meet me on my lunchbreak on Friday.'

'I thought you didn't get a lunchbreak?'

I felt my phone vibrate. It was Instagram, notifying me that I had a new follower called 'PrinceAbel_93.'

He had stalked my pictures from as far back as my au pair days in Spain. He'd slid into my dm's, too, sending me a picture of myself that I had taken on the beach in Australia with Naomi.

'You are all kinds of beautiful.'

I grinned to myself and put my phone away. I was meeting him Friday. It was decided.

* * *

'I need to leave the office for a bit. I won't be long.'

Daniel raised one eyebrow and Hayley pursed her lips. They both knew it wasn't for a client meeting. They never happened on Fridays.

Neither of their expressions warranted an explanation for

why I was leaving, other than that if I did it again then I would be judged, scrutinised and quite possibly beheaded. This was clearly my one time 'get out of jail' free card. I grabbed my bag and scurried out the office to go and meet Abel. As I headed past reception, Jennifer shot me a frosty glare. It was extra icy. She was like a watchdog.

'Where are you going?'

'Mind your business,' I snapped, tossing my hair. 'Don't you have nails to file?'

Since receiving praise from Kristen that I was thriving at the company, I had gained enough confidence to rise above office bitchiness. I knew my worth. It was time for the world to.

I had arranged to meet Abel at a café near the office. I did ask if he minded going to another coffee shop given that he worked at one, but he said it didn't matter as long as it involved seeing me again. Since he had stalked me on Instagram, his messages had become increasingly intense. He was texting me late, saying he thought romance was dead until I had scribbled my number down on the back of a loyalty card. He had asked for my star sign and sent me a screenshot of our romantic compatibility. He referred to me as his 'English rose' and had sent me three red love heart emoji's before I'd even woken up. Naomi thought it was sweet. Max thought it was hilarious. Lily thought it was psychotic.

Abel was already sat at a table when I arrived, dressed in a bright blue Lycra two-piece. He looked like a model for a wetsuit campaign.

'Sorry I'm late,' I said, kissing him on either cheek. 'I had to wrap up a client call.'

'Don't stress. I'd wait for you forever, babe.'

I quickly realised the intensity of Abel's texts was matched in person. He kept complimenting me on how beautiful I looked, when really, I was frazzled and had period pimples.

It was technically a first date, but somehow, I didn't feel too nervous. A few days ago, Abel was just Deli Guy. Now, he was Abel. Ethereal Abel. A six-foot four statue god with muscles in places I didn't know existed.

'Sit opposite me, babe,' he smiled. 'I want to look into your eyes properly.'

Just then, the waitress brought over a tray with green juices and a granola pots.

'I ordered us something healthy. You said you needed to load up on the vitamins.'

'That was thoughtful.'

Abel smiled. 'You were confident giving me your number the other day.'

'I don't know what came over me, to be honest. It's usually my friend Lily, who–'

'I liked it.'

I giggled. I didn't know how to receive Abel's intense energy.

'You're cute when you laugh.' He stroked my nose and brushed his thumb against my cheek. 'Like, seriously cute.'

'Thanks.'

'Your beauty is mesmerising.'

'Thank you…'

'And your eyes. Spellbinding.'

Abel looked deadly serious. I didn't know what to make of his compliments. I began asking him typical first dates questions: Where are you from? Do you have siblings? Travelled much? Perhaps it was because we'd texted so much already that Abel wasn't interested in talking about himself. He either brushed off the question or deflected it back at me. The guy wasn't a fan of small talk – his only appetite was for the here and now. He wouldn't stop staring at me.

'What colour are your eyes?'

He slid the granola pot towards me, encouraging me to

eat. I picked up my spoon and tucked in, feeling his gaze bore into me as I ate.

'Hazel.'

I looked up at Abel's gaze, uncompromising and gentle. We both knew he had queried the colour of my eyes on purpose. He wanted to give himself a proper excuse to stare into them without looking like a weirdo, although either way, he did.

'I think your eyes are more green than they are hazel,' he said softly. 'That's rare, you know. Only two percent of the world's population has green eyes. It makes you even more of a mythical creature.'

It sounded as if he were reciting Keats or Shelley. I felt Abel's hand gravitate towards me, as his fingers slid into the spaces of mine. The intimacy felt a little startling.

'Look at your hands!' squealed Abel. 'They look so cute against mine.'

Comparing hand sizes is a fool-proof flirting tactic. I played my part and held mine up against his, pretending to chuckle at how small it looked. Really, I was more concerned at getting back to the office. I felt my phone vibrate. My heart sunk when I read Hayley's message.

'Where the fuck are you? You had a client call at half one and you missed it. Daniel's fuming. You can't just leave whenever you feel like—'

I panicked instantly. The last thing I wanted to do was compromise my position at the ATC.

'I think I had better get going,' I said, taking my hand back protectively. 'I've got work to finish and I'll be in trouble if I'm late.'

'Can we meet again this weekend?'

'I'm busy this weekend.'

'After work sometime?'

'Maybe,' I smiled, grabbing my bag. 'I'll let you know.'

'I hope you will. I'd love to see you again, my sweet English Rose.'

I gave him a quick hug goodbye and headed back to the office. It was a more abrupt departure than I had intended for, but I was panicked. My mind began to run rampant over thoughts of Abel as I headed back to the office; his body, his hands, his voice – the tender way he looked at me. It was a forgotten feeling of romance, which I hadn't experienced since Kyle. It didn't feel peaceful like it had done with him.

It felt totally inconvenient.

* * *

Despite my best efforts, I fell for Abel. He was thoughtful and brought me lunch to work every day. I'd get a call from Jennifer around noon, informing me that there was a bag waiting for me at reception. She'd demand I hurry down to get it as she was a vegan, and apparently the smell of bacon made her think of piglets being tortured. Abel had left me a sandwich, juice and a handwritten note scribbled on a napkin. It was simple things at first, like 'I hope you smash your meeting today!' and 'I miss your smile ☺', but as the days went by, the messages became deeper. Abel started writing things like 'you deserve the world, and I hope it's me who gets to give it to you' and 'I feel as if I could climb Mount Everest with you by my side.' I developed a habit of sneaking out the office, telling Daniel that I had to collect medication for a recurring yeast infection, when really, I was going to frolic around with Abel for twenty minutes against a wall. It was sickeningly pathetic, but I couldn't help it. I enjoyed the attention too much.

'I am never going to hurt you,' he said one day, kissing my neck. 'I promise.'

Gradually, the napkin notes transpired into chocolates, cookies and hampers. It was behaviour I'd witnessed between Kyle and Toni – but on an extreme level. Abel would leave large wicker baskets for me at reception containing cellophane wrapped sweets and treats. It became a weekly occurrence.

'You need to check before ordering things like this into the office,' snapped Jennifer. 'Some of us are dairy intolerant and allergic to nuts.'

'It's not me ordering them. Quite clearly they're gifts.'

'So you don't take my allergies seriously?'

'I didn't say that.'

'There's a box of donuts here right now with peanut butter frosting on top. Peanut butter! I could die, Verity.'

I'd wander down to retrieve whatever Abel had brought me and leave them on the communal table for people to help themselves. The gifts were always decorated in red ribbon, so it became increasingly obvious to the whole office that I was receiving male attention. Hayley pointed it out one afternoon whilst breaking into a giant heart-shaped red velvet cookie. 'People are gossiping about you, and I thought you should hear it from me first.'

'Saying what?'

'Speculating on your secret admirer, of course. Deli Boy.'

In the evenings, I received not hampers, but Shakespearean sonnets. Abel would send me lengthy paragraphs, declaring his feelings for me as if I were the love of his life and the world was ending tomorrow.

'My love for you surpasses the quantity of every grain of sand in God's creation, which seems to be revolving at triple the speed since my eyes met yours,' read Lily. 'Bloody hell. You've only known the guy a few of weeks.'

'Extreme, I know.'

'Extreme doesn't cut it. He put his dick inside you last

week and said 'Thank you.' I mean, do you want me to go on? Because I can.'

'Abel's just sensitive,' I bashed. 'He wears his heart on his sleeve.'

Lily pretended to throw up. Admittedly, her reading of Abel's text had sort of made me want to do the same. I think I was getting 'the ick.'

Today was Friday, and my lunch bag from Abel included a banana with a message written on the skin asking me to meet him outside at three o'clock. Daniel had grown suspicious of my constant desk hopping, but I had to tell Abel in person that we were moving too fast.

'I'm just going to pop to the pharmacy.'

'Again?' asked Daniel, rolling his eyes. 'Are you dying, or something?'

'It's my yeast infection,' I whispered. 'It's flared up again.'

I twitched in my seat for dramatic effect to make the excuse more believable. Daniel looked utterly repulsed, but it was a clever excuse. Any medical problem relating to female genitalia is never something a man can dispute. As I approached the deli, Abel was waiting for me outside with the largest bouquet of roses I had ever seen. They were long stem – I was sure of it. I held them in my arms, inhaling their sweet scent. Finally, I was the girl who was receiving roses. I'd watched it be Toni, and now it was my turn. I should have felt infinitely more elated than I did. All I could think about was how I would smuggle them back to the office without anyone noticing.

'I think I love you.' Abel's tone was low and intense. For a mad moment I thought he was going to get down on one knee and propose to me with a diamond ring. 'It's ok if you don't feel it yet,' he said, grabbing both of my shoulders. 'I know you will soon.' His eyes suddenly began to water. He looked overcome with emotion.

'What's wrong, Abel? You've gone all serious.'

'I am serious. I'm scared you'll break my heart.'

Frankly, I didn't know what to say. This was clearly not a good time to suggest we hit pause on our situationship.

'Don't be upset. I'm enjoying getting to know you.'

'Shall we go to the cinema tomorrow?' He chirped. 'They're showing the thriller movie of that book you like.'

'I'm not sure. I might be at the office till late. I keep making up excuses to leave my desk to meet you…'

'But I've already bought the tickets,' he wept. 'I got VIP seats and everything!' My phone started ringing. It was Hayley calling me.

'Calm down, Abel, ok? I'll see what I can do.'

* * *

I thought I would be able to hide the roses at reception, but Jennifer was having none of it.

'We're not allowed to store personal belongings behind reception. It's company rules. Sorry.'

She wasn't sorry at all. Quite the opposite, in fact. She sat back on her chair with one eyebrow raised, delighting in watching me struggle with the bouquet. I started to panic. I didn't know what to do. The cookies and cakes were one thing, but roses were a different story. If Hayley and Daniel saw them, I'd be outed and the truth behind my pretend pharmacy trips would be exposed. I decided to rush back outside and squash them in the nearest bin.

'I'd be scared, if I were you,' muttered Jennifer when I returned. 'Last time a girl snuck out to meet a guy, it didn't end well. Her name was Madeline.'

'What happened?'

Jennifer shrugged. 'Last I heard, she's an au pair in Spain.'

* * *

The atmosphere was uncomfortable when I met Abel for our cinema date the following evening. I knew I had to call the shots, and I sensed Abel wouldn't take it well. He was waiting for me outside Trafalgar Square with a giant teddy bear. It was almost half the size of him. He turned the teddy bear's head and waved either one of its arms, putting on a squeaky pretend voice. 'Hello! My name's Buttercup.'

'Enough, Abel.' I pushed it away, agitated. 'You can't keep buying me all this stuff.' He looked offended.

'What's wrong, baby?'

Once upon a time I'd longed to be called 'baby.' Now, it was just making me gag.

'Nothing's wrong,' I snapped. 'I just don't know where I'm going to put it, that's all. We'll look nuts carrying a giant teddy into the cinema.'

Sure enough, we did. The man was demanding we pay for an extra seat to facilitate it.

'Can't we just put it on the floor?'

'We can't put him on the floor, Verity! How would you feel if I did that to you?'

The ticket man stared at us blankly, as if we were putting on a comedy show. I couldn't help but feel that he was gaining joy from watching Abel and I squabble. It was probably the highlight of his evening. 'It's practically the size of a human,' said the ticket man. 'You either pay for an extra seat, or I can't allow you into the screening.'

I looked at the teddy with its chubby arms popping out either side of its round tummy. It had a red bow wrapped round it's neck with a heart shaped pendant that read 'be mine.' I felt the same way towards it as I had done about the roses yesterday. Resentment.

'I'll pay,' said Abel. 'Go on up and choose some snacks. Maybe we can get Buttercup a little bucket of popcorn!'

By the time Abel and I had found our way to the correct screen, we looked as if we were moving houses. Between us, we had my handbag, two buckets of popcorn, a hotdog, a box of sweets, Fanta frozen and a giant teddy bear.

'Why are cinema's so dark?' I hushed, going inside. 'We may as well be blindfolded.'

'We're row M, babe.'

'Row M? Why couldn't you have picked a more convenient letter of the alphabet? You knew I was coming from work.'

I was being exceptionally cranky. I think I was due on my period. I hoped to god I was, because it was nearly a week late. The last thing I needed was a pregnancy horror; with Abel of all men. As we trudged up the steps trying to locate our seats, I fell over and bashed my knee. I spluttered the popcorn all over the floor.

'Ouch!'

'Baby! Are you ok?'

'The film has already started,' sneered a woman from the side. 'Stop ruining it for the rest of us!'

When Abel and I eventually found row 'M,' we had to ask the couple next to us to shuffle along and accommodate for the giant teddy bear.

'His name's Buttercup!' said Abel to the couple, as if the teddy bear were our child. God knows what he'd be like if we really did have a child. Please let my period come. As we settled into the film, Abel's eyes were more fixed on me than the movie. He stared at my side profile the entire time with intense fascination, utterly love-struck.

'Watch the movie,' I whispered, nibbling on the hotdog. 'You're missing the good parts.' Abel didn't take his eyes off me. It was intense and uncomfortable. The more obsessed Abel became with me, the more obsessed I became with work. My mind began to spiral over client admin, the ATC next month and the opinions of Daniel and Hayley. My behaviour over the last month had slacked, and I longed to reverse time. I became so entangled with regret that by the time the film had ended, I had missed the plot entirely.

'What did you think?' asked Abel, as the credits went up. 'Better than the book?'

'It didn't do it justice. Film versions never do.'

Abel's eyes began to puddle with tears. A single tear plopped down his face.

'What now, Abel?'

'You're just so clever when you speak.' He sniffed, dabbing his eyes with the end of his hoodie. 'I'm in love with how your mind works. I'm so lucky. I just can't believe it when I look at…'

I gripped onto Abel's arm suddenly, shrieking with pain. 'Ouch!'

A sharp, stabbing sensation rippled throughout my entire uterus. My boobs began to throb and my knickers felt wet.

'Sorry, Abel, but we need to get going. I think my period has just come on.'

He looked panicked, clearly seeing this as an opportunity for him to swoon in and save the day as my knight in shining armour. 'Do you want me to carry you, beautiful?'

'No,' I blushed. 'It's just a bit of blood. I don't know if you're aware, but it happens to a woman every month.'

Abel grabbed my bags, took the teddy and pulled me right out my chair, hurrying me down the stairs.

'Excuse me, everyone! My baby girl isn't well.' He turned to face me. 'It'll be ok, beautiful. I've got you.'

Huddles of people began to stare as we shuffled past them, making our way out the door. Abel was displaying the compassion of a husband supporting his wife in labour. It was over the top, making my pain worse.

'Is she ok?' asked one woman. 'Do you need an ambulance?'

'Verity?' said Abel. 'Do you think we should call one?'

I was starting to have a flashback of my date with Pablo. The memory of the Spanish waiter came flooding back – thick, fast and nauseating. I felt as if I was in the café again.

'It's just a period pain,' I snapped. 'Of course we don't need an ambulance.'

Admittedly, I wasn't convinced. I hadn't experienced pain quite like this before. The dull ache spread across my legs, rippling through my entire back. I had leaked blood on my tights, too. I could feel it dripping down my legs.

Eventually we made our way out of the screening. Abel began pacing around the entrance trying to book an Uber. I knew he was being protective. All he wanted was to care for me. I crouched down against the wall, burying my head into my hands.

'It'll be here in five,' said Abel. 'Hold tight.'

My mind began to ruminate over uncompleted client work and all I had to catch up on next week. The more I thought about it, the worse the pain got. My stomach throbbed, as if it were punishing me for being such a hopeless romantic and getting caught up in an Abel whirlwind.

I felt my muscles weaken as I flopped to the side.

'Baby!' Abel screamed, rushing over to me. 'Let me help you…'

'Please, just stop!' I tried to push him away from me, but it was too late. I toppled onto the carpet and blacked out.

* * *

I woke up to the sensation of Abel's hot breath tickling in my ear.

'Verity?' he whispered. 'Oh, thank God you're awake! We're in Brixton, at my place.' I opened my eyes, jolting at the sight of a giant teddy bear next to me. 'What the…'

'Buttercup!' laughed Abel. 'I brought him for you earlier, don't you remember? Perhaps you're suffering delirium, beautiful.'

I think I was. Everything felt like a blur. All I could remember was Abel pacing the cinema entrance, trying to book an Uber.

'What happened to me?'

'You fainted,' he said. 'I was so worried, you know. I didn't know what to do.' I noticed a guitar propped in the corner. Abel saw me look at it and smiled. 'Let me serenade you better, baby. It'll help.'

He picked it up and sat on the end of the bed, fiddling around with the keys.

Oh god. Please don't sing. Please. Ok… nope… too late. Abel had broken into a re-rendition of 'If You're Not The One' by Daniel Bedingfield an octave higher than the original. I didn't think that was even possible, but unfortunately, it was. For someone with such a deep voice, Abel's vocal cords were ear-piercingly high. I shuffled up, trying to regain a sense of equilibrium. Pain rippled through my stomach again, reminding me I had come on my period. Shit. Had I leaked onto the sheet? I lifted the duvet to check as Abel continued singing. I sighed with relief that his bedding was still clean. All was well.

… Except it wasn't. Abel was erupting into full on tears as he reached the bridge of the song.

'Abel!' I interrupted. 'Why are you so upset?'

'There's something about the lyrics in this song. It reminds me of us. I can't believe I've found you, Verity…'

Abel buried his forehead close to mine, smothering me with kisses. Like a trigger, my brain began to stew with how much I had to do at the office. Frankly, I wanted to go there now to make a start with it all. I had to end things with Abel. It would break his heart, but it was now or never.

'I don't want to do this anymore.'

I paused. I was waiting for Abel to crumble into a blubbering mess, but he seemed calm. It was the opposite of what I had expected from him. It made me feel guilty.

'It's work at the moment. It's full on, I have no time, I–'

'You don't need to explain,' he said. 'I understand.'

It would have been easier for him to scream – to cry, to lash out at me, to demand answers. At least then I'd be able to reconcile my decision with the fact he was too intense, too emotional, too smothering. That's how a heartbroken person is supposed to behave. I would know, because I usually am one. The role reversal felt strange.

'You have a lot of love to give,' I mumbled. 'Your affections are better spent on someone else – someone who can truly appreciate them.'

Abel paused for a moment. 'The problem with you, Verity, is that you're so used to bad men who pretend to love you that you barely recognise the good ones who really do.'

I didn't know what to say. Abel was speaking to me like a wise therapist.

'Don't ever feel that you didn't deserve my love. You deserve the love of a good man more than any woman I know. You just don't know how to receive it.'

I never saw Abel again after that night, but his words were significant.

Chapter 8 – Grant Black

Six weeks later
Kill & Kontent PR, Clerkenwell

'Good news, sunshine,' said Daniel. His eyes were glued to his computer screen and his fingers were moving manically against the keyboard like live fish caught in a net.

'What?'

'Your week's holiday has been approved.'

Thank God. I was dying for some off.

'You could use a week to recharge,' chipped in Hayley. 'The circles beneath your eyes look like the shadows of two dead bats.'

Daniel looked over as if he was thinking the same thing. 'Hibernate, meditate, masturbate – I don't care.'

I stared at the reflection of my face in my computer screen. Hayley was right – I looked exhausted. The last month at the office had been strenuous. I'd thrown myself back into work; early starts, late finishes, meeting as many clients as possible. Since the Abel fiasco, I'd been determined to regain everyone's respect, and had subsequently pushed myself harder than ever. Later that night, I tried to tempt Lily into coming away with me to a spa for a few days. 'Can't we save spa trips for when we're divorced and forty-five?'

'But I need a break,' I wailed. 'We could go to one of those fancy retreats in the countryside – somewhere rural, near Pipford!'

'Somewhere near Pipford?' Lily turned her nose up. 'No thank you.'

'Oxford, Buckinghamshire. There's loads of getaways round there. Just for a few days…'

I knew it was a firm no. Lily was just as busy I was. She'd been staying at the studio until the early hours most nights this week, on standby in case she was flown off to work on a music video in Hong Kong. There was no way she'd budge.

'Let's go out this weekend instead. Have a real blast – just like the old days.'

'Chelsea?'

'Good thinking. I still have Dex's number. He's liked every single one of my Instagram posts since the Caleb night and replies to my stories with the flame emoji. If that doesn't qualify for a free table in VIP then I don't know what does.'

I shuddered at the thought of Caleb in his single bed and leather thong.

'Perhaps we should try somewhere different,' I said. 'What about The Bluebird?'

'Perfect!'

* * *

By the time Saturday night came round, I wasn't just ready for a blast. I was ready for a full-blown thunderstorm. It had felt like forever since Lily and I had gone on a proper night out, frolicking around as Lilian and Vivian. I'd missed us being partners in crime, wild, giddy and loose, when our only concern was whether we would make it to our house viewing in Mayfair the next morning. I was nostalgic for that phase of our friendship again, and had a strong urge to dismantle the drudgery of my work schedule with a spark of something new and exciting. I put on my favourite black bodycon dress with a daring red lip and rocked up to The Bluebird with Lily at around nine. Chelsea was a bustling hub of glamorous, beautiful people. I looked around the bar at the clusters of twenty-somethings gossiping noisily over cocktails at tables. We had never been to The Bluebird before, but it was number seven on Lily's notes page of London spots to try. We still had seventy-three to get through. Everyone in Chelsea looked as if they had stepped out of Forbes or Vogue. They all seemed to know each other, to know something about somebody; and the somebody they knew something about looked as if they knew something wild and revolutionary. I felt like an imposter. Lily, on the other hand, was confidently ordering us champagne at the bar as if she was a regular. The waiter presented us with two glasses of champagne, which we sipped immediately.

'We forget to cheers,' gushed Lily, holding up her glass. 'To getting drunk, kissing strangers and waking up in hotel beds that aren't ours.'

We both downed the champagne as if it were a magical potion that was going to transform Lily's toast into a reality.

'I can tell you mean business tonight, Vee. You haven't worn a red lip in ages.'

'I have a theory that when a woman wears red lipstick, she becomes invincible. She gets femme-fatale superpowers. Toni, for example, wore MAC 'Ruby Woo' on the night she stole my boyfriend.'

We knocked back another glass, patiently waiting for something to happen; something crazy that would add a splash of colour on the canvas of our youth. Within ten minutes, Lily was starting to get twitchy. She said she wanted our dresses to get the attention they deserved, and no one had looked over to us since we arrived.

'Shall I call Novikov to see if they have any tables left?'

I glanced around the room, feeling my gaze shift towards

a much older man sat alone at the bar. Lily caught me looking instantly.

'Come off it, Vee. He's ancient.'

'He's sexy.'

'He's old. You're not gonna go over there, are you?'

'I don't know. Should I?'

'No. He could be married.'

'He's not wearing a ring. Look.'

We both glanced over. The man was staring into space with a vacant gaze through a pair of tinted aviators, sipping on a glass of amber coloured liquid I could only assume was whiskey. The sleeves of his white shirt were rolled up. He was covered in tattoos. I noticed Lily study them from afar. Tattoos were a well-known aphrodisiac when it came to her taste in men. Perhaps she was struck by his nonchalant air of confidence, too, for he was sat alone without a damn to give. Intrigue was making its way over to us like the faint beginnings of smoke from a deadly warning fire.

'Eleven-eleven; make a wish!'

Lily was superstitious whenever it was eleven minutes past the hour. She made her wish, morning and night, no matter where she was or who she was with. It was a habit she had maintained since she was thirteen. In fact, she attributed all her success to the fact she had never forgotten a time where she didn't say it, even if it was during a eulogy reading at a funeral. This was a true story when Lily was sixteen. Her mother had never forgiven her for being so starry-eyed and selfish. Lily had forced the saying onto me, but unless I am with her then I'll forget to say it. Maybe that's why my love life has failed more epically than hers.

We both closed our eyes, wishing, I think, for the same thing. 'I'll admit it, Vee. That man doesn't look half bad for his age.'

'Told you.'

'I think we should go and talk to him. He might be useful.'

'Wait!' I said, grabbing onto her arm. 'Do you think he wants to be disturbed?'

'Who the fuck cares?'

* * *

One hour later, the three of us were chatting away like old friends. The man's name was Grant Black, and he was the sharpest, wittiest most amusing man I had ever spoken to. He'd written a book on the avoidance of marriage – a notion which seemed to relate to Lily's free-spirited way of thinking and the ongoing failure of my romantic experiences.

'If there was any love, trust or belief in marriage, there would be no need for marriage in the first place; and there would be no divorce, either. Really, it is an unnecessary item on the shopping list of life.'

I sat there, quietly observing Grant like a star-studded speaker at a concert hall. I was enjoying listening to him speak, even if I did look like a placid lemon. Lily, on the other hand, was talking louder than usual, flicking her hair in a way I'd never seen before and finding things funny that she usually didn't.

'The shopping list of my life is long,' she giggled. 'I might have to get married, just so I can fund it all with tasty divorce settlements. I'll need at least three or four. One won't cut it.'

'Divorce turns nightmares into a reality and reality into a nightmare. It is a travesty; but then again, so is marriage.'

I giggled at Grant's wit. I don't think Lily had caught onto it yet.

'I want a Louis Vuitton jewellery case, a diamond encrusted Cartier watch and a house in the Hamptons by the time I'm thirty. Failing that, Bermuda.'

'That's some list,' Grant said. 'I think you should choose things that are more expensive.' Lily laughed, touching his arm. 'Will you be on my Instagram story?'

Before Grant could respond, Lily had opened her phone camera. She began firing Grant with questions I was thinking but didn't have the guts to ask. It turned me from an observational lemon into a profusely apologetic one.

'Have you ever been married?'

'Once. Now widowed.'

'You can't ask that, Lily.'

'Have you got a girlfriend? Some hot young chick?'

'No.'

'Shut up, Lily!'

'What's up with all your tattoos?'

'I wanted to piss my father off.'

'Sorry about her, Grant…'

'If you're retired, what do you do every day?'

'Read books, enjoy coffee and sunbathe naked.'

That one got us both.

Lily's questionnaire continued for another round, when I realised Grant wasn't all that fazed by her audacity. He found her cheekiness endearing, which admittedly made me a little jealous. We learned that Grant resided in Malibu California as a scriptwriter, but only when he felt like it. He had been retired for ten years, and spent a lot of time travelling. He was passing in London fleetingly to visit a relative. There was no job he hadn't done, no country he hadn't visited, no restaurant he hadn't dined at. His life was like a colourful patchwork quilt. I wanted to learn every square.

'What about you, Verity?'

I blushed. 'What about me?'

'Well, I know about Lily's world. What about yours?'

I didn't want to share details of my PR life. I was more than happy to sit and listen to Grant speak. Hearing his stories was like falling in love with a new song by an artist you never knew; going to their concert for free, and hanging out with them backstage after.

'Verity likes poems and books and black and white romance movies,' blabbered Lily. 'She's been working as a junior executive at a PR firm for almost six months.'

Grant brushed Lily off, asking me what I'd do if I didn't work in PR and anything was possible.

'Write, eventually.'

I blushed crimson red. I'd never said that out loud before. Whether it was to appear more interesting to Grant, or compete with Lily, I did not know.

'Write?' mumbled Lily. I felt the heel of her shoe kick mine from beneath the table. 'Since when do you write?'

I'd never admitted it to anyone before, but writing was something I had longed to do since I was a girl. Secretly, I had hoped the universe would pave the way for me to start it somehow, but life kept throwing hurdles my way. Australia, Stanley's, Kill & Kontent and a series of London dating disasters with a limitless capacity for failure. Writing hadn't happened for me yet, but I lived in the hope that it would.

'When I write, I could do it forever and ever. When you think about it, writing is a lot like kissing. If you're writing the right book, or kissing the right man, then both have a way of making time stand still.'

I wasn't making much sense. I think it was the champagne taking over. Lily rolled her eyes and told Grant that I often get these poetic outbursts when I'm tipsy, and to take it with a pinch of salt.

'Verity's a dreamer,' snapped Lily. 'She's a lover of Luhrmann.'

'Lily's a visionary. She's a sucker for Scorsese.'

'Or Brian De Palma. *The Unforgettables. Scarface.* Those are two of my favourites.'

'Lily has seen *Scarface* seven times,' I said. 'Can you believe that?'

'Which one are you, Grant?' Lily held her phone camera up to his face again. 'A visionary or a dreamer?'

I don't know why we were addressing Grant by his first name so much. Lily and I had always taken mutual solace that neither of us would fall out over a man, because we were both attracted to completely different types. Our only exception was a gay fitness instructor at our boxing class. Handsome older men like Grant were unchartered waters to us both. I wasn't sure if even Lily had enough nerve to go there. I wasn't even sure if I did.

'I don't like love stories,' said Grant. 'I like stories about love.'

'I'm sure you know all about love,' said Lily. 'You know, being so much older and all that.' Grant laughed. 'I am old. I'm fifty-four.'

Lily tossed her hair back, downing half the glass of her champagne in one sip. 'When I'm fifty-four I hope to be retired in LA, draped in pearls, sipping on margaritas in pink waterfall coupes with two pet tigers on the lawn.'

Lily dragged my arm away from the table, summoning me to the bathroom. I didn't have the chance to excuse myself to Grant, but he didn't seem to mind. I think he was enjoying our company.

'Do you really need the loo?' I hushed. 'I was enjoying chatting to him.'

'I can tell. I think you should go for it.'

'Really? I don't want to stand in your way...'

'You saw him first! Besides, he's fifty-four. This is more of a Verity type of experience than a Lily one.'

I paused.

'He'd treat you well, Vee. Older men always know what they're doing in the bedroom.'

Lily was whispering, even though we were alone. I think her encouraging me to pursue a man thirty years my age was so scandalous that it had to be whispered. It was the wildest thing either of us had ever done, and probably would ever do. I couldn't act on Lily's advice without drinking more champagne. When we returned to our table, Grant had left, leaving all the champagne on the table. There were three half-drunk bottles. Lily was about to help herself to more when the waiter appeared. He read the look of panic on our faces and laughed. 'The gentleman has already settled the bill. He left a note for you on the table.'

Sure enough, there was a small business card in the middle. Lily grabbed it as if it were life- changing mail that had just arrived through our front door.

For the red head who likes to write as much as she likes to kiss.

Meet me tomorrow. The Connaught, Mayfair, at noon. I'll be waiting at the bar. x GB

'Holy shit. Are you gonna go?'

I felt lemon-like again. I didn't know how to answer Lily's question. It felt as if I had been taken hostage by a plethora of strange, sharp emotions; ones I'd never felt from any interaction with any man before. Intrigue. Fear. Disgust. Grant was only five years younger than my own dad. Was I normal? Did I have daddy issues? What even are daddy issues? Lily stood there, watching my mind spin. There was no way she'd let me talk myself out of going. She lived vicariously through my love life. Often, it was entertainment for her.

'You have to go, Vee! This is a once in a lifetime opportunity.'

My doubts were strong, yet they diminished to irrelevant speckles of dust against the weight of temptation that meeting Grant again presented. I read his note again, feeling myself unfurl like the petals of a rose with the longest stem in the world.

* * *

The following morning, I woke up early. I had drunk a little too much, but I hadn't forgotten the note. I reached for the card on my bedside table and studied the writing again to see how it looked in daylight. I marvelled at the long, loopy letters as if studying a rare artefact from a history museum.

I felt nervous on the way to meeting Grant. It was different from the standard pre-date jitters I had experienced with other men, with the dainty flutter of butterflies in your belly. This was stomach-churning, intestine-dancing terror. I arrived to the entrance of the hotel promptly, and was greeted by a friendly London porter.

'Good afternoon, Madam.'

'Good afternoon,' I said, feeling my heart pound against my chest. 'I'm meeting someone inside at the bar.'

He smiled. 'Do go in.'

It was really happening. I was shaky as hell. To my left was the hotel terrace restaurant, comprising of cream and silver table décor which evoked a French Riviera ambience. Bright light glistened through large double doored windows, as guests laughed over champagne flutes and tiny portions of Michelin star cuisine. It was spectacularly elegant. I caught a glimpse of myself in a tall mirror behind the reception desk, questioning whether I had made the right outfit choice. Suddenly, a man in a grey overcoat appeared behind me, grinning. I felt the blood rush from my head and took a short, sharp breath. It was Grant. I turned to face him, noticing his distinctive air of sexy composure. He smiled, knowingly, as if he had an invisible stethoscope attached to him and could somehow hear how fast my heart was beating. It hadn't resumed to a normal rhythm since I'd left my flat. He leant in to kiss my cheeks.

'I'm so pleased you made it,' he said, taking my arm and guiding me over past reception towards the hotel bar. 'How are you?'

'Fine,' I squeaked, feeling my lower lip tremble. This was an emergency for my nervous system. In fact, I seemed to have become my nervous system. We were one, triggered by the incredibly attractive Grant Black.

'You seem a little tense,' he said gently. 'Am I making you nervous?'

'I rushed to get here, that's all. This place is magnificent.'

I looked around the hotel, trying to think of impressive and intellectual observations; perhaps comment on the paintings, the interior, the history. Anything that would make me sound older and more sophisticated. I tried, but the words didn't come out. I was too nervous. 'The Connaught is one of my favourite spots when I come to London,' said Grant. 'This city will always feel like home. It's got that warm, earthy nostalgia about it. Full of beautiful idiots and brilliant lunatics, as Wilde said.'

I didn't want to ask which I was. Both, perhaps. 'Are you from London originally?' I asked.

'Buckinghamshire.'

Before I could tell him that I was too, we were approached by a waitress.

'Your table is ready, Mr. Black.' Grant put his hand on my shoulder, escorting me through to the bar. He was cool, capable and impeccably groomed, and carried himself with a gentlemanly ease that I had never seen in any man before. Although older than me, his sex factor was undeniable, and he would never lose it. I felt proud to be seen with him, and found myself wanting people to notice us and speculate on our relationship. From the outside in, I could be anyone. His secret long lost daughter from his one-time affair with a 90s supermodel. An upcoming actress for his latest Hollywood movie. His lover, his soulmate, his muse. With Grant, I'd take anything. I could be anything.

He pulled out my chair when we arrived to our table. No man had ever done that before. I tucked myself in, glancing round the room. It was very dark. Leather chairs surrounded candlelit tables against a dazzling backdrop of vintage spirits and wines. The smell of incense permeated the room, warming the atmosphere yet making it oddly wintery for July. I took the menu from the waiter and put an olive in my mouth. I regretted this instantly. Removing an olive stone from your mouth is hard to do elegantly, especially on a date. It can sense your fear. Grant read my embarrassment, placing his hand affectionately on my left thigh. Other couples were dotted around us, glancing over and whispering. I felt like standing up and tapping my fork on my wine glass to make an announcement.

'I AM OK! DO NOT BE ALARMED. I WAS NOT PAID TO BE HERE. I AM HERE BY CHOICE.'

I locked eyes with a woman sat at a table with her husband several meters away from me and Grant. She was the type of elegant that made pearls look sexy. I quickly turned away, staring down at Grant's hand on my leg. He rubbed his thumb against it slowly. I felt my knickers dampen. I was desperate for a distraction and felt scared to look him in the eye, so I decided to open the menu and start browsing the options.

'What are you going to have?'

'I can't decide between the pancakes or French toast,' I sighed. 'What do you think?'

'Pancakes?'

'But then I can't have the French toast.'

'Have the French toast, then.'

'But then I can't have the pancakes.'

Grant laughed. 'Are you always this indecisive?'

'I'm a Libra. It's written in the stars.'

I sat back on my chair, catching Grant glance at me up and down.

'I like your legs.'

'I like your style.'

He grinned, rolling the sleeves up of his shirt to expose his tattooed arms. I don't know whether he was trying to draw attention to them on purpose or whether he was just warm. Either way, I was struck by how muscular they were. To be honest, I was slightly relieved. I'd had it in my head that every man past the age of fifty cares less about their body than they do about darts and Brexit. I don't think Grant could have cared less about either. He was too Hollywood. I traced my finger lightly over a small eagle etched on his left hand. I didn't tell Grant that it looked like the Pipford school crest.

'What about all your tattoos? Do they mean anything?'

He looked at his arms and then back at me; and in a quiet voice, he said: 'After years of thinking about it, I'm still not sure. I think I might be suffering from extreme vanity. Or severe-self-hatred. Or both.'

I watched Grant smile as I toyed with the image of how interesting he would look naked, covered in writing and pictures and squiggles. His candour made him a sexy and refreshing human being, who, frankly, I hadn't anticipated to feel so attracted to. I had a hard enough time comprehending that Grant Black was his actual name. I've always envied people who have colour names. Like Ruby, Scarlet or Emerald. Grant Black suited him down to the ground. Just then, the waitress appeared to take our order.

'Welcome to the Connaught bar,' she smiled. 'Have you decided what you'd like?' Before I could open my mouth to speak, Grant was doing it for me.

'Tea for two, please. Plus, the pancakes and French toast. We'll go fifty-fifty on both.'

The cliché rang a bell. I remembered that Kyle had said ordering mains and going fifty-fifty on both was the hall-mark of a good relationship on Hinge. At the time, I had lusted over the two of us ordering pizza and pasta at his local Italian, asking the waitress to bring an extra plate, gig-gling at how cute we were – conforming to number one on the list of annoying things that couples do. This scenario never transpired into a reality. In hindsight, I think Kyle had just written it there to sound cute and goofy. Now I was doing it with a man thirty years my age for brunch. It was an infinitely better situation than my former self could have imagined.

'I'll take the eggs and avocado too, please.'

'Of course,' said the waitress, scribbling Grant's order down like a diligent student. 'How would you like your eggs cooked, sir?'

'Perfectly.'

I watched confusion spread across the waitress' face. Grant closed the menu and handed it back to her before she could ask him which variation of 'perfect' he had meant. I felt sorry for her that she'd have to guess. If it were me, I would have cried out the back.

'Tell me about you, then, Verity.'

Sentences gushed out my mouth effortlessly like unapol-ogetic thuds of rain. Talking to Grant was easy; it filled me with that wonderful type of high you get from talking to someone you have just met yet feel you've known for-ever. My favourite thing about Grant was that I laughed a great deal more than I spoke with him, and if that's not the loveliest sign of compatibility then I don't know what is. We spoke about everything; Kill & Kontent, Pipford, Leeds, Australia, politics, poetry and books. Grant listened to understand – he didn't listen to respond. Everything that came out my mouth was met with genuine curiosity, as if it were the first time he had ever heard anyone lament the woes of the PR industry, the shackles of a quintessential boarding school or the brilliance of F. Scott Fitzgerald. The conversation flowed like ripples in a calm sea. We were just two corks bobbing along in the current, without care or concern of where it would take us.

I quickly became conscious that I had spoken about myself too much. The last thing I wanted to do was reinforce the Instagram obsessed reputation us millennials exhibit in the world, and Lily had done a prized job of showing it last night. I paused to let Grant speak about himself. His life in the 90s was fascinating; after writing scripts for BBC dramas, he went on to produce and star in Hollywood films. He had also dipped in and out of fashion, owning various boutiques in London specialising in custom made coats and lingerie.

'The secret is saying yes to every job and figuring out how to do it once you've got it. Not the other way round.'

Grant's outlook seemed to contradict everything I had ever been taught. Nowadays, we have to be fluent in Mandarin, have run the London marathon and have five years' experience under our belts in the industries of every entry level job we apply to.

'I'm just going to pop to the ladies' room.'

'No problem,' smiled Grant, leaning back on his chair. 'I'll settle the bill. Meet me by the hotel entrance.'

I walked round to his chair and planted a kiss on his cheek, wrapping my arms round his neck. Showing physical affection towards him now came with unthinkable ease. As I headed to the bathroom, I realised that sex with him would be inevitable. I wanted him, intensely, and I didn't know how I felt about it. What does it feel like to have sex with an older man? This was different to the novelty of dating a thirty-year-old when you're twenty-one. The idea seems alluring, but the reality is that they're just grownup boys with their own flat, a fancy coffee machine and a more elite gym membership than you. As I sat on the toilet seat, I began listing all the celebrity age-gap couples I could think of in search of some miraculous reassurance that I was normal. Michael Douglas and Catherine Zeta-Jones. George and Amal Clooney. Kris Jenner and Corey Gamble. Ok, I thought to myself. So maybe I'm not a total freak. It occurred to me that I hadn't messaged Lily, Naomi or Max to tell them I was not only safe, but head over heels, too. I made a WhatsApp group with the three of us, titled 'DICKSAND.' If you're unfamiliar with this term, it is used to describe the intense attraction a woman feels shortly after meeting a guy she fancies. Her mind gets sucked in like quicksand to the point of insanity.

Verity: SOS guys. I'm deep in.

Max: Him, or the boot of his car? Two very different things.

Verity: Him. He's so fucking cool. He helped with the script of Cold Feet.

Max: Can you ask him if James Nesbitt is actually hot in person?

Lily: He's not, Max. Confirmed. Met him at an E4 event once.

Verity: Guys? I'm freaking out about what his penis might look like.

Lily: You won't be thinking about that when he's inside of you! ☺

Lily: Even if you wanted to marry him he wouldn't let you.

Naomi: Love is love and age is but a number! Release your expectations and have fun.

Grant was waiting for me at the main entrance of the hotel. He was sat down on a leather armchair, scrolling his phone. I paused for a moment, taking in the mad, magical absurdity of this situation. When he saw me walking over, he put his phone in his pocket and pulled me onto his lap.

'Do you like chocolate?' he asked, taking a strand of my hair, twirling it around his finger.

'I love chocolate.'

'Good,' he said. 'Because I'm taking you to Rococo.'

* * *

I slept in on Monday with the joyful reminder of a week's holiday ahead of me. I looked up at the large box of truffles resting on my bedside table and grinned to myself, reminiscing over Saturday's experience at Rococo. Grant had marched straight to the counter and chivalrously demanded that I have 'One of everything.' I opened them and put a large praline straight in my mouth. Since meeting Grant, the mundane reality of my life was on standstill. All I knew was that he was getting a flight back to LA in forty-eight hours, and we had dinner plans together this evening. I reached for my phone lazily, seeing I had a WhatsApp message from him. He had sent it one minute ago. The urge to open it instantly was overwhelming, and frankly, I didn't think twice. The great thing about dating an older man is that you don't have to worry about playing it cool, Lily had said once, because you are forever a hot young novelty. It's a liberating mindset.

Grant: I need Lily's number.

I felt my heart sink. Lily. It was always Lily.

It all made sense. She was confident in a way that I wasn't. She had flirted with Grant at the bar on Saturday, and the two of them had spoken far longer than him and I. I had always sensed there was something disarming about Grant, and this was it. He was an older man, taking advantage of me just so he could have his wicked way with my sassy best friend. The chocolates, the long lunch, the romance. He knew I would tell Lily all about it so that she would subconsciously desire him. It had been a performance on his part – a ploy to get closer. I was just a prop to aid him in the process. Grant remained online. I could practically feel him staring at me through the screen of my phone.

Grant: I know you're reading this. I need it now.

Verity: Why do you need it?

Grant: Don't you trust me?

I sent him Lily's number and buried my head into my pillow, blasting out Kelly Clarkson in a desperate plea to the universe to go and fuck itself for putting Grant Black in my path. What a great big cosmic joke.

* * *

The rest of the day went by slowly and painfully without a word from either Grant or Lily. I ended up cleaning, polishing and arranging anything and everything I possibly could – including the cutlery draw. It was incredibly out of character. As each hour passed, my brain conjured a new scenario of how they might be spending their day together. Twelve o'clock was brunch at The Wolseley. Two was shopping in Bond Street. Four was afternoon tea at the Claridge's. Of course, it was gloriously sunny outside, which made the image of the two of them together even more vivid and painful. It was coming up to half past four now. They were probably on their second glass of champagne at some fancy hotel. Maybe Grant would take Lily to The Connaught, too. Maybe they were having sex. Mondays tended to be quiet for Lily. The bulk of her work was taken up on weekends at various gigs, interviews and performances. Apart from the two hours of phone calls she did at an independent coffee shop in the morning, she was usually free. She told me that she wouldn't be home until later today because she had errands to run. That said, if a man had sprung upon Lily's scene then things like ASOS returns and a nail appointment would take a back seat. Combined with the intensity of Grant's charm, I was resolute that there was no way something wouldn't be happening between the two of them, even if she had encouraged me to 'go for it' on Saturday night. Grant's sex appeal was undeniable to any woman. Lily wouldn't have been exempt from feeling it too.

It was painful waiting around at home. I decided to take a long walk to the park, leaving my phone at home. When I returned an hour later, I had a message from Grant and a missed call.

Grant: Change of plan for tonight. Meet me at St Pancras station. Sorry if you have to change direction. Get there for 6 pm, sharp.

My heart raced, as I entertained the possibility that I had got the wrong end of the stick between Lily and Grant. It's no secret that my brain is guilty of jumping to conclusions like it's competing for a gold medal. Despite the scenarios I'd played in my head, the pull was still there. I still wanted to see him. Fuck it, I said to myself. Just go. I quickly showered and had a brief meltdown on what to wear. I missed Lily. I wanted her here to help me. I couldn't find my favourite top or jeans, and time was of the essence. I settled for a dress, tights and boots and made my way to King's Cross station.

All I could remember about St Pancras was the WHSmiths with good snack options, Hotel Chocolat and a fancy champagne bar by the Eurostar. Maybe we were having a drink there before dinner. Plausible, but it still seemed odd, given that we were on the other side of London. I messaged Grant to let him know that I'd arrived at the station, and was waiting in the middle. It was eerily quiet, apart from a man playing Ludovico Einaudi on the piano. I knew the piece well. 'Nuvole Bianche' was one of my favourites. I jumped, feeling someone leap up behind me with their hands on my shoulders. When I turned around, I saw it was Lily.

'I hate it when you jump up on me like that,' I snapped. 'What are you doing here?'

'Nice to see you too.'

Without apologising, she opened her rucksack and thrust my passport in my hand, handing me a small bag filled with what felt like a pair of jeans, socks and toiletries.

'You'll need all this. I had to rummage around your room a bit when you went to Sainsbury's.'

'Wait. What? You were spying on me?'

'Only for your own good.'

I felt guilty. I had accused Lily of unforgivable things in my head. She had obviously been playing the trusty friend, caught up in some plan with Grant, hiding in the bushes and waiting for me to leave the house so she could steal my passport. But why?

'I need to go. Tash's studio session starts in fifteen.'

She wrapped her arms around me and gave me a tighter squeeze than usual. I watched her dash off, feeling my phone vibrate. It was Grant calling.

'Where are you?' I asked urgently. 'What's going on?'

'Did Lily give you your passport?'

'I just met her. Is that why you needed her number?'

'Yep. She was very obliging. I'm waiting for you now, at the champagne bar.' I walked over to the escalator, feeling a wave of excitement.

'Before you meet me, I want you to remove your underwear.' I felt my heart thud. 'What...? Why?'

'Don't ask questions. Just go to the ladies' room and do as I say.'

My whole body felt flushed, pulled into some mad, erotic trance. I never thought the evening would pan out this way, but that was Grant for you. Everything was surprising.

He was waiting for me on a bar chair with a bottle of champagne and two glass flutes. It was wonderfully quiet – as if we were the only two people in the station, venturing to Paris, our undiscovered secret from the rest of the world.

Grant poured me a glass of champagne, presenting me with two first class tickets. I couldn't believe it.

'Paris?!'

I tried my best to sound surprised. I was, of course, but looking at Grant made me wonder less about Paris and more about what he was going to do to me once we were there.

'Paris indeed. For twenty-four hours.'

He raced his hand against my leg, pausing at the juncture. My whole body tingled.

'You did as I said,' he whispered in my ear. 'Good girl.'

I melted. This, right here, was romance.

'Our train leaves in half an hour.'

I reached for his hand, interlocking my fingers through his.

'Thank you, Grant. This feels like the most perfect dream.'

* * *

Grant and I spent the entire journey talking and laughing like two kindred spirits. It never felt like there was enough time to say all the things we wanted say and ask all the things we wanted to ask. The best part of the whole journey, though, was that no matter what we spoke about; no matter where the conversation drifted to; Grant never let me forget that I had no knickers on. I would be deep in some story, some opinion, and Grant would interrupt me with the sensation of his hand against my thigh. The Eurostar was the birthing place for my obsession with his hands. They were sexiest hands in the world, and we hadn't even kissed yet.

We arrived at the Gare du Nord at approximately nine o'clock; or as Lily and I like to call it – sexy dinner time. Grant had arranged for a car to collect us and take us to the Hotel Costes. Lily had gone last year with her music management company, and didn't stop talking about it when she got back. She described it as an enchanting place with a Moulin Rouge like aura to it, filled with unconventional people with unconventional jobs doing unconventional things. I think it was because she had ended up in the suite of a Scandinavian DJ at 3 am playing a game of 'Would you rather?'

We arrived at reception and were handed the key to our room, inspired by the glamour of the Rue Saint-Honoré district. Jazz music floated along each corridor we passed through, painted red with velvet curtains. Grant held onto our key, turning around to smile at me as he led me through this magical crimson maze. Eventually, we arrived to our room on the third floor, overlooking the bustling glitz of the city. Grant dropped his bag down on the floor and, for the first time, leant in to kiss me. It felt startling yet so easy.

'I want this to be special for you,' he whispered.

'It already is.'

Grant pushed opened the door, and in doing so, unlocked the magnificent grandeur of the nineteenth century. The room was furnished with lavish cream and crimson furniture. I walked around, mesmerised. He must have paid extra for it, because it was enormous.

'This is sensational,' I said, stroking the gold tassels of the curtains. They overlooked a small, outdoor terrace with a table and two chairs. I pictured the two of us sat there the following morning, sipping on coffee and eating croissants.

'Wonderful, isn't it?' he smiled.

I looked over to him, slumped on the bed as if he were part of the furniture. Grant was Paris. He belonged here. Everything that surrounded me brought me back to him. From the velvet furnishings to the trio of brass candlesticks placed on the chest of draws. Every item was an emblem of his romance, his charm, his decadence. I had to have him now.

I wandered over to him on the bed, feeling the weight of his body press against mine. He edged himself on top of me and began undoing the buttons of my blouse. I watched his hands move with a strong urge to feel them inside of me, but Grant was moving slowly, with intention. He gently pushed my hair back and planted kisses down the side of my neck, working his way down towards my chest. I let out a small moan. Five minutes later, his head was buried between my legs. Ten minutes later, I was riding him, amazed that sex could feel like this.

'I'm going to come,' he gasped, flipping me onto my back. 'Any second.'

I clung onto his shoulders, wrapping my legs around his waist, feeling the warm, tingling sensation spread inside and take over my whole body.

'Yes...yes...' I moaned, feeling myself come again as he, too, finished inside of me. We both lay in a silent euphoric trance, Grant's head resting peacefully against my chest. I didn't want to break the moment. It was Grant who did, standing up to blow out the candles. He came back into bed and nuzzled into me. It was the first time in my life I had ever experienced an orgasm, but I didn't let him in on this. I just fell asleep in his arms.

* * *

I woke up to Grant sat on the edge of the bed, showered, fully dressed, typing an email on his phone whilst sipping on a cup of coffee. His suitcase was tucked neatly in the corner of the room. Reality hit that Grant was flying home tonight. I shot up instantly.

'Morning, baby.'

'What time is it?' I shivered, feeling the chill of the morning breeze against my bare skin. The curtains fluttered aghast as Grant stood up to pull the windows shut.

'Half ten. I ordered you breakfast whilst you slept.'

He wandered across the room to bring me a silver platter of coffee and pastries. He looked slick as ever, dressed in black jeans and a simple white t-shirt. A wave of lust stirred inside me beneath the sheets.

'Eat,' he said, placing it on the duvet. 'I want to show you Paris.' I took a bite into a fresh pain au chocolat. It was still warm.

'Did you enjoy what I did to you last night, Verity?'

I froze, taken back by the blatant tone in which he'd acknowledged our intimacy. I replayed how it had all begun; his slow caress of my leg, the neck kisses, his head beneath my legs. I looked him in the eyes. I was sure he was replaying the same tune. He walked over to the bath-tub and switched on the taps, collecting a sponge and two mini bottles of bath gel from the bathroom. I tingled, watching him pour liquid into the bath as steam began to waft around the room. It smelt like sweet mulled wine. I sipped my coffee, watching Grant undress and step into the bath. He settled into the foam, closing his eyes. The tap was still running. I got out of bed to join him, tipping my toe into the water.

'Jesus! Are your baths always this hot?'

Grant laughed, reaching out his hand to immerse me into the hot water. I leant back, resting my head against his chest, relaxing.

'This bath gel smells like Christmas.'

'Pomegranate, amber and cinnamon. I drown my apartment in the stuff,' he laughed.

'And my car.'

Grant kissed the top of my head, splashing me with the bubbles. It was like something from a film; both of us wet, soapy and naked. I don't know about him, but I was smitten. He slowly ran his hands through my hair, wetting it.

'I love your red hair. Don't ever change it.'

'I would never.'

He reached for the bath gel, squeezing it into the palm of his hand.

'Would you lean forward for me?'

He brushed my hair aside and began rubbing the gel in deep, circular motions against my back, working his way into my shoulders. He took more of the gel, pulling me against his chest, lathering it against my décolletage. I felt my pulse quicken, imagining where this might end up. I wanted him more intensely now than I did last night. Grant began ravishing me with his hands. Somehow, I was more sensitive in daylight. It made everything more real. My moans were unstoppable.

'You like that, don't you?' he whispered in my ear.

'Yes,' I gasped, arching my back. The ends of my hair were dripping wet. Grant released the plug and let the water drain, moving his hands against my ribcage and down towards my hip bones.

'How badly do you want me to touch you?' he muttered. 'Tell me.'

He slipped his finger inside me, caressing my clitoris all over again. I closed my eyes, moving my body against the friction of his finger as he went in deeper.

'It's not like this with other guys, is it?' he hushed in my ear.

He was right. It wasn't. It wasn't at all.

He stopped suddenly, standing up from the bath. 'I want to take you against the wall.'

I stepped out and made my way to the side of the room, pressing my hands against the wall. Grant grabbed hold of either of my breasts and pushed into me in deep, aggressive thrusts. The sensation was sharp; on the cusp of pain, but I was too wet for anything to hurt properly. 'Get down on your knees,' ordered Grant. 'Now.'

Hearing him say that turned me on unspeakably. After Joe raped me, I was convinced I'd never like this type of aggression, but with Grant, I did. I'm not sure why. Every intimate moment we shared was a gateway of sexual discovery to me, as a woman. Grant came in my mouth hard, without warning, as I swallowed his release.

I enjoyed that bit too.

* * *

Grant and I spent the rest of the afternoon strolling around Paris with a shared refusal to acknowledge the inevitability of separation. We shopped at the Boulevard Saint-Germain, where Grant purchased me a silk camisole that I'd admired in the window of a small clothing boutique. We then visited the Galerie Vivienne, where I bought two new books: one on the poetry of Oscar Wilde, the other on the wit and wisdom of Leo Tolstoy. Grant and I had discussed over lunch how much we loved his writing – especially *Anna Karenina*.

'The beauty of Tolstoy is his ability to depict the subtleties of human character. There's that line in Anna which I love. He stepped down, trying not to look at her, as if she were the sun, yet he saw her, like the sun, even without looking. It's understated genius.'

'I like Hemmingway, too. And Fitzgerald.'

'The roaring twenties, huh?'

'The glitz, the glamour, the release of inhibitions,' I beamed. 'Of all eras, the twenties charm me in a different kind of way.'

'They slipped briskly into an intimacy from which they never recovered.'

'Gatsby,' I smiled. 'What about, April is the cruellest month. Breeding lilacs out of a dead land, mixing memory with desire, stirring dull roots with spring rain…'

'Easy,' laughed Grant. 'T.S. Eliot. The Wasteland is mind-numbingly long, though, and fucking depressing. I think he lost the point of what he was trying to say after the second stanza.' The epic guessing game of lines from poets and books of the 1920s continued for the next hour, and I cherished every second. The intellectual tussle I had with Grant was like nothing I had ever experienced.

'You should pursue writing, you know.'

'Don't be absurd. I can't.'

'Do you think that's what Fitzgerald would have said? Or Hemmingway?'

'No, because they were the greats.'

'They were great because they were wild enough to believe they were,' said Grant. 'Consider it at least. Work takes up almost a third of our adult life.'

'Not in your case. You're retired.'

'I'm serious, Verity. Your days on earth are limited. Don't waste them doing something that doesn't set your soul on fire.'

I decided I would pack the Tolstoy book discreetly in Grant's case before he left later that evening as a gift. I also picked up the giant box of macarons for Lily that we always promised we would buy each other if either of us ever went to Paris with a man on a whim. I don't think either of us thought it would ever actually happen. The fact that it had was wild.

As the evening drew in, Grant and I sat in a comfortable silence on two chairs in the Jardin du Luxembourg, facing the most perfect candy floss clouded sunset I had ever seen.

'You'd think by now, on my twenty-fourth orbit around the sun, that the novelty of a pink sky would have worn off slightly, but it hasn't. Sunsets still leave me speechless.'

Grant laughed. 'I'm on my fifty-fourth orbit, and even I'm still surprised by them.'

I checked my phone briefly. It was coming up to half past five. We'd have to head back to the hotel soon, otherwise Grant would miss his flight.

'I've had the most wonderful time, you know. I don't want to it to end.'

Grant paused, staring up peacefully at the sky with a neutral expression. I longed to know what he was thinking. All I knew was that he thought the sunset looked nice.

'We should head back soon,' said Grant eventually, checking his watch. 'I can't miss my flight.' I felt hurt that he hadn't said anything about us. My heart began to swell with emotion.

'Aren't you sad about us leaving one another, Grant?' I clung onto his face, desperate to feel connected one last time. 'You haven't said anything about us leaving one another.'

'You know,' I continued, nuzzling into his neck, 'I could have you now – all over again. Let's go back to the hotel and have another bath... let's fuck each other one last time...'

'Stop, Verity!' said Grant, pushing me off him. 'You're behaving inappropriately.'

Do not cry, I said to myself. Whatever you do, do not cry. Of course, telling yourself not to cry is the surest way to make crying happen. Tears started to gush down my face helplessly. 'Please don't cry,' said Grant, taking a red hand-kerchief from his coat pocket. 'You're making me feel like a bastard.' He dabbed gently at my eyes. Even in my sobbing state, I couldn't help but notice how soft his handkerchief was against my cheek; as if its sole purpose was for wiping away the tears of broken-hearted women.

'I can't help but fear that you've got ahead of yourself, Verity.'

'You don't secretly have a wife and kids, do you?'

'God, no! Is that seriously what you think of me?'

'No. I was just trying to lighten the mood.'

Grant laughed. 'You're a wonderful girl, but you know we can't...'

'I think I've fallen for you, Grant. I tried, but I couldn't help it. You shouldn't have swept me away so much.'

'But I was always clear with you that my visits to London were infrequent and sporadic. You knew this all along...'

'What if distance wasn't an issue? Then would you?'

'Then would I what?' Grant sighed, taking a slow, steady pause. 'Attempting anything long distance will get unbelievably messy, and I believe in the beauty of your future too much to let that happen to you.'

I knew he was trying to say the right, adult things, but selfishly, I wanted him to hold me in his arms. I wanted him to tell me to stop crying. I wanted him to book me on his flight back to LA with him – or at least open it up for me to go and visit him again. I wanted the ridiculous solution that made no sense; not the sensible one that was better for me in the long run.

'I have loved every moment we shared this week, but this will never be able to be a serious relationship. I know you're young, but you're an intelligent girl, and are no doubt mature enough to understand the reality of this.'

I sat there, quiet. Grant was fifty-four and lived in Malibu. I was twenty-four and lived in London. He was right; the notion of a relationship between us was ridiculous. Still – I had wanted it to be true. Desperately. He cupped my face in his palms.

'You're full of life and have life ahead of you. I've lived mine. Go at yours with your arms wide open.'

I'm not sure what Grant was getting at. It felt like I was getting ghosted but with a heads up. As we wandered back to the hotel, I made peace with the fact that maybe he was right. I had to appreciate this experience for what it was – an experience. A spontaneous, crazy, once in a lifetime experience. Sometimes, that's how dating works. It hurt now, but I knew I'd be ok. I looked down at the Laduree box. All I wanted was to see Lily and dive into them with her in our pyjamas whilst watching *Sex and the City*.

I packed my belongings in silence when we arrived back to the room. When Grant went to the bathroom, I slipped the Tolstoy book into his suitcase.

It was gone midnight by the time I arrived back to London. My phone had died on the tube home, but as soon as I charged it, I had a message from Grant.

'Life did not stop and one had to live.'

A quote from the book you left me. Thank you. Sweet dreams. X

Chapter 9 – Patrick

One month later
The Annual Tech Conference – Canary Wharf

Arriving ten minutes early for things was an ingrained habit since my Pipford days. Exam, job interview, work event; I always endeavoured to be ten minutes early. Somehow, I thought it would make the outcome more successful. I would pass the paper, land the job or get the client. Learning from Lily that this ought not to apply to dating, where it was fashionable to be late and keen to be early, had been an impossibly hard pill to swallow. To me, it just looked like bad manners.

It was the morning of the ATC, and to increase my chances of the event going well, I had doubled my arrival time to twenty minutes early. This was quite clearly a principle applied by absolutely no else in the tech industry, for the conference centre was scarce. I wondered if I had got the day wrong. I decided to triple check with Daniel. He would think I was insulting his intelligence since I had already checked twice, but still. I was panicked.

'What is it, Verity? You're not lost, are you?'

'No. I'm here, waiting to go in.'

'Already? The event doesn't start until ten. I told you ten. It's not ten yet, is it?'

For once, I think Daniel had told me the correct time, but the fact that the only other person in the building was a maintenance man with a mysterious bucket and duct tape was making me unsure I was in the right place.

'That's what the email invite says. 10 am at the Webforce Centre. Except there's no one here, Daniel.'

'That's because you're an Early Eileen,' he sighed. 'You're such a goody two shoes that it's a wonder how you even found yourself in PR. Go and have a cigarette.'

'You know I don't smoke.'

'Right. Well, go and wait outside.'

'I would, but it's raining.'

Daniel sighed again. 'The ladies' room, then? I don't know. Masturbate, meditate – I don't care. You're supposed to be good at these networking things. That's why we fucking asked you to go!'

He hung up the phone. To my relief, a tall suited man walked through the door accompanied with two women. They were all smartly dressed and looked very important. I rushed over immediately, holding out my hand.

'Hi! I'm Verity Ellis – an account executive from Kill & Kontent.'

'Patrick,' grinned the man, shaking my hand. 'World Events Research. Or "We R", as the millennials say – the events company who organise the ATC every year.'

I laughed. He seemed warm and friendly – unlike the other two women. Up close, they looked like Jennifer's evil triplet counterparts with attached iPads round their necks.

'This is Alexa and Marie.'

I didn't have a clue who was who, but I smiled politely anyway.

'Where did you say you're from?' asked one, opening up her iPad. 'Kill & Kontent?'

'That's right.'

'How long have you been waiting?' I shrugged. 'Half an hour, maybe?'

She smirked at me. She was far too big for her boots given that she was the nightclub door girl of the tech event world. I didn't like her one bit. I sensed Lily wouldn't be keen either. More people from their events company started to clamber in with tables, chairs and crates of glasses, walking up a set of stairs from the foyer to prepare the hall. Their arrival triggered a bustling army of men, too, dressed in grey suits with ties of varying garish designs. They were tech journalists; several of whom I recognised from my previous stalking at Kill & Kontent. I noticed one in particular from Buzzchain, whose name was Woody Humphrey. Even with my existing connections at other publications, he was notoriously difficult to pin down. I had been trying for ages.

'Guess we better get mingling,' smiled Patrick. 'See you around, perhaps.'

Kill & Kontent had given me the task of charming a jungle of highly respected tech wizards from all over the world. A common misconception about people in the industry is that they are a bunch of smarmy, dead-end nerds in glasses who fumble about coding, robots and software growth. The reality is that everyone in tech oozes intelligence, glamour and success that even the sassiest of PR girls would find intimidating. I looked down at my leaflet and saw that Woody was one of the headline speakers. He was due to be speaking in five minutes' time on 'Future Trends in Television Segmentation,' talking about digital specifications in gadgets that would dominate the tech market in the next five years. I made my way to the front of the podium so I could be in ample position to chat to him as soon as he'd finished.

As I waited, I caught a glimpse of Patrick from across the room. I'd been flustered this morning when I met him, meaning I must have missed how incredibly attractive he was – especially in a suit. Naomi and I are convinced that a man in a suit has magical aphrodisiacal properties. Suits turn average men into handsome ones and handsome men into gorgeous, glorious breeding machines; even through the eyes of a raging feminist, like Lily, who doesn't want children. Watching Patrick laugh with a colleague was causing an implosion in my ovaries. He looked like some sort of dream pinup husband; powerful enough to run a business, reliable enough to support a child and sexy enough to thrill his wife. Damn. What a catch. He glanced over in my direction. I turned away, conscious that I was lusting after him in a room of people. Stop this. This is not a bar. You're here to work. Woody Humphrey got on stage, took a sip of water, and began bellowing into the microphone. He spoke with an American accent, which seemed to elevate his commanding presence into something more Hollywood.

'I'm excited about the future of television, and you should be too...'

Several minutes into the talk, Patrick wandered over to join me at the front. Seeing him walk over to where I was made it difficult to concentrate on what Woody was saying.

'... this can all be attributed to the growing gaming sector; something which requires HD compatibility...'

I did my best to focus, but it was hard. Patrick was stood right next to me, and I was filled with the strong sense that he was about to whisper something inappropriate into my ear. Whatever stir he was igniting between us was inconvenient. If I missed the point of what Woody was saying then I wouldn't be able to make a meaningful contribution to his speech when it finished. My career depended on this talk. Now was not the time to generate some flirtation between me and an attractive man in a suit. If Patrick or I moved any closer, then our fingers would be touching. I shivered, feeling the sensation of his breath tickle my ear. 'What are your predictions for the future?' he whispered. 'Do you think we'll have televisions for eyes?'

I giggled from beneath my breath. 'Actually, I think we'll morph into robots.'

'And listen to heavy metal!' he chuckled.

That was an official dad joke. It was then that I knew Patrick was a certified Mr Napkin Head from *The Holiday*. Not that that's a problem. Everyone loves Mr Napkin Head. I observed Patrick's face more closely. Perhaps the most obvious feature was his conspicuous blue eyes, filled with a warm, happy glint. He wasn't sexy like Grant, dashing like Kyle, or athletic like Abel, but was nevertheless handsome in his own goofy kind of way. Not charismatic because he was attractive; but rather, attractive because he was charismatic. Sometimes, those men are the hottest in the world.

'Fancy a drink at the bar when this is done?'

'I can't. I need to hover round here for a bit.'

Suddenly, everyone began clapping loudly. There was even an occasional cheer, commemorating some genius insight that I would have been able to ask Woody about had I not been so distracted by Patrick. We both succumbed to a half-hearted round of applause, although frankly, neither of us had caught the gist of what the speech had been about. I felt disappointed in myself. Members of the audience gathered to form an informal huddle around Woody. It was my time to shine. I would have to swoop in and wing it.

'Take this in case I lose you.'

Patrick slipped his business card into the pocket of my blazer and dashed off. I quickly noticed that everyone gathered around Woody was female, most likely from other PR agencies. They were over talking over each other, trying to get his attention. I'm sure he was loving it. Woody was the sleazy tech guy who Hayley had warned me about from the very beginning. I decided to be brazen. I shuffled past them to get as close to Woody as I possibly could.

'What are your predictions for the future, Woody? Will humans have televisions for eyes or morph into full on robots instead?'

It was a low blow attempt at regurgitating Patrick's joke from earlier. It didn't matter if Woody laughed or not: I just had to get his attention. To my delight, he was grinning.

He stepped down from the stage, walking over to me. The other two girls rolled their eyes and dispersed out of sight. I think I had scored.

'Televisions for eyes?' said Woody. 'Give it a hundred years or so, and we'll probably be able to govern satnav through eye lens.'

'That's if we're still driving cars.'

He laughed loudly, looking me up and down.

'Where you from, babe?'

'Kill & Kontent PR. I'm representing Livewire.'

'And do you reckon the increasing prevalence of OLED in domestic applications shows its appeal over the "on paper" higher specifics of QLED?'

My mind blanked. I froze, then I panicked. Shit. I told myself to relax, to bluffer it.

'Er, well, I suppose it's… erm…'

Why was I stumbling? I had researched this stuff meticulously before the event; analysed all the details in considerable depth, just in case it came up in conversation with someone like Woody. It didn't get bigger than him, and I was blowing away my chance flimsily like the fluff of a dandelion.

'Well?'

'I guess I hadn't really thought about it.'

He raised his eyebrows and looked down at his watch. I had officially blown it. I was furious at myself.

'Better run. Good talkin' with ya, kid.'

* * *

For the short series of days that followed the event, I had allowed the image of Patrick in a suit to fester in my memory. I had pondered, I had daydreamed. I had even masturbated. Lily had encouraged me to get a vibrator after I told her I had experienced my first ever orgasm with Grant. She said the attachment had come from oxytocin; the 'love' hormone women release during sex and labour which makes you feel all connected. At least that would explain my dramatic farewell to Grant in the Luxembourg gardens. The man had gone down on me and it had felt so sensational that I was convinced I was in love. Really, I had just orgasmed. What a stunning revelation. The reviews on the vibrator I purchased sounded life-changing. One woman said it had made her unintentionally 'dick sober,' and she hadn't felt the need to go near a penis for three and a half years. Of course, that wasn't the intention with Patrick. The small spark of chemistry between us at the ATC had awakened my appetite for something greater. I ended up texting Patrick on the number he had left on his business card, and we had agreed to meet at a sushi restaurant this evening after work. At first, I didn't know if it was for business or pleasure, but the fact that neither of us could really be of any benefit to each other in the professional sense of things assured me it was the latter. That, and the kiss face emoji he'd sent me following a 'looking forward to tonight' text.

As I headed onto the tube to meet Patrick, it occurred to me that for the first time in my life before a date, I didn't feel nervous. Maybe it was because I had been on so many that I was starting to get used to it. Or, it was down to the fact I had met Patrick under the refreshing clarity of everyday life circumstances as opposed to the alluring darkness of a drunken bar. You couldn't get more real than meeting someone at a work conference. There had been no alcohol induced pretences – no 'I wonder if he'll recognise me when he's sober' concerns. He had seen professional, 10 am Verity, and a small stir had still ignited between us. The grounds couldn't have been more promising.

Patrick was already there when I arrived at the restaurant. He smiled brightly when I walked in, eyes glistening. God, he looks good. The mental image of him that I'd masturbated over had now transpired into a real-life situation. Seeing him in person again made me feel hot and bothered.

'Good to see you, Verity!' He kissed me on either cheek as I sat myself down on the bar stool. 'How are you? Long day? You look great. I ordered you martini. Rose flavoured, if you can believe that. It's got this wonderful pink tinge to it. Look!' He held it up excitably, inspecting the petals floating on top like a kid delighting in their new pet goldfish that they'd just won at a fairground. 'I didn't know if it's what you'd like, but I thought it looked good. I ordered one for myself, too. It's nice actually; nice and refreshing. Still, it has that deceptive sweetness to it which makes it rather palatable for something that is probably very alcoholic...'

It was obvious that Patrick was nervous. He began to erupt into short, goofy bursts of incessant blabbering on random topics; work, the weather, politics, his family. Patrick's energy was high and he wasn't stopping for breath. When the waiter came to take our order, he demanded half the menu.

'... Sorry,' he said, pausing from a useless story about a US client who had overshared details about his wife's liposuction. 'I'm on a bit of a high today.'

'I gathered. Did something good happen?'

'Not as such. It's a condition I have called hypermania.'

'... Oh.'

'Means I get these sudden waves of euphoric energy.'

'I see.'

'Inflated self-esteem; that's another one. Oh, and racing thoughts.'

'Yeah. I got that one.'

'Excessive money spending, no need for sleep, total lack of inhibitions, a risk taker...'

'You sound like a catch. I'm glad I came.'

He laughed. 'I prefer to be as open about it as I can. Emma told me to be transparent when I branch out into the dating pool again.'

'Who's Emma?'

'My ex-wife.'

'I didn't know you were married.'

Patrick nodded. 'Divorced, as of last year. Childhood sweethearts.'

'That's shit. I'm sorry.'

'Don't be. I'm the third bloke in my group. The modern destiny of marriage is disaster.'

'Funny you say that. I recently met someone who convinced me of the same thing. They described marriage as an unwavering, illogical and ill-thought-out belief on the existence of fairy tales.'

Patrick laughed. 'Try divorce.'

'I've heard that's a bitch too. Apparently, it turns nightmares into a reality and reality into a nightmare.'

'Yep. It's a long, bloody war – especially when a kid is involved.'

'That's what Grant... I mean, yes – they said that too.'

I think we had both overshared on things we shouldn't have. I'd let slip about Grant, king of orgasms, and Patrick had let slip out about his ex-wife and divorce gloop. For some reason, neither of us let it bother the other. It was quite nice, actually. Just then, a hundred small dishes of Japanese cuisine appeared. I awkwardly shuffled back to make room for it all. It was an embarrassing amount for two people.

'Reckon we overdid it slightly?'

'Don't be silly. There's no such thing.'

Time passed quickly with Patrick. We laughed, we giggled, we flirted, we exchanged views and entertained new ones. The fact he had been so honest with me about his condition hadn't put me off in the slightest. If anything, I was turned on by his vulnerability. The refreshing openness, the raw, heartfelt honesty, the total lack of game-playing that being with a divorced man presented was all new and exciting. There's no denying that Patrick was bruised, but maybe that would warrant someone worthwhile of my affections. Maybe I could help him. It was getting on for half past eight when Patrick announced he had to head back to Kingston and resume childcare duties.

'I'll piss Emma off if I'm late. I have Harry three nights a week and every other weekend, you see.'

'Sweet.'

'He's a great kid, Harry is. He's got his dad's humour and his mum's brains. Let me show you a picture.'

He held up a Facebook photo of the two of them stood outside the front porch of a cottage. Patrick was suited and beaming proudly, kneeling down next to his son on his first day of school holding a reading bag. It looked like the glistening front cover of a sales brochure selling you the nuclear family dream.

'He's got your eyes.'

'You think so?'

'Yep – and grin. How old is he?'

'Seven.'

Patrick paused, looking at the photo with a warm glint in his eye. 'It's funny you mention his smile. I always thought that was Emma's.'

We paid the bill and set off to the tube station. It was on a random street corner of Tottenham Court Road when

Patrick grabbed me tightly in his arms and kissed me. It wasn't slow or tender – it was rapid, whole-hearted and explosive. He pressed me against the window of a shop and began planting urgent kisses against my neck. My masturbation dream was coming to life. This should have felt like an erotic storm, but all I could think about was the look in Patrick's eyes when he had mentioned… Emma.

'Stop for a moment, please.' I stepped back, edging Patrick off me. 'I need a moment.'

'I'm moving too fast, aren't I? Fuck – I'm sorry. It's the alcohol. It never bodes well when I'm one of my highs. I just fancy you, Verity. I mean look at you, you're so young, so sexy, the pheromones between us, I can't even–'

'Do you still love your ex-wife?'

Patrick paused, frowning. He was thinking deeply about his answer, which I appreciated. If he'd given me a flat out no, then I'm not sure I would have believed him.

'My feelings toward Emma are complicated. She's the mother of my son.'

I sighed, adjusting my bag. 'You know, Patrick, maybe this isn't such a good idea after all…'

'Don't be like that. We've only been on one date.'

'Right. And I'm not prepared to be some hot young anchor you clutch onto in order to muster through the wreckage of your divorce. No offence, but it sounds like a teenage breakup on heroin. One you're not over.'

I had been a Lily level of sharp-tongued. Patrick looked hurt.

'I just mean that it's ok if you're not over her. It's something I could understand. But if that's the case, then it wouldn't be wise if…'

'It's done with Emma. Totally done.'

I paused. 'Are you sure?'

'Papers are signed, court proceedings are finished, custody battle finalised. It's over. It has been for a while.'

Whilst I wasn't a forty-year-old man at the finishing line of a messy divorce battle, I still knew the disheartening throb of life not going to plan. The gruesome feeling of a plot twist, hurtling you right to the bottom of a sewage pit, leaving you to claw your way up as you try not to drown. The worst part of it all is watching the world around you carry on as normal – seeing people sail through life easily, smiling like clowns. I'd felt it after Joe raped me in Australia, acting for weeks as if nothing had happened whilst navigating a new life in London. I'd felt it again after Kyle had left me for Toni and our relationship had piddled to a stop. Believing that life is going one way and watching it change direction can be agonising.

'I don't crave Emma anymore. I don't want her, I don't desire her. I haven't for years; not since we were in our twenties...'

'Why did you have Harry, then?'

'Harry was the final straw, and sadly, the one that broke the camel's back. The lack of sleep, the arguments, Emma's sacrifice of her career... we thought having a baby would fix our problems, but all it did was make them worse.'

I nodded sympathetically.

'Please don't write me off, Verity. You have to believe me when I say that I'm ready to date again.'

I kissed him properly this time, when I felt his phone vibrate in his pocket. It was Emma calling. 'I'm on my way, Em. I'll be there in an hour. Ok, ok... yep. Mmhm. Got it. Getting on the tube as we speak. See you soon.'

'Go, Patrick. I don't want to keep you.'

'Tonight has been unexpectedly amazing. I'm happy we did this.'

He kissed me one last time and rushed down to the underground. I watched him trip over an escalator stair and apologise profusely to an old lady behind him. He blurted out some long-winded apology that he was late to see his son. The fact that Patrick's apology for his clumsiness would only make him more late was the very thing that made him so endearing.

The old lady chuckled along, asking Patrick questions. She was certainly drawn to him. I knew that on some level, I was too.

* * *

I hadn't expected my time with Patrick to transition into anything beyond a string of casual dinners and the occasional evening smooch down side streets of central London. I thought the novelty of him would wear off quickly, but somehow, it didn't. The lustful post-work dinners and flirtatious drinks at bars erupted into something entirely unexpected – that was, a steadfast friendship, comparable to my bonds with Max, Naomi and even Lily. For the first time in my dating life, I was depended on, and I liked it. Patrick leaned on me in a way no man had ever leaned on me before; calling me for long talks about his family, his job, and his mental health. All the tiny irrelevant details of his day, that, to an ordinary person, would be incredibly boring, were to me delightful intricacies and nuances of some great story. I found myself looking forward to our conversations every night, never wanting them to end.

'We've been talking for two hours.'

'Two hours and twenty-seven minutes. I like it.'

'You're good at this talking stuff, you know. I've been having CBT for years, and not even my therapist explains stuff to me as well as you.'

I laughed. 'I'll have to start charging you soon.'

'… Or I can repay you in other ways.'

It had been over three weeks since our first date, and

Patrick and I were still yet to sleep with each other. Our intimacy hadn't transpired beyond midweek kissing in central London after we'd finished work. I was sure we'd covered Bond Street, and maybe even Marble Arch, too. Sex wasn't through lack of trying. Somehow, the timings hadn't worked out; Patrick could never come back to Streatham on nights he had Harry, and I could never go to Kingston on nights I had to be at the office for 7 am. After Abel, I wasn't about to make the same mistake of putting a man before my career.

'Let's meet this weekend.'

'I thought it was yours with Harry.'

'Daddyyyyyy! I want a treat from the snack drawer!'

It was Harry wailing. He sounded as if he were on Patrick's lap. The closeness made me feel a little jarred.

'Wait till Daddy's finished speaking to Auntie Vee. Do you have a snack drawer, Auntie Vee?'

I hadn't met Patrick's son yet, but I always detested it whenever he forced me to play happy families down the phone. I felt too young to adopt a maternal-like bond with a seven-year-old, and I didn't fancy the role of a cool auntie, either.

'Can we drop the Auntie Vee thing, please?'

'Sorry.'

'You sound busy. We can talk another time.'

'Go and watch cartoons whilst Daddy finishes with Auntie – with Vee, I mean. I'll join you soon, sausage.'

I don't know why Patrick called his son 'sausage.' It was a hideous pet name that was starting to give me a mild form of 'the ick.' He had said it to me over text, once; a simple message that read:

Goodnight sausage.

It had sent Lily's brain hurtling and made her stomach go queasy. She couldn't understand why I was still speaking to Patrick as a result of it. I told her it would be too petty to write him off just because he had called me 'sausage,' although Patrick said the term so frequently that even I was starting to have doubts.

'I can swap weekends with Emma. I want to have proper time with you.'

'Sure,' I said. 'Just as long as I'm not messing things around. The last thing I want to do is infringe on your family affairs.'

'You'd never be,' he said softly. 'I want you, Verity.'

I paused in my bed, feeling all of a sudden aroused. I decided to make the most of it.

'What are you doing right now?' asked Patrick.

'Lying in bed. Talking to you. Horny.'

Patrick paused for a short moment. I heard his footsteps walk up the stairs. 'What are you wearing? Are you naked?'

'I can be.'

I briefly put the call on mute and shuffled myself out my skirt and tights, pulling my blouse over my head, removing my knickers. I shouted Lily's name to double check I was alone in the flat.

'Back, and fully naked. I'm all yours.'

'Touch yourself, then.'

I sighed. 'You need to stimulate my imagination a bit first, Patrick. You can't just charge in with the clit rubbing stuff.'

'Right – of course,' he mumbled. 'Imagine I'm there, rubbing your...er... tits.'

'Tits? Do you have to call them tits?'

'Fine,' he blustered. 'Caressing your... full breasts. Your soft mounds. Is that better?'

'No! Too Austenian.'

Patrick began to stutter down the phone. It wasn't my intention to humiliate him, but thanks to Grant, I had learnt exactly what I like in the bedroom. I was sexually liberated.

'It's been a while since I've done this, Verity. You'll have to bear with me.'

'Hence I'm guiding you. Nipple play doesn't do it for me. Can you say something else?'

'Why don't you… lie back and imagine I'm kissing your neck.'

'Better.'

'I'm working my way down to your chest, kissing your stomach, racing my hands against your ribs at the same time.'

'Yes… this is good…'

'I work my way down to your hips, racing my tongue against your inner thigh.'

'… Fuck…'

Fuck, indeed. Fuck, fuck, and fuck again, because all I could think about was Grant fucking Black. No. No. No. Go away. Stop. Actually… don't stop. Please. Keep doing what you're doing, yes… just like that, Grant…

The image of Grant slouched on top of me muttering sexy things in my ear came back, just as explosive as when I had met him. I began touching myself, not needing to even rub that hard. I closed my eyes, remembering the feeling of kissing Grant, the feeling of his breath against my neck, the feeling of him inside me, on the cusp of an orgasm again…

'Verity? Are you still there?'

'… Ahhhhh!' I broke out into a mad, frantic release. 'Yes… Gra… ahh… mmm.'

'Jesus, Verity! Are you ok?'

I retrieved the phone, panting. I had been embarrassingly loud. Patrick's ego had probably swelled to the size of a swimming pool inflatable.

'Sorry. I was in another world.'

'Wow! I am good.'

I laughed nervously.

'I can't wait to have sex with you now,' he gushed. 'It's going to be… as you say… wild.'

'Daddy! Where are you?'

'I better go, sausage. I'll see you Saturday.'

Patrick ended the call. I stared up at the ceiling, longing to be stained with Grant's sweet, soapy smell again. I reached to my drawer for my vibrator and thought about him on top of me in Paris for an hour longer until I fell asleep.

* * *

Patrick couldn't swap his weekends, so we settled for the following one instead. I met him on Saturday around noon at West Hampstead. It was a beautifully sunny day – not hot, but lukewarm. I imagined Patrick and I would resume our normal routine of passionate street-corner kissing, but in a park, with the addition of a long lunch and sex at his place. At least that was the plan. Patrick was already waiting for me on the platform when my train pulled in. I had never seen weekend Patrick before, only business Patrick. He was dressed in jeans, converse and a checked shirt. He looked oddly proud when I stepped off the tube – like a dad watching his child do flips on a bouncy castle at a family barbeque.

'You didn't need to collect me, you know. I'm perfectly capable of finding the station exit myself.'

'Sorry. I was just excited.'

He pulled me in close and gave me a long, urgent kiss. I felt Patrick's boner press into me.

'Jeez. Already?'

'I'm remembering that phone sex we had the other day,' he whispered in my ear. 'Hot, wasn't it?'

I hesitated, remembering the way I'd thought about Grant on the phone – the way I'd kept on thinking about him ever since. I kept hoping I would feel some sort of guilt, some sort of remorse over the fact it was his body I was imagining and not Patrick's, but it never came. The only thing that was coming was me, multiple times a day, and the more I expected guilt, the more it inspired lust. Hayley even commented that I had a 'glow' about me and that my hair looked extra shiny. The Paris sex scene was more alive in my brain than ever before, and I was addicted to it. I thought about it constantly, all the time, every day. I had even done it in the dentist toilets whilst waiting for an appointment last week. I was halfway through when they called my name, and came out of the cubicle with a face as red as a cherry tomato. When the vibrator had dropped out of my bag on the way in to the dentist's room, I was a full-on plum.

The mental movie was always the same, on repeat. It was always Grant. I had thought about reaching out to him again, but decided against it every time. I was involved with Patrick now, and it felt like a form of emotional cheating. That said, masturbating over him whilst on the phone to Patrick didn't feel far off.

'Are you hungry?' I said to Patrick. 'Because I could eat a horse.'

* * *

We found a quaint, country-style pub down a cobbled street. As soon as we sat down, Patrick assumed the behaviour of a horny schoolboy trying to get laid.

'I could fuck you right now.'

'Patrick! Keep your voice down.'

He moved our glasses of wine aside and leaned forward, picking up my hand and kissing it passionately.

'Ever since that phone call, I've not stopped thinking about you. I could take you right here, right now against this table. Really pound you hard, ravish you from behind...'

The idea of Patrick taking me against the table made me shuffle in my seat, and not in a good way. He began rubbing my palm against his face, closing his eyes. I had done my own research towards Patrick's condition, and knew that an overactive sex drive was a common symptom of hypermania.

'Are you having an episode?'

'Possibly. It's like sneezing; I can't predict what triggers it and I don't know when it's going to happen.'

Just then, the waitress came. She was petite, blonde and beautiful.

'Hi guys! Have you decided what you'd like to eat?'

I caught Patrick subtly check her out. I don't know if I was paranoid because of the previous disaster with Kyle and Toni, or whether I was just in one of those tetchy moods where I was being overly sensitive. It was most probably an amalgamation of both, with a good pinch of premenstrual stress. I was due on any day now, so it was good timing Patrick and I had chosen this weekend to consummate our 'love.' What was left of it, that was. Patrick was ogling the waitress as if she were a hot prize up for grabs at a parents' raffle evening. The dad vibes were coming at me from all angles, and I was overcome with 'ick.'

'We'll have the fish and chips, please,' I said. 'And the chicken pie.'

'Good choice,' she gushed. 'Are you one of those couples who go halves on your main courses together? Cos that is so utterly adorable!'

She was incredibly squeaky, on par with Patrick's level of enthusiasm. I handed the menu back to her, hoping she'd disappear and leave us alone.

'Thanks, but we are not one of those couples.'

'I think you guys look cute together,' she beamed. 'Actually, sir, you remind me a lot of my brother.'

Despite not knowing anything about the waitress' brother, Patrick let the comment go to his head. I think it was less about the brother comparison and more about the fact the waitress had addressed him as 'sir.' Patrick liked people who supported his illusions of self-grandeur. It was another symptom of his hypermania.

'Is your brother also a supermodel with a fantastic bod and world-class chat?' he chuckled. 'Actually, I suppose you couldn't refer to him in that way, could you? That'd be a bit weird. You'd be sexualising him. Not that it'd be bad if you did. That might be what you're into. If it is, that's fine. I don't judge. I mean, I can objectively state that my sister, Veronica, is beautiful, but it doesn't mean that I…'

'Jesus, Patrick!' I cringed. 'Shut up!'

I looked up at the waitress expecting her to be mortified, but oddly, she didn't seem to mind at all.

'He gets these… outbursts,' I muttered. 'Sorry.'

'You do?' shrieked the waitress. 'That's just like my brother! He suffers from bipolar disorder. He rambles like you do when he's on one of his highs.'

'I'm hypermanic, actually.'

'I'm depressed. And I have S.A.D. It's better now we're in summer, though.' I didn't know what S.A.D. stood for, but Patrick seemed proficient.

'I hear light therapy helps,' he said.

'I have anxiety, too,' smiled the waitress. 'That said, I'm better at managing my attacks these days thanks to mindfulness. It's turned my world around!'

She spoke about mindfulness like a Jehovah's Witness speaks about God and Psycho Joe spoke about crystals. I'd tried mindfulness before and found it fidgety and unhelpful.

It just wasn't for me. Patrick, however, was buying into her every word. I couldn't help but feel that there was a time and a place for these sorts of discussions. I'm all for debating the importance of mental health, but Patrick and I were supposed to be on a date.

'I keep telling Verity to try mindfulness again. She suffers from panic attacks, don't you sausage?'

'No way!' beamed the waitress. 'Anxiety allies!'

'Panic pals,' giggled Patrick. 'I'm loving this convo, guys. This is how mental health should be spoken about.'

'I totally agree,' smiled the waitress. 'If you want, I can totally recommend you guys this app. It connects you with people in your area struggling from different mental health conditions. We can all link on it – check in on each other weekly. One guy even suffers from dendrophobia.'

'What's dendrophobia?' I asked.

'A fear of trees!' squealed the waitress. 'I can't believe I didn't know about it. I felt so ignorant.'

'We don't want to download the app,' I snapped, getting up from my chair. 'I'm going to the bathroom.'

When Patrick and I headed back to Kingston on the train, he was singing the waitresses praises, whose name, we learned, was Paige. Preachy Paige.

'Don't you just love normalising mental health with strangers? Opening up the dialogue, doing the work. It's just so refreshing, isn't it? I thought Paige was great.'

'I didn't. She didn't know when to shut up.'

'What's gotten into you?' frowned Patrick. 'You've been in a strop ever since we left the pub.'

'I told you not to discuss my panic attacks with anyone, Patrick. It's personal. I opened up to you in confidence. I mean, a waitress in a pub? Really?'

'The whole point is reducing the stigma enough so that they stop becoming such a big deal, just like Paige said.'

'I'd prefer if you didn't say her name.'

Patrick didn't apologise. Instead, he embarked on one of his lengthy mental health monologues, as if he were doing a speech on a TED talk stage.

'Reframe how you view panic, Verity. See your attacks as a normal part of you, just as you would hay-fever, or a migraine or a nut allergy. We could even give them a name or something. You know, just like people name storms.'

'But I'm not a storm.'

'That's right,' he winked. 'You're a hurricane.'

I rolled my eyes at Patrick's attempt to be all poetic and romantic. If Grant had said it, then it would have had the desired effect. Suddenly, he was all I could think about again.

'Sometimes, Patrick, I think you'd prefer me if I was more fucked up.'

'That's obscene.'

'It's the truth. You enjoy talking about mental health and comparing notes with others. It's how you connect with people. You enjoy the tussle, the conversational vigour. That's when you feel most alive.'

Patrick frowned. We spent the rest of the journey in silence.

By the time Patrick and I arrived back to his place, I was fraught with sexual frustration, having let my mind run wild with thoughts of Grant on the train.

'Let me give you a tour.'

'Screw the tour,' I muttered. 'Take me now, just like you wanted to at the pub.'

I leaned my arms against the kitchen island, knocking over a pot of water and colouring book at the same time. There was a painting on top of it – presumably one Harry had done. Thanks to my clumsiness, it was now completely sodden. Patrick despaired.

'Harry was working on this all morning! It's all ruined now.'

'I'm sorry,' I said, kneeling down to help salvage it. 'We can put it back on the table to dry.'

'It won't work,' said Patrick. 'The sunbeams have all smudged and the stickman's hair has gone all fuzzy.'

I sighed, looking at the picture. I hadn't seen the before version, but I'm sure there wasn't much difference from the one I was looking at now. I wanted to reassure Patrick that it was hardly the work of Picasso, but reminded myself that anything a child draws for their parent is sacred and regarded as such. I remember when I had made my mother a necklace from string and dry pasta at primary school. She'd pretended to be delighted, as if I had just handed her a diamond neck wreath. I was only eight years old, and even I knew she was faking it. 'Does it really matter, Patrick? You're making an awful lot of fuss.'

'Of course it matters,' he snapped. 'You don't get it, do you? Since the trauma of the divorce, colouring has been Harry's little creative outlet. A lot of people use art to heal. Especially children.'

I didn't know what to say. Patrick began cleaning up the mess on the floor, laying out the soggy painting to dry on a copy of the *Times*. I tried to help but Patrick pushed my hand away.

'Just leave it. Make yourself at home on the sofa and I'll join you in a bit.'

I reached for my bag and wandered along the hallway, feeling more like Harry's annoying teenage sister as opposed to his Dad's young date.

Despite his messy divorce, Patrick's home exuded pristine, family perfection. I had expected there to be odd socks everywhere, empty mugs lying around; sufficient evidence of a struggling father trying to get it together, but it was the total opposite. Everything was in place and immaculate, smelling of fresh laundry and flowers. On the living room mantelpiece was a series of black and white pictures of Harry when he was a baby. I spotted one of Patrick, Emma and Harry as a family of three; Emma radiant and beaming with Harry in her arms, Patrick overcome with joy from seeing his new-born smile for a picture. Emma was a beautiful woman. Although the picture was in black and white, I could see from her freckly complexion and light eyes that her hair was a similar shade of auburn to my own. Her and Patrick looked so complete, so whole. It looked like the type of happiness that people spend their lives searching for.

The picture next to it was more recent, no older than a year or so. The three of them were wrapped up tightly in hats and scarfs on a windy beach on some coastal town of the UK. This time, neither Patrick or Emma was smiling. They looked vacant, and really, really tired. I edged closer, staring into Emma's eyes, searching for some sort of pain to insinuate that things had maybe started to go wrong in her marriage. According to Patrick's timeline of events, it would have been around the time of this picture being taken when they did. I jumped when he burst through the door, embarrassed that he had caught me looking. Patrick walked over behind me, wrapping his arms around my waist, swaying gently from side to side. 'That picture was taken in North Devon last year. It was where Emma and I got married.'

'Does it not hurt to have all these pictures up?'

'Not at all. The child psychologist said exposure to our original family unit will help Harry adjust to the new one. It's important for him to grow up with the belief that he's still part of something, you know?'

Patrick began kissing my neck. I relaxed into his touch, closing my eyes, feeling his hands rub against my waist and up toward my chest.

'See?' he whispered. 'It's just like how I described over the phone that time…'

Why did he have to say that? Now all I could think about was…

I turned around and pushed Patrick onto the sofa, furiously unbuttoning his shirt whilst grinding on his crotch. I began kissing his neck, trying to catch his cologne, hoping that it would somehow match the distinctiveness of Grant's scent. Maybe it would if I tried hard enough. I would have to use my imagination.

'Slow down, Verity. You're behaving like an animal.'

'You were desperate for me earlier.'

'Yes, but I don't like fast and furious sex. I like it slow. I want to make love to you.'

He knelt down on the floor and began pulling off my trousers, kissing me tenderly from the ankles up. I lay back onto the sofa and closed my eyes, pretending I was in Paris again.

'Apocalypse pending! Recalculating… Apocalypse pending!'

I jolted out my skin at some robotic action toy with a revolving head walking to the sofa.

'What the fuck is that?!'

'Zed Ex, the Super Robot Zombie! He's the world champion in Robot Riots. Perhaps he wants to join in.'

'Not funny, Patrick.'

'Sorry,' he laughed, switching the toy off. 'I thought Harry had taken it with him to his mum's.'

'Talk about ruining the moment,' I mumbled. 'The thing nearly gave me a heart attack.' Patrick tended back to my calf, pulling my knickers down at the same time. He plunged his finger inside me, swirling it around in aggressive, frantic motions.

'What did I tell you about diving straight in?'

'But you're so wet already,' smiled Patrick. 'Would you like me to go down on you?'

'Don't ask me. Just do it.'

He quickly unbelted his jeans and pulled his t-shirt over his head, pushing me down on the sofa.

'Excuse the dad bod. I'm still working to shift a few pounds.'

'I don't care, Patrick.'

I spread my legs apart and shuffled back. Thankfully, his sofa was L-shaped and big enough to accommodate for the both of us, unlike Caleb's single bed. Spacious environments made mid-sex glitches less awkward. I watched Patrick go down on me slowly, hoping the image of his head between my legs would fill me with desire. Sadly, it didn't. I found myself restless, wanting the whole thing over with as quickly as possible. I didn't care about pleasing Patrick. I wanted to come for myself, thinking about Grant. I urged Patrick to stop.

'I was in the middle of something there.'

'Skip it,' I said, pulling Patrick into me and wrapping my legs around his waist. 'Let's just have sex.'

'I should get a condom from the bathroom, then. Wait there.'

He wandered upstairs whilst I reached for my phone in my bag. I had a message from Lily, who had been to some work lunch at The Connaught. She had sent me a photo of a stack of pancakes with raspberry coulis – the exact ones I had ordered with Grant. I looked at them lovingly, remembering how they had tasted. I heard Patrick's footsteps and put my phone away hurriedly. He dangled the condom in his hand triumphantly.

'Found this guy at the back of my cabinet next to an old packet of antidepressants.'

He fiddled around with the condom like a nervous teenager about to have sex for the first time.

'Sorry,' he giggled. 'Like I said – it's been a while.'

'Do you want me to…'

'It's alright,' he said, securing it in place. 'I think I've got it.'

He toppled back on top of me and began grinding against my body in an odd, uneven rhythm, resembling a drunk seal stuck on the edge of a rock in a gale force wind. It was so freestyle and out of synch with my body that it was easier for me to just stare at the ceiling and do nothing. As Patrick got more into it, I realised I'd have to fake it. I quickly got the hang of it; the ebb-and flow of panting, the frowning, the flicking of the hair when we switched positions and I went on top. It felt like conducting a live orchestra to a bunch of musicians who were pretending to play the instruments. It was a disaster.

'Do you like that?'

'Mmmhmm.'

'I think I'm going to come… ahh… yes… fuck… EMMA!'

I froze, staring down at Patrick's face which was scrunched up like the skin of a dried prune. Whether from pain, pleasure, or guilt – I did not know. I waited for his jizz-filled high to settle back down and watched his brows furrow with embarrassment.

'Jesus,' he frowned. 'I'm so sorry.'

I quickly got up from the sofa and began putting on my clothes. My ego felt bruised, but equally, I could hardly judge the man. He may have mentioned his ex-wife mid orgasm, but I had masturbated to Grant on the phone the other week.

'It's fine.'

'It is so not fine. It can't be, for God's sake. I just mentioned… I mean, I called you… fuck.'

'Do you still love her?'

Patrick froze. I didn't want to look at him, so instead, cast my eyes on the condom. It lay on the arm of the sofa like a dead tadpole.

'You already asked me that.'

'Well excuse me for asking again.'

Patrick sighed. 'No. I don't love her.'

'But you miss her.'

'Everybody misses somebody.'

'Doesn't mean you mention their name during sex, Patrick.'

He sat down on the sofa, resting his head in his hands. Oddly, I didn't feel angry towards him. Given the intensity of my thoughts about Grant, it would have been too irrational, too unjustified. I could tell Patrick was horrified, and I wasn't going to hold it against him.

'I'm sorry, Verity. I'm a mess.'

I looked up at the family photos again, observing Emma.

'You dated me because you wanted to relive the glory days with your childhood sweetheart, didn't you?'

'What?'

'I'm not stupid, Patrick. The woman's a redhead. There's not that many of us lurking around these days.'

Patrick hesitated. 'There was a similarity between you both, yes. Especially when I first met you at the ATC. Seeing you felt like being twenty-five with Emma again. There was this pull to you that made me feel reborn…'

I rolled my eyes. 'Jesus.'

'Pretty, fucked up, I know.'

Patrick was right. It was fucked up. But so was my obsession with Grant. Maybe Patrick and I were just as bad as each other.

We decided to stop seeing each other later that evening over a long phone call. It was, as breakups go, pleasantly civilised.

'I'm no expert, but I think you're supposed to call me a dick and block my number.'

'Too cliché.'

'Why are you so nice, Verity?'

'I wasn't always. Sorry for what I said to you on the train earlier. It was spiteful. I was in a weird frame of mind.'

'Forgiven, always. Can we stay friends?'

'As long as you view me as Verity as opposed to the twenty-five-year-old ghost of your ex-wife.'

'Deal.'

'Daddy! Where is Zed Ex, the Super Robot Zombie?'

'Take care, Patrick.'

Chapter 10 – Sammy

Six months later
London Cocktail Club, Liverpool Street

'How many muscles are in a cat's ear?'

God help me. As far as dodgy opening lines go, this one takes the cherry.

'I don't know,' I sighed, taking a long sip of my drink. 'How many?'

'The whole point is that you guess.'

'Fourteen?'

'Not quite. Try again.'

He looks like an absent-minded professor and has a moth hole in his t-shirt. I've also identified four crisp crumbs in his beard. I am certain they are the remains of a tangy cheese Dorito. 'Ten?'

'Nope.'

'Look, I don't mean to be rude, but I'm waiting for someone, and–'

'The correct answer is thirty. Thirty muscles in their miniature triangular ears! Can you believe that?'

Please someone save me from crisp crumb man. Someone. Anyone. Please…?

'I'm a comedian out of work. Sorry about the bad jokes.'

I didn't respond, hoping to God he'd take a hint. It didn't work.

'How about we debate something else. Do you agree that the centre of an After Eight tastes like toothpaste?'

I didn't think this guy's chat could get any worse, but I was wrong.

I scrambled into my bag for my phone. Lily said she'd be here at ten and it was now half past. We were supposed to be meeting to celebrate my work promotion, but there was no sign of her. I was going to kill her for making me suffer like this.

'Excuse me, but I have to pop to the ladies room.'

'Can I buy you another drink?'

'No.'

I shuffled off my chair and headed to the toilets. My head felt light. I had already guzzled back two gin and tonics whilst waiting for Lily. I was tipsy.

I walked into a more promising male stranger, head first.

'Woops! Sorry.'

'Don't be,' he smiled. 'It was my fault.'

I quickly checked him out. He was dressed in vintage jeans and a baggy retro sports jacket with the blonde hair curtains of a Backstreet Boy. These days, it's cool to look like you're from the 90s.

'You were trying to escape that weird guy at the bar, weren't you?'

'Yes.'

'I was watching you.'

This guy was cute. He reminded me of Dazzling Derek from my uni days.

'Do you know who the strange man at the bar is?' I asked.

'No, but he came over to me and my mates earlier and asked if we thought whether the centre of an After Eights tastes–'

'Tastes like toothpaste? Yep. He said the same to me.'

We both glanced over at crisp crumb man. He was

sucking at the lemon from his drink, gnawing at the rind like a squirrel.

'I did think about coming over to save you.'

'You should have. I would have been eternally grateful.'

'It was too amusing watching you suffer,' he laughed. 'Sammy, by the way.'

'Verity.'

My phone suddenly vibrated. It was a text from Lily, explaining that she wasn't going to be able to make it after all due to an emergency work incident at the studio. I wasn't going to let it stop me celebrating. I was here, dressed to the nines as the new senior account executive of Kill & Kontent PR. It had taken Hayley leaving for me to get the role, but still. I was happy as a clam.

'How do you feel about getting drunk and dancing with me till 6 am?'

Sammy grinned and leaned forward, whispering in my ear. 'That's if you can keep up with me.' After three rounds of tequila shots, dancing to ABBA and making out with Sammy in the smoking area, I had found myself at an underground basement rave in Vauxhall. Everyone was high off drugs and looked fresh out of uni, sweating, grinding and gurning. It reminded me of being a student with Max again. I felt incredibly out of place. This wasn't how I had imagined the night to go.

'I feel too old to be here,' I said, grabbing hold of Sammy's hand. 'Don't you?'

'Live fast, die young!' shouted Sammy, jumping up and down to the music. 'You're only as old as you feel!'

I looked at him in a drunken, sweaty frenzy, wondering how old he was. My guess was twenty-two. An odd choice for me, given that I usually date older guys, but I was too drunk to question whether getting caught up with him had been a good idea or not.

There was little use in talking further. The music was deafening and the lights were flashing luminous colours. I looked up and felt the whole room spin. It was safe to say my raving days were well and truly over. I checked my phone. It was ten to two in the morning.

'I think I'm going to head off,' I shouted in his ear. 'It was good to meet you.'

'Wait!' he yelled. 'Let me come with you.'

Sammy and I stumbled back in an Uber to Streatham. We kissed in the back seats the whole way there. When we arrived to my front door, he had turned suspiciously quiet.

'Are you ok?'

'Fine, thanks.'

By the time we had settled down in the living room, Sammy's nerves hadn't subsided. The poor guy was jittering. I turned the lights up brighter to take a closer look at him, offering him a glass of water.

'You didn't take a dodgy pill or something, did you?'

'No. I'm just nervous.' His teeth were chattering against the glass. 'You're like a proper woman, you know. Not a girl. A woman.'

It sounded as if he were singing a rendition of an old Britney song. I didn't entertain his mumbling. Instead, I sat down on the sofa and started kissing him again. He removed my jacket and pushed me down on the sofa, fondling my boobs, staring at them with fascination. 'God you're sexy,' he gawked. 'What did you say your name was again?'

'Verity. I told you three times already.'

This is precisely why I don't have one night stands anymore.

He knelt up and began unbuttoning his jeans, distracted by a note on the table. It was the note that Grant had left me from The Bluebird night, which I had treasured as a keepsake of our time together. I had been studying it fondly earlier on today, examining the perfect swirls of his writing. To my dismay, Sammy picked up the note and began reading it out loud.

'For the girl who likes to write as much as she likes to kiss….'

'Leave it!' I snatched it from his hands, feeling weirdly protective of it. 'It's personal.'

'Sorry.'

As Sammy toppled back onto sofa, all the change fell out of his pocket. He looked embarrassed, getting up to retrieve all the pound coins that were scattered on the floor. I thought the only people who carried change nowadays were elderly people who didn't trust contactless payment or kids who weren't old enough to own a debit card yet and wanted to buy sweeties. I didn't know how he had managed to fit so many coins into his jeans. It looked as if he had unleashed a piggy bank.

'Sorry,' he blushed, scarlet red. 'I didn't mean to make a mess.'

He began kissing me again, moving his body against mine. I was distracted by the edge of something sharp, digging into my waist. I moved my hand against the pocket of his jeans and pulled out his ID card. I took a closer look at his face with the date 25/01/2001 beneath. I looked up at Sammy, who looked like a startled lamb. The guy was eighteen.

'Fuck! Why didn't you tell me how old you were?'

'Embarrassed, I guess.'

'You do know I'm older than you, right?'

Sammy grinned. 'I could tell. You were dancing to Shania Twain like a single mum at a wedding.'

'Exactly how much older did you think I was?'

'Dunno,' he shrugged. 'Thirty, maybe?'

'Thirty? I'm twenty-five, thank you very much.'

What a waste of my collagen subscription and avocado eye cream. I suddenly felt furious at the Instagram influencer who had promoted it. Her cream had the opposite effect.

'Age doesn't bother me, babe. I like older women.'

This guy sounded like a mini-Caleb in the making. He had to go. Now.

Just then, Lily messaged me to say she was on her way home. If she saw me half naked with an eighteen-year-old on the sofa then she'd think I was having some sort of breakdown. To be honest, I was starting to think that I was.

'I'm mature for my age,' pleaded Sammy. 'I can locate the clit. I promise!'

'No offence, Sammy, but not even forty-year-old men can locate the clit. Take it from me.'

'Can't you let me try?'

'No! Go and be a fuckboy on girls your own age. It's a rite of passage.'

I didn't let Sammy anywhere near my clit. In fact, I forced him to leave in such a hurry that he left all his change behind. I decided I would keep it for myself in the name of babysitting money. When Lily burst through the door half an hour later, I hadn't moved from the sofa. I was filled with despair. Meeting eighteen-year-olds at raves? What had my life come to? 'Christ, Verity. You look rough as hell.'

'That's what happens when you get ditched by your best friend and end up at a rave in Vauxhall. Thanks a bunch for standing me up. I've had the worst night of my life.'

'A rave, in Vauxhall?' Lily raised her eyebrows. 'Don't make me laugh.'

'I met a guy. He just left.'

'What?'

'He was eighteen. The end.'

Lily's jaw hadn't dropped so low since I told her Caleb lived in Uxbridge and slept in a single bed.

'Please don't tell me you had sex with him, Vee…'

I shook my head. 'Found his ID just in the nick of time.'

'Fifty-four and eighteen. You go from one extreme to another.'

We both stared at each other, wondering whether my dating life was a cause for concern or hysterics. I don't think either of us knew the answer.

Chapter 12 – Nate

Three weeks later
The Goat, Fulham Road

'I think you should stop dating for a while.'

Naomi was concerned, and with good reason. At some point, all the dating disasters that had spun cyclically over the last five years had to stop. From a crystal worshipping rapist to a toy-boy from Uxbridge posing as a Rolex obsessed trader – the cluster of my romantic catastrophes were never-ending. They were engrained in the laws of the universe, governed by science, and most frighteningly, always to be expected. I couldn't rely on Naomi, Max or Lily for direction, or even my career for distraction. If the woes of my dating life were going to stop, then it had to come from me.

'I'm not suggesting you never date again. Just have a break. Go on a yoga retreat. Climb a mountain. Meet some monks in a temple or something.'

'I had always lusted over a hot bald man, you know. A bit like Jason Statham. Just me?'

'Just you.'

I was being tongue and cheek, but Naomi's concern had deepened.

'It's not natural to keep lurching from one man to the next, Vee. Don't hate me, but I've spoken to Lily.'

'That's never the start of a promising sentence.'

'We're both worried about you.'

Since meeting Kyle all those years ago when I first moved to London, I hadn't stopped for air. Reflecting on the sequence of events that had occurred since was like examining the chronicles of a bloody war in a history text book, each chapter filled with messy, gritty, surprising details. I had to take a breather. I would, I told myself. Just after my date with Nate. I was waiting at a bar in Fulham, twiddling my thumbs. I had never been stood up on a date before, but Nate was fifteen minutes late, so it was looking like an increasingly possible scenario. I had matched with him on a dating app. He was a thirty-five-year-old kickboxing instructor from Parsons Green; a rugged French lothario with sparkly green eyes and a scar on his chin which made him look as if he were from the Italian mafia. Max, Lily and Naomi had each said conflicting things when I had presented them with a picture of Nate stood in a leather jacket next to a motorbike.

'Fuck me! I'd ride him into next Tuesday.'

'He looks like a newly released convict who just served a ten-year prison sentence in Eastern Europe.'

'He'll break your heart and make it look sexy.'

I checked my phone and applied more lip-gloss, staring at the note Grant had left me that time at The Bluebird. I always kept it in my purse. I studied it occasionally, almost always before a date with someone else. It was a torturous habit which I don't know why I did. I guess it was soothing on some level. There aren't always answers to the oddities of human behaviour. I heard a loud motorbike engine outside. I looked out of the window and saw a man parking up, dressed head to toe in black clothing. As soon as he removed his helmet, I could see it was Nate. The sight of him made my stomach flip. I downed the remaining wine in my glass and stared down at my phone screen to avoid eye contact with the waiter. He had already asked me twice if I was ok and whether I wanted a complimentary bread basket. I must have looked like a hungry spinster. Nate was faffing around with his motorbike outside. I watched him adjust the collar of his leather jacket and secure the bike with a chain. It was like previewing an upcoming gangster movie starring a dark and dangerous heartthrob hero. When the bar door swung open, he ignored the waiter and strode confidently towards our table, smiling. It looked as if he were coming to rescue me from… well – everything, really. 'Sorry I'm late.' Nate was clearly parched. He swung back an entire glass of rosé as if it were water. Everything about him was strong; his voice, his posture, his smell. Flamed citrus peel and leather. I liked it.

'You look nice,' he grinned.

'Is that an attempt to rectify the lateness?'

He tilted his head back, drinking more wine. Nate had an earthiness about him; a rugged physique which made him look as if he had acquired his strength from lifting trunks of wood in a forest as opposed to pumping dumbbells in the gym. He possessed the attributes of a wild animal and the might of a caveman.

'You're lucky I'm still here. Ten minutes later and I would have been gone.'

'Then I would have come looking for you on my bike.'

I looked out at his Harley-Davidson. 'You couldn't pay me to ride that thing.'

'You'd always be safe with me,' he laughed, gently brushing his thumb against my knuckles.

'I promise.'

Something about the warm coarseness of his hand enveloped me with the strong sense that he was right.

* * *

Unless you'd rather be at home watching Netflix, first date feelings will generally fall into one of two categories:

Sweet, excitable butterflies which leave you feeling light and giddy.

Gut-wrenching terror with the strong sense your life is about to turn upside down.

Kyle had been one. Grant had been two. Nate was a glorious blend of one and two. I saw him again for another date the following week, and our chemistry was difficult to ignore. Nate's sexiness was found in the rare interplay between strength and sensitivity; his grit against his gentleness; the fieriness in which he approached his life against the soft way he tended to the people in it. He had moved to London from Nîmes in the south of France eleven years ago, and had experienced life from primitive, humble beginnings.

'My mum was a teacher, my dad a bus driver. He used to take me to work with him sometimes as punishment for my reckless behaviour,' he laughed. 'I'd sit there, silently, watching him lose his temper with traffic on the road with the rage of a lion. He was terrifying, but strangely, I looked up to him.' Nate paused. 'He died when I was fifteen on a motorbike accident. It crushed his skull. The doctors said it was the most gruesome injury they had ever seen.'

'Jesus. That's awful.'

'The brain is delicate, you know,' he continued. 'I always thought the heart was our most vulnerable organ, but seeing how my dad died, and how my mum grieved – it made me think it could be the brain.'

I thought then of Patrick, who told me he had recently fallen into a cycle of depression and left his job. It was only speaking to Nate like this, earnestly with his eyes, that I wondered what that must have felt like.

'I would go to school and come home to the blinds all

shut in the house. Daylight through the curtains brought her to tears. I think it reminded her that the world still had to carry on, you know?'

Neither of us spoke for a short moment, until Nate decided to change the subject.

'Do you enjoy PR?'

'I don't think anyone enjoys PR. They just enjoy how it sounds to a room full of people. Adrenaline, attention and fancy brunches with strangers.'

Nate laughed.

'What else do you like to do?' he smiled. 'Away from work?'

'I write.'

'Really?' said Nate. 'About what?'

'Everything, really. It's the only way my brain sits still. Do you write?'

'Never.'

'Read?'

'Not enough.'

'Movies?'

'Of course.'

I laughed. 'What's your favourite?'

'*The Lion King*.'

'I wasn't expecting that.'

'No one ever does,' Nate shrugged. 'Disney films are full of life lessons if you pay attention.' I noticed that Nate never liked to show his teeth, closing his mouth quickly whenever he finished speaking. He had done it in previous pauses of our conversation. I think he was embarrassed that they were a little crooked. They say that your imperfections will be someone else's favourite part of you, and in Nate's case, it was. Whenever Nate tried to conceal his smile, I found it endearing. It was drawing me further into him, and as we carried on talking, I gradually felt our chemistry shift into something more palpable. Maybe it was our pheromones taking over, for we were now flirting helplessly, toying with each other's hands. Whatever it was a strong force, infinitely bigger than the room were in. Bigger than the couples on tables, their muttering, the plates of food and the glasses and the changing of cutlery and the faint background music. It was bigger than even time and reason, for we had only known each other a few days. Nate relaxed his hand on my cheek and caressed my eyebrow with his thumb, leaning across the table to kiss me. It was messy and inelegant, but I'd been wanting to do it for ages. We smashed a glass and knocked cutlery on the floor in the process. Neither of us cared. I walked round, treading the sole of my boot into a shaft of glass. I sat on his lap and his tongue softened in my mouth like a whole tablespoon of rich butter. It was a full serving of a kiss; all-consuming and rich. The type that sweeps you away in a single moment and makes romance novels of the past seem real rather than corny. Lily said the best kiss she ever had was at 2 am in the Indian ocean with a stranger when she was travelling (until she got stung by a jellyfish). Max's was with Tom on the sofa, waiting for a Chinese takeaway, for no reason, he said, other than that it felt like the beginning of everything mingled with a sense of coming home to himself. Mine was now, with Nate, in this restaurant, with cutlery on the floor and glass everywhere and suspicious looks from waiters. I was sure there would be no greater one like it.

'You know,' said Nate, with my arms around his neck, 'I think what writing is to you, is what boxing is to me.'

'What do you mean?'

'Well, it's that thing that keeps your brain in check from the chaos of the real world, isn't it? That necessary sort of escapism.'

People were staring at us, caught in a passionate, murmuring frenzy. I couldn't blame them. I would have stared, too. We were pent up with the type of lust most often reserved for people who meet for affairs.

Sexual chemistry like this was a well-established Grant Black symptom that I hadn't expected to feel again, unless by some miracle we found our way into each other's lives and embarked on round two of some tumultuous Parisian escapade. This didn't feel all that important anymore, especially after a kiss like that. Eventually, we were interrupted by the waiter who came to clear the glass. After we paid the bill and made our way to the door, he came running out after us.

'Madam!'

I looked around and saw that he was holding Grant's note. My heart began to pound from fear that he was going to read it out loud like Sammy the teenager had done.

'This fell from your pocket as you left. I assumed it was important.'

I took the note from the waiter's hand and stared down at it. The l's and y's were my most cherished part. I always thought they made Grant's words look less like writing and more like operatic chords dancing on a sheet of music.

'You can throw it away,' I said, handing it back to the waiter. 'I don't need it anymore.'

* * *

Six weeks later, I fell in love with Nate.

Of course, it wasn't the first time. There had been Kyle, and Max in my uni days. I had fondness for Patrick, tenderness towards Abel, and infatuation with Grant. However, there was something about Nate that was different from all the other men I had dated. This time, I was in love; consuming, unquestionable, adult love, which seemed as if it had infinite potential to actually go somewhere and impact my life in the way I had always dreamed of. I thought falling in love would be like getting run over by a taxi in a New York street. It would take me by surprise, make my whole head spin and leave me gasping. Really, it was the opposite. Falling in love with Nate was the softest, safest, easiest thing in the world, like the realisation of a snowflake landing in your hair. He was so gentle with my heart that I wondered why I had ever thought about quietening it down.

Nate lived with his brother, Joshua, in a small two-bedroom flat in Parsons Green. They shared a bond that I quickly became in awe of. The depth of their closeness was quintessentially Mediterranean. They loved that little bit harder, hugged each other that little bit tighter and always ate dinner late and together. The problem of one was the problem of the other, and their love was unwavering and concrete. I felt more at home in their family dynamic than that of my own. Naomi said it was beautiful. Lily said it was weird. Max said it was Freudian.

We curled up on the sofa and spoke about how our days had been. We laughed at small things, like how Nate always put two teabags in his cup to maximise the flavour and how the volume of the TV always had to be on an even number. Nate would mock my inability to finish hot drinks and set a hundred phone alarms, whilst I would laugh at the way Joshua spent longer on his hair in the bathroom than I did and once thought you could travel to New York by the Eurostar. Nate and I shared a bond which felt like it would never split, even if you went at it with the spears of two hunting knives. The precise moment of falling in love with him arrived a week later. We were out for dinner at a restaurant owned by his friend, and he had reserved the entire top floor for us. Unfortunately, I had caught the flu.

'I should take you home. You're not well, Verity.'

'At least wait for the food to come. You went to so much trouble.'

'Forget the food. There will be other times.'

Nate gave me a ride home on his motorbike. He told me to hold onto his back tightly and not let go. I wouldn't recommend riding on the back of a motorbike for the first time with the flu. Even with Nate driving slowly, it felt like my guts were going to fall out of my ears. When we arrived at my flat, he carried me inside up to my bedroom. It was the lift my dad used to give me after a late-night car journey. I would fall asleep on purpose, just so I could be carried up inside and put to bed. Nate trudged up the stairs and wrapped me up tightly into the duvet, spooning medicine into my mouth, kissing my hair. He was like a sedative, calming everything in me that was bewildered and confused. Although poorly, I was filled with a burning desire to tell Nate how I felt about him.

'I think I love you.'

The words came spluttering out of my mouth with an unfortunate trail of the orange medicine. I had sort of wanted Nate to lay down topless so I could tickle the words on his back and make him guess what I had spelt. However, I was a shivering, sneezing wreck, half asleep. It wasn't going to happen. If it were Grant, then I would have panicked that I looked like a zombie. With Nate, I didn't care so much.

'Excuse the delivery,' I wheezed, as Nate wiped my mouth. 'I wanted it to sound nicer.'

Nate removed his jacket and cradled me until I was almost asleep. When I glanced up at him, he was beaming.

'You shouldn't stay here,' I whispered. 'I might make you ill.'

'Don't be silly. I'm indestructible. It's my job to protect people.'

Of course, Nate did get ill. That following weekend, he was supposed to be coming to a housewarming party with me in Balham. He had to cancel last minute because he couldn't get off the sofa and felt as if he had been hit by a bus.

'Take this,' I said, pouring the medicine on the spoon. 'It's the same one you gave me last week. It tastes quite nice, actually. Sort of like a melted fruit pastel…'

'I love you too.'

'What?'

'I love you, Verity.'

Deciding to ditch the party, I kicked off my shoes and snuggled up to Nate on the sofa. We lay there, tangled in each other's bodies with the TV on, watching our love bleed into the room like daylight in the crack of a blind.

* * *

'I got an email from our gas company. We need to send them a meter reading. Can you sort it by next week?'

Lily had been busy working in LA since I had met Nate, and we'd gone a lot longer than usual without speaking. I hadn't been home for days. Half of my wardrobe (and part of Lily's) was on his bedroom floor. She was currently in a footballer's mansion in Beverly Hills. Now was clearly not the time to tell her this.

'I'll be back tomorrow,' I said. 'I'll do it then.'

'Back tomorrow? Where are you?'

'Nate's place.'

'Who's Nate?'

'French Guy.'

'Oh. Him. You haven't moved in already, have you?'

'No. I just hang around here a lot. You know I hate being in the flat when you're not there.' Lily paused.

'Spoke to Esme the other day. She said you didn't show up to her housewarming on Saturday.'

'I wasn't feeling all that great. I had the flu.'

'Gross.'

Lily began video calling me. When I answered, she was holding her phone up on the edge of a swimming pool.

'Holy shit. I need a tour!'

'And I need details of French Guy. Are you an official couple?'

'Well, we've said "I love you," which means we must be. Right?'

'Wrong. You're not a couple until you have had "the chat." You know – the exclusivity talk.'

'Yes, but if you've already said "I love you" then the exclusivity talk doesn't count. I mean you've declared love, for goodness' sake. Love! It doesn't get bigger than that.'

'This isn't a Fitzgerald novel, Vee.' Lily frowned at me with a pitiful look in her eyes. 'Sometimes I worry about you. All those movies you watch; all those books you read. They distort your vision towards the reality of modern dating.'

'But I thought saying "I love you" changes the game – maybe even ends it!'

'No. It complicates it.'

* * *

I had dated more men than Lily, Naomi and Max put together. I should have known better than all of them that dating wasn't a simple game, but with Nate, it felt like it was. I told myself that all the years of romantic disasters had been for a purpose – they were guiding me to him. I thought he was the summit of the ridiculous, comical mountain; the destiny to it all. The finishing line of some ridiculous dating marathon that had gone on for far too long. I took Lily's advice and decided to have 'the chat' with Nate one night after sex.

'What are we, Nate?'

'Don't ask me that. You know I hate labels.'

I shuffled away from him, stubbornly taking more of the duvet with me.

'Come on, Verity. What would you like me to say?'

'I was sort of hoping you'd ask me to be your girlfriend. I mean, now that we've both said the L word…'

'But I don't want a girlfriend.'

'Then what the fuck are we doing?'

I shot up in a naked fluster, feeling like the mad woman in the attic. Nate looked like a frightened child who had just found me in an unfortunate game of hide and seek. My mother always told me there's nothing scarier to a man than an angry, crying woman, and I think she was right.

'I don't get it, Nate. I've stayed round here every night this last month. I sleep with you, I eat with you, I wake up with you every morning. We do everything that couples do.' I positioned myself back on the end of the bed, wrapping the duvet around me. 'Plus, there's the fact that we love each other,' I whispered. 'Isn't there?'

'Of course there is. But I can't have a girlfriend, Verity.'

'Why "can't" you?'

'Because…' Nate began to stammer. 'Because commitment terrifies me. It terrifies me to death.'

'Do you realise how ridiculous you sound?' I snapped. 'You're thirty-five years old.'

'You don't get it, do you? Your childhood was all sunshine, cupcakes and rainbows, but I grew up in a house of plates smashing, affairs and arguments about money. Your dad is a teddy-bear. Mine was a fucking maniac.'

'My parents are divorced, Nate. I'm aware my beginnings

were more privileged than yours, but my life hasn't been all hunky dory. There are things about me which you don't know.'

'This isn't a pity party.'

'I didn't say it was.'

Neither of us said anything for a moment. It was the first time we had argued properly.

'My ex was crushed when our relationship ended, Verity. Eleven years, and I ripped her heart to shreds. I can't bear the weight of hurting someone like that again. The responsibility of someone's heart in my hands is overwhelming. Somehow, yours comes with more pressure than the average persons. I don't know why. You're just so... delicate.'

'You'll crush me a hundred times more by giving me some weird replacement, which is what this is. You do know that, don't you?'

'Well then I'll stop.'

Neither of us spoke for a good five minutes. Nate tried to hug me, but I pushed him away. He began to cry. Frankly, I felt angry at myself for not finding the man more pathetic. I wanted to feel rage at him for leading me on, fury that he had wasted my time; but I couldn't. I wanted to make reasons for his excuses and excuses for his reasons. I didn't want to let him slip away. I loved him too much.

'I would be a good girlfriend, you know. I'd love you just the right amount, however much or little you need. Just tell me what you need, and I'll be it. I'll be whatever the hell you need me to be.'

Nate didn't say anything. He was sat on the edge of the bed, biting his lower lip.

'You have to be careful with love, Nate. Sometimes we only find it once.'

I knew I was sounding desperate; convincing Nate of something he didn't want. The most dignified thing to do would be to leave. I threw on my clothes and began packing my bag, scanning for only the important things, like Lily's bra and bracelet, which she'd kill me for losing. If Nate and I really were going to end things, then I would have to come back for the rest of my belongings once the dust had settled. I hovered by the door, feeling tears trickle down my face.

'Can't we at least try?'

Nate didn't say a word, but he didn't need to. Sometimes, there is such thing as loving someone too much. It is then that you are at risk of saying too much, too.

I left his flat, half hoping he would come running out after me. The wait time for an Uber was seven minutes, just like it had been when I left Kyle after the threesome disaster. And just like Kyle, Nate never came running.

* * *

Forgetting Nate would be hard, Lily said, but not impossible. It had been three weeks, and I had gone through the usual breakup routine with her, Skyping Max and Naomi in to all the ceremonious events. The deletion of Nate's number, eating ice cream out of the tub, singing along to female power ballads and watching episodes of *Sex and the City* on repeat. I was even getting close to cutting a fringe, but Lily reminded me that any haircut done out of heartbreak would most likely be one I would regret.

She kept comparing Nate to Big from *Sex and the City*; the older guy who positions himself as the great love of Carrie's life, yet is emotionally unavailable and will never give her a relationship. This comparison just made me miss Nate more. I always rooted for Carrie and Big. I saw romance in their tumultuousness. Lily just saw reality.

'See!' said Lily, pausing the screen. 'The guy even has an issue with her leaving her toothbrush in the bathroom. His fear of commitment is on another level.'

'They get married in the movie, though. He proposes to her with a black diamond.'

'On the condition that they spend three days a week apart to accommodate for Big's commitment issues. He's such a man child.'

'Maybe if Nate and I had an open relationship, then it would work...'

Lily burst out laughing. 'You'd have about as much success in an open relationship as I would in a convent. You're not cut out for it, Vee, and that's not something you should change.'

'But if it was what Nate wanted, then maybe I could be happy; come to terms with it somehow. After all, Grant said monogamy rhymes with monotony...'

'You're not still obsessing over that fossil, are you? His favourite chocolate from Rococo is a pear liquor. He couldn't be more ancient if he tried.'

I burst into tears again. Sometimes it was unclear what I was crying over; Nate, or the general disaster of my dating life. My tears were becoming almost routine, along with the 'best friend' speech Lily gave to try and console me after.

'I wish you could see yourself from my eyes. Then you would know that you're worthy of a loyal, loving relationship. Don't sacrifice your standards. Don't deprive yourself of what you know you're worthy of.'

She even held me up in her mirror, forcing me to recite 'self-love affirmations.' She'd seen it on Instagram; apparently, it's supposed to reprogram negative subconscious beliefs about yourself and rewire your neural pathways. I tried, but I felt ridiculous. I can't believe the tactics people come up with these days. I didn't want to fix the pain, or even talk about it. I just wanted to sleep. Lily lay in bed with me before I dozed off, listing things about Nate to try and make me get 'the ick' over.

'Remember what I said to you once, Vee…'

'I know, I know. 'The ick' is more powerful than love. You can fall out of love, but you can't fall out of 'the ick.''

'Right,' she said, opening her notebook. 'So, let's start with his looks. He was a Slick Rick with an accent and a chain. Kind of sleazy when you think about it. Oh, and he got Botox.'

'Everyone has Botox nowadays.'

'Fingernails?'

'Fine.'

'Feet?'

'Surprisingly nice.'

'Mirror selfies?'

'He doesn't have Instagram.'

'Strange for someone who spends forty-five minutes on his hair in the bathroom.'

'That was his brother.'

'What about that time he choked on a calamari ring? Surely that must have given you "the ick."'

'Nope,' I sighed. 'It just made me really, really scared. I thought he was going to die.'

'In hindsight,' said Lily, 'maybe it would have been better he had.'

No matter how hard she tried, she couldn't get through to me. No one could; not even Kristen, who had given me a sympathetic hug in her office when I told her I was going through a break up over someone I was never actually in a relationship with. These days, she said, that that is the only type of breakup there really is.

* * *

Two weeks later following a concert with Lily at the O2, I heard from Nate. We had ended up backstage with a group of producers from LA. It was a prime networking opportunity for Lily, to which I had been granted a free best friend pass. We were all sat on chairs around Hollywood mirror lights, drinking beers from a minibar whilst debating frozen yogurt toppings. The music industry is like that, Lily said once. The more random the conversation topic, the more likely a connection will develop. She had once slid in the DMs to the manager of the most famous rapper in the world recommending him the poetry of Langston Hughes, after he posted an Instagram story saying he liked jazz music and New York. He sent her a Harrods gift card for an obscene amount of money in the post a week later, offering Lily an exciting work opportunity. Lily changed the topic to our '2019 New Year's Eve' nominations. On the first New Year's we spent together, we mutually agreed that we loathed it. It was a torturous event, always disappointing. As a result, we formed a new tradition. Every year, we would come up with awards for different categories in our lives. 'Best Outfit,' 'Worst Date,' 'Most Iconic Moment,' 'Biggest Wet Wipe.' Abel and Patrick were up for two of them. Lily had put herself up for one.

I had deleted Nate's number, but when it flashed up on my screen, I recognised it instantly. Before Lily had forced me to remove him from my phone, I had sneakily memorised it by heart and reserved it in the same part of my brain as the words on Grant's note. I don't know why. In case of an emergency perhaps, like a burglary or theft if I was ever alone in the flat and Lily was in LA. If that ever happened, I know Nate would beat the criminal to death, sweep me up in his arms and tell me it was all going to be ok. The warm press of his embrace was always a feeling of safety. Either that, or I'd text to wish him a Happy Christmas next month. Happy Christmas texts are always acceptable to receive from an ex, or a sort of ex. In fact, they're expected. You can disguise your reaching out to them as a polite seasonal greeting. I could only see the first couple of lines of Nate's message, which read:

Hey Verity. I hope you're well. I just wanted to say that I've been thinking about you. About your eyes, mainly, and the way you make me...

Instantly, I felt as if I had been plugged in and lit up like the wired lights of a Christmas tree. A deep sense of relief followed, cocooning me with the familiar Nate feeling that everything was all going to be ok. It was as if he was in the room again, holding me close, telling me that our break up had been a foolish, ill-thought-out decision. I hadn't read the rest of the text, but I knew that whatever it said would finally make me sleep peacefully again. Nate and I were going to work things out. Lily, ever suspicious, caught on to my change in mood. She dragged me furiously out the room, away from all the producers.

'What's got into you?' she said, closing the door. 'You're looking at your phone in there like Dopey the seventh dwarf.'

'I'm just a little drunk off the beer.'

'Liar.'

She grabbed my phone and saw the message on my screen, reading it out loud:

'"Hey Verity. I hope you're well. I just wanted to say that I've been thinking about you. About your eyes, mainly, and the way you make me laugh. I miss you. Can we meet for a coffee to talk?" Pathetic.'

I paused, feeling hurt that she wasn't happy for me. 'You don't need to be such a bitch, you know.'

'You think after just two weeks he's going to have miraculously worked through his issues and provide you with a committed relationship? I don't think so.'

'He just wants to talk, Lily. I haven't said that I'm definitely going to get back with him.'

'No, but you will.'

'And what would so bad if I did?' I felt the anger in me rise. 'Why are you so fucking passionate about it?'

'BECAUSE I CARE ABOUT YOU!'

Neither of us said anything for a moment. For someone so unfiltered, Lily rarely shouted. It took both of us back.

'I love him, Lily, and when you find love, you have to go at it with all you have. Only a fool would deny the will of their own heart, let alone that of the person who loves them too.'

'And only an idiot would make the same mistake twice. I can't watch you get hurt again, Vee. He turned you into a fucking wreck.'

Lily began to cry. I tried to comfort her, but she shook me off.

'Maybe I should go.'

'Maybe you should.'

I left the arena with no particular sense of where I was going or how to navigate my way back to the tube. It was dark and confusing, but I didn't care. I stumbled around in the pitch black, high from Nate's text. I felt as if I could gallop the ten-mile distance between Greenwich to Parsons Green right now, leap into Nate's arms and laugh at how pointless our month long break up had been. We'd destroy each other's mouths and make love on the kitchen island for hours, knocking everything over on the floor, just like the urgency of our very first kiss. Maybe I really could turn up at his place tonight; answer his text in person and take him by surprise. He'd still be awake when I arrived. Mediterranean people don't sleep until late. However, Lily's words stuck with me. Deep down, part of me knew she was right. It was unlikely that Nate had resolved his commitment issues in two weeks. He was thirty-six, set in his ways, and proba- bly unable to compromise. There was a risk he would hurt me again, and if he did, it would be the ugliest heartbreak in the world. I didn't follow my head, of course. I never really understood why people did. It's such a boring option. Instead, I ran with my wonky, clumsy heart and replied to Nate, agreeing to meet him for a coffee next Sunday.

* * *

A month isn't long enough for someone to age, especially when they've had Botox. Still, I had expected Nate to look different. A little wearier; perhaps. Dishevelled, with more stubble than usual. Maybe even chubbier, or dramatically gaunt. In the short time I had been with Nate, I had done most of the cooking. I had half hoped he'd been living off Uber Eats without me, or maybe even nothing at all, so heart-broken that he'd just let himself wither away. I wanted the sorrow of missing me to have eaten him up, just like it had me. I wanted the pain to be obvious, but it wasn't. It wasn't at all. Nate looked as if he'd just got back from a two week trip to the Maldives. He was glowing and smelt like freshly picked lemons, looking devastatingly handsome in a soft blue shirt that I had never seen before. Coupled with the bottle of rosé in the ice bucket, the sight of him made me crumble.

'It's good to see you again,' he smiled, pouring me a glass. 'How have you been?'

'Shit, to be honest.'

'Well you look lovely.'

'I thought we were meeting for coffee,' I said, taking off my jacket. 'If it was wine then I would have worn something else.'

'You look perfect in everything you wear,' he said, lightly touching my hand. 'I've always thought you were that rare balance between cute and sexy, you know. That hard-to-find combination which every man wants.'

'Cut the crap, Nate. What is this?'

'What's what?'

'This. Why did you text me?'

He paused, giving me the broken look I had been waiting for. I couldn't tell if he was putting it on or not.

'I've missed you. Isn't that enough?'

'Not really.'

He buried his head into his hands, struggling with what to say. I didn't try and prompt him. I wanted to watch him suffer.

'This last month without you has been torture.'

'It doesn't look like it. You're all tanned and glowy.'

He leaned forward, grabbing onto either one of my hands.

'Please, Verity. I need you.'

'You know what I want, Nate,' I mumbled. 'Commitment. I thought you brought me here to tell me you were finally ready to give it to me.'

Nate laughed nervously, as if the mere mention of the word was enough to make him sweat. 'You make it sound scary, like some legal contract.'

'Hardly. That's what marriage is.'

'Marriage?' Nate spluttered his wine out at the word. I stood up, handing him a napkin. I think part of me was still traumatised from the calamari incident.

'We can work through your fears, Nate,' I said, wiping his mouth from across the table. 'We can un-heal your trauma. I'd even come with you to counselling. Don't hate me for suggesting it, but maybe it would help...'

'Stop making a fuss,' he hushed. 'People are staring.'

'It never used to bother you when people stared at us. I actually used to think you got off on it slightly.'

We both took it in turns to sip our wine, not speaking for a moment. Eventually, it was Nate who did. 'This last month has been hell. You know that, don't you?'

'How bad was it?' I said. 'I want to know.'

'That's fucked up,' smirked Nate. 'Are you being serious?'

'Yep. Tell me how it tore you apart.'

'Let's just say that even getting the groceries was difficult.'
I paused. 'Did you cry?'

'Sometimes. Did you?'

'Almost every night.'

'Come here.'

I walked over to his chair and sat on his lap, nuzzling into him. Couples began looking at us suspiciously, from the shock of two people canoodling at a restaurant in raw daylight. I melted in the embrace of his arms, like I always knew I would.

'Fuck,' he gushed, nuzzling into my neck. 'I've missed your smell.'

'I've missed yours too.' I choked, feeling my eyes water. 'You should have just called me, Nate. I sat in my bed, missing you every night. Why didn't you just call me?'

'I thought about it. I kept wanting to, but I stumbled every time. I didn't know what to say.'

'And what about now?' I looked deeply into Nate's eyes, gently caressing his face. I could see he wanted to smile, but was trying to hide his teeth again. I was comforted by the reappearance of this quirk.

'Well I think we'd be foolish to not give it another go,' he grinned. 'Don't you?' I squeezed him tightly, feeling at peace again, never wanting to let go.

'Did you buy a new shirt just to win me back?'

'Maybe,' he grinned, ever so slightly smug. 'Did it work?'

'Did it hell.'

We kissed, picking up exactly where we had left off after our first date. Just like that, Nate and I began seeing each other again. I never let Lily in on it, but there was still a part of me that ruminated over our argument at the concert, making me question whether it would work or not. Whenever my brain engaged with this scenario, I squashed it down. At no costs did I want to imagine Nate breaking my heart again. If he did, it would tear me apart more deeply than the first time. I wasn't sure I could go through all that again.

* * *

Lily and I had grown distant since Nate and I got back together. If I accidentally said his name, she would block her ears like a child.

'It's fucked up what you're doing, you know.'

'You don't have to agree with everything I do, Lily.'

'I mean it. You're going to get hurt like you've never been hurt before. If you thought last time was bad, just you wait.'

'Nate and I…'

Lily blocked her ears, so I shouted over her.

'Nate and I are going to work through his issues, you know. We're going to get him help for his trauma.'

Lily released her hands, bursting into a fit of laughter. 'I love how he frames his playboy ways and refusal to commit as trauma. Really, he's just trying to lure in women who think they can "fix" him. You've gotta give it to him, Vee. The guy's a genius.'

'You don't know anything about him,' I snarled. 'Nate has had a difficult life.'

'I know that he destroyed you once and he'll do it again. This time, your heart will feel as if it has been ripped out your chest and smashed together in a blender.'

'You're so crude with everything you say.'

'What I say is the truth. You defend him like he deserves it. He's a piece of shit.' I felt my eyes prickle with tears.

'Deep down, I know that rumour is eating you up alive.'

Apparently, a mutual friend of ours called Mia had recently found Nate on Hinge. I had attempted to justify it through arguing that it was within the month period where Nate and I hadn't been together. Sometimes expired dating profiles hang around on the app for ages, even when they're not active. It doesn't necessarily mean anything.

At least that was the narrative I was going with. Lily said she had the screenshots as proof, but I hadn't wanted to look.

'I'm going to Nate's for a few days. I think it's best if you and I have some time apart.'

'Have fun getting your heart broken.'

'Oh, I will!'

* * *

My hands grasped tightly on the edge of the table as Nate thrust himself inside me from behind. It was the first series of days we had spent together since rekindling our relationship, and it was safe to say that our sex had changed. It always started in the flat lobby, right before we had even put the key in the door of Nate's flat. The urge was so strong that we would barely even bother undressing each other. Tender intimacy had transformed into wild, relentless fucking. Gentle neck kisses, whispers of 'I love you' and post-sex cradling beneath the sheets had been replaced with aggressive thrusts, tongue throttling and hair pulling. It was no longer sex between two adults, but rather, two humans who fucked each other with the unbridled enthusiasm of mating animals. I felt not like me, but some sex-crazed creature, driven by instinct, hunger and fear that everything with Nate was in jeopardy of crumbling apart.

'I need the bathroom,' I muttered, stumbling over the loop of my thong. 'Be back in a moment.'

I sorted my face out and caught myself staring at Nate's bathroom cupboard. I had never bothered rummaging through his possessions before. Although we were never in an official relationship, the connection between us in those early days had always felt relatively secure. Nate's love had been a force of protection and instilled me with a feeling of unquestionable safety. It was only now that paranoia was beginning to spark in my mind. Nate had seemed sincere about us making a go of things again, and I hadn't wanted to question it. I had been quick to defend him to Lily and Mia when he had been discovered on that dating app. I told them that he was single during that month, and it would have been perfectly reasonable for him to have dated other women. But was he still? My mind began to analyse the subtle changes in Nate's behaviour; the way he always checked his phone after sex in a way he never used to, the difference in the way he touched me, the fact he hadn't said he loved me since the day he had begged to get me back. Like a scavenger, I opened the bathroom cabinet and began scanning for clues. I didn't need to try very hard. Standing proudly before my eyes in height order was a female deodorant can for 'sensitive skin,' a purple bottle of perfume named Russian Nights and a tube of Sainsbury's nail varnish remover.

My heart began to hammer. The air felt thick to swallow. I reached for the perfume and squirted it into the air, somehow thinking it would make the atmosphere more breathable. I coughed instantly at the stench of candyfloss, cherry cola and stale liquorice. Sickeningly, it reminded me of Toni's scent on the night of the attempted threesome. Was Nate cheating on me? I took a deep breath, trying to rationalise. There was a chance that the items belonged to a girlfriend of Joshua's, although the more I thought about it, the more unlikely it seemed. He was currently out of

London, visiting their mother in France. I had received no knowledge from Nate that Joshua was even dating, let alone had a girlfriend. In fact, Nate used to joke that Joshua was notoriously unlucky with women and had the flirting skills of a fumbling politician. It was Nate, the older sibling, who was the lucky one. He was the star-studded womaniser; the age-defying lothario; the sexy French guy who rode a motorbike around Parsons Green in a leather jacket and looked hot as Death Valley even when taking the bins out.

'Verity?' he shouted. 'Are you ok in there?'

'Fine, thanks! Just freshening up.'

As soon as I got out the bathroom, I pretended that I had to go back home as a matter of urgency. Nate tried to grab me, but I quickly pushed him off.

'Lily's upset about something. I have to go and be there for her.'

'I thought you guys weren't friends?'

'Never believe women when they say that.'

I kissed him goodbye and decided to walk back home. It would take me two hours to walk from Fulham to Streatham, which seemed like the perfect amount of time to simply think.

* * *

I was halfway home in Clapham Common, when I pulled up to a tree with a strong urge to collapse to the ground and burst into tears. The thought of Nate with someone else was suffocating, and since seeing the toiletries in the bathroom, I couldn't get the image out of my head. Presumably, this girl was the aggressively feminine type. She wore a deodorant smelling of a 'floral bouquet,' painted her nails red and embodied the smell of Russian Nights. What even happens during nights in Russia, anyway? Do women prance around

St Petersburg square in fur coats drinking vodka on the rocks, staining their glass with red lipstick? Do they gallivant around ice rinks, porcelain and perfect, like Kitty in *Anna Karenina*? Or do they reside in mystical castles with roofs that look like giant marshmallow twists, tending to their baby chihuahua's with princess manes of hair? Who was this girl? Was she bewitching, like Toni? Petite, like Naomi? Sassy, like Lily? What did she give him? But more importantly – what did she have that I didn't? All I could think about was Nate frolicking around with some Russian goddess, the smell of her perfume on his skin, his bedsheets, his towels. I tried to think back to his flat, wondering if there had been a smidge of evidence that I had missed somehow. I re-entered it all, room by room, feeling sweaty and sick. I crouched down, breathing deeply, when I felt the hands of a stranger tap me on the shoulder. I turned around and was greeted with the concerned expression of an old lady.

'Are you ok there, dear?'

'I'm fine,' I mumbled, standing up. 'Just a little dizzy, that's all.'

'You look ever so pale. You ought to go and get yourself a nice hot chocolate. Do you need some money?'

'Money?' I was hurt that I looked homeless enough for her to have asked so confidently. 'I'm fine, thank you.'

I staggered back onto the high street and felt my stomach growl as I walked past a local coffee shop. I hadn't eaten anything all morning. I wandered in and ordered a hot chocolate with marshmallows, thinking some sugar would give me the energy to think more clearly.

'£6.50, please.'

'£6.50?'

'Well, duh,' sighed the barista. 'The chocolate is non-dairy, infused with salt from the Himalayan mountains, topped with an organic marshmallow and melted with a blowtorch.'

'I get the picture,' I snapped, rummaging for my bank card. 'Thanks.'

To my horror, it wasn't in my bag. Panicking, I tipped it upside down and sprawled the contents out all over the floor. There was everything, from tampons to dirty knickers and an abundance of mini fragrance samples Lily used to collect me from events. We both always agreed they were useful tools for nightclubs, dates and 'staying at guys' houses.

I suddenly had an intense longing to see her and repair our friendship. 'Excuse me, madam, but I'm going to have to ask you to move to one side…'

'Forget it,' I sneered, shoving everything back inside my bag. 'I'm leaving.'

* * *

My phone was on minimal battery, so I had to think quickly. I retraced my footsteps from when I had arrived at Nate's place earlier this afternoon. As usual, we had barely said a word to each other before rushing into sex. It had taken place in his kitchen this time; he'd held me against the counter, shoving my tights down to my ankles, pounding me furiously. I played back the memory of our sloppy sex scene, trying to solidify the small details. I briefly remembered chucking everything that was in my hand on top of Nate's microwave. The items had been my phone, Nate's keys and, thank god, my card holder. I sighing with relief. That's where it was. On top of the bloody microwave. I used the remainder of my battery to book an Uber back to Nate's place. I would dash in to retrieve my bankcard and head straight home to make amends with Lily. We would cuddle up on the sofa and resolve all this chaos. Her patience was thin, but when all was said and done, she was a perfect friend. She'd help me figure out what to do, how to handle it, how to play it all. She'd almost definitely know everything about Russian Nights perfume, in the same way she had known all about the difference between long and short stem roses from when they had been left on Toni's desk that time.

'Anywhere here fine?' asked the driver, as we pulled onto Nate's road.

'Yep,' I said, hurrying out the Uber. 'Thanks.'

I ran over to Number 28, desperate to get back home and sort things with Lily. The door was ajar when I arrived. I let myself in.

'Nate? Are you in? I forgot my bankcard. Idiot, I know. I think it's on top of your microwave.' He shot out from his bedroom suddenly, clean shaved and freshly showered.

'It's here,' he smiled, handing it to me hurriedly. 'Found it when I was clearing up.'

He was wearing that soft blue shirt and stank of freshly cut lemons again. Although I was in a rush to get back, it was hard to resist him looking so sexy.

'You didn't need to come all this way, babe. I would have dropped it off to you later on my bike.'

Suddenly, Nate's phone buzzed from the pocket of his jeans. He looked at the screen, panic stricken, as if he had just received an anonymous text telling him he was positive for chlamydia.

'Nate? Are you inside?'

The soft hush of a female voice echoed along the hallway. Her heels clicked right to the front of Nate's door, which was still half open. I turned around, feeling my heart drop to the pit of my stomach. Stood in front of me was a slim girl with caramel hair, olive skin and big brown eyes. She was wearing gym gear with no obvious intention of working out, matched with a pair of boot heels. I didn't study her face long enough to analyse whether she looked Russian or not. I was too paralysed.

'Georgie! I thought you weren't coming here till five?'

'Meh. I got bored.'

I was in a state of shock. Nate and his side chick, Georgie, going about their vulgar Sunday night rendezvous as if I were invisible. I looked at both of them in a desperate search for clarity, but their faces were a blur. The only thing that made the situation real rather than some nightmarish scene from a psychological thriller was the thud of my heart. I could hear it beating in my ears.

'I'd been gone for an hour, Nate,' I trembled. 'One hour.'

Nate didn't say a word. I turned to face the girl, expecting her to be filled with rage, preparing to slap Nate round the face. She looked frighteningly ok, as if she were expecting me to be here. The situation was all of a sudden obvious. As usual, I was the last to catch on. Nate was cheating on me, two weeks into our fresh start, and I was the poor scorned woman. Classic. I felt my eyes clog with thick pools of water. Tears spilled down my face, plopping into the crack of my cleavage. Nate, on the other hand, had the disturbing calmness of a stoned clown in a theatre about to perform live heart surgery. He was half laughing, half attempting to comfort me.

'Technically, Verity, we never discussed...'

'We discussed everything, you narcissist.'

The words heaved out my mouth as if my guts were being strangled with bleach. I ran past Nate and out onto the road in search of a place to shatter properly; somewhere I could howl in private. It must have been seven minutes straight I ran for, sweeping past cars and families and babies in prams and trees and motorcyclists. Eventually I found an empty car park. I collapsed to the pavement and let out a shrill, sloppy, retching howl, amazed at what my body was capable of. Lily said if I thought last time was bad, wait, because this time would be worse. She was right.

It was the most exquisite heartbreak I had ever known.

One year later

It might seem strange to look back on my dating life with a full heart as opposed to a damaged one, especially when I never found love. I ought to be jaded, perhaps; a little bitter, fraught with cynicism, ready to warn the next generation of fresh-faced singletons to protect their hearts and steer clear of dating apps which boast every type of man possible. But I'm not. And I won't.

You see, whilst my experiences with these men were varied, colourful and rich – from the epic Grant romances, to the shattering Nate heartbreaks – I have come to realise that finding the right man was never what it was all about. It was about finding me.

When I first embarked on the tempestuous seas of the London dating scene, I was a devout believer in the fallacy that my life would be better off, if not complete, with a man by my side. What I ultimately learned was that (for me) this was an outdated, boring and ill-thought-out narrative which women have been conditioned to believe for centuries without really asking whether there was another way. As it turns out – there is. It is fun, crazy and fucking wild.

As I discovered, most men you will date in life are full of surprising details that you will never suspect. Some good, like the six-foot Swedish stuntman I matched with on Hinge last week who has royal connections in Monaco; and some not so good, like Joe who had a secret girlfriend in Bali, and Kyle – the sensible Surrey boy who hosed his house plants down in the bath on Sunday mornings and wanted to introduce a threesome into our relationship with my marketing coordinator. Whilst these experiences hurt, they unearthed a strength in me that I never knew existed, and reminded me that surviving something which has every reason to break you will be the hallmark of your resilience.

I realise now that the demise of one relationship was a gateway to new people walking on new paths, who in turn, presented me with opportunities I never thought possible. Learning to let go of one person allowed me to be open to every new person I met. It was a revelation. I now see my dating life as a vast learning paradise, filled with realms of discovery in the form of people who inadvertently armed me with the weaponry to navigate the chaos of the modern world.

Sometimes, you have to be reminded numerous times of why someone is wrong for you, just like I was last year when I saw Nate with another girl and felt as if my guts were about to splutter out of my chest in the middle of a car park – they didn't, and now I have, at last, got over him.

Love is a cruel game, especially for the hopeless romantics among us; but we cannot overlook the fun to be had along the way. Dating doesn't have to be a long, treacherous ordeal of pain and despair. It can be filled with unexpected hilarity and spontaneous bursts of joy; cupcakes, roses, brain concussions, and orgasms coupled with random trips to chocolatiers and foreign hotels. For every wrong guy you date, there will be a downright iconic story that will follow. My first date with Pablo all those years ago may have resulted in an overnight stay in a Spanish hospital, but it taught me that dating can be freeing, light-hearted and fun.

Pablo wasn't the Enrique Iglesias 2.0 my former self had set her eyes on, but it didn't matter – I discovered tapas and paella, and improved my Spanish through being an au pair (and also learned that I never want children, which is an unexpected relief).

I suppose the same rung true with Caleb; I got to sample a picnic from Fortnum & Mason, and then have a loud music, wind in your hair, sing your heart out spin in a fancy Jeep Wrangler whilst trying to work out how to get someone to tell me something they didn't want to tell me.

Thanks to Abel, my email is still registered as part of a subscription that occasionally sends me chocolate truffles wrapped in cellophane with a pink ribbon bow. Whilst his sweetness still haunts me, it is a reminder of how it feels to be adored by someone; even if it did coincide with the development of my career at Kill & Kontent, where I am now an account manager.

I never saw (or even heard from) Grant again, but I had a seventy-two-hour whirlwind with a sexy older man and discovered what an orgasm feels like. In Paris. For a short time, my heart was entirely aflutter for a man who made me feel like a woman from a black and white movie; and now, I won't settle for anything less.

On the other hand, Sammy may have turned out to be teenager, but Lily and I used the change he left behind to tip a cute waiter at a café the following weekend. For the first time in her life, Lily took a leaf out of my book and scribbled her number down on the back of a loyalty card. The two of them went on a date, until Lily got 'the ick' after he posted six mirror selfies on Instagram in twenty-four hours and pronounced Givenchy as Giv-enchy.

Sometimes, dating is just dating. And that is ok. Perhaps the image of a successful woman should depend less on her ability to find the right man and more on the actual journey instead; how open she is, how fearless she remains, and how much she takes from the experiences that will ultimately shape her as a woman. Failing that – they will at least make her laugh with her friends, and those will be her enduring memories.

Dating is a wild and exciting adventure, and you never stop learning; about yourself, about the world, and most importantly, about other people. Naomi and Max were (and continue to be) my steadfast anchors. They are there for me when I need it most, filling me with a sense of home whenever I speak to them or see them.

To ensure I never retreat too far into my old, dreamy self who sees the world through rose-tinted glasses, I have Lily; the vehicle who continuously drives me down the road less travelled. As the two of us adjust to our new flat in Notting Hill and delve into the latter half of our twenties as single women, we are becoming increasingly confident and optimistic about what the future holds. Thanks to social media, which preaches girl power and female independence, the ripe old age of thirty just doesn't feel that scary anymore. In fact, Lily said the other day that she imagines her thirties will be like her twenties, but with a bigger bank account, a wider wardrobe and a greater capacity for orgasms.

Times are changing. We have a voice, we have a platform, we have opportunities to grow and shine and develop. Our dating lives are all part of this new found liberation, and I have Lily by my side to continuously remind me of that whenever I grow weary.

Looking back, I'm really happy that I took that leap and dove in head first with arms wide open and heart fully exposed. Did it hurt? Sometimes, of course. Did I learn something? Did I gain something? Did I grow? Yes. Yes. Yes. Would I do it all again? Absolutely! Every single date, drama, disaster and delight made my life mine, and most of all, it helped me understand who I am and how to navigate the unpredictable ocean ahead of me.

And that's a skill that serves a woman for a lifetime.

CPSIA information can be obtained
at www.ICGtesting.com
Printed in the USA
LVHW031646260122
709009LV00004B/6